THE *MIRACLE* YEARS

What I Learned about God, Miracles, Life, the Paranormal, and Why We Are Here

by

Norma Locker, Msc.D.

"There are only two ways to live your life. One is as though nothing is a miracle. The other is as though everything is a miracle."
Albert Einstein.

TELEMACHUS PRESS

THE MIRACLE YEARS: What I Learned about God, Miracles, Life, the Paranormal, and Why We Are Here

Cover Designed by Rick Midler

Cover Art by Rick Midler
http://www.rickmidler.com

Published by Telemachus Press, LLC
http://www.telemachuspress.com

Visit the author website:
http://www.NormaLocker.com

ISBN # 978-1-937698-11-9 (eBook)
ISBN # 978-1-937698-12-6 (paperback)

Version 2013.10.31

Printed in the United States of America

10 9 8 7 6 5 4 3 2 1

PRAISE FOR
THE MIRACLE YEARS

As author of eight books, a Hall of Fame Speaker and former 20 year nationwide President of Hearst Newspapers—it has been my privilege to see and witness abundant talents, who share those talents abundantly. Dr. Norma Locker's impressive book is a mirror of her impressive life and wisdom. Readers are in for an ocean of marvelous insights—destined to bring each life and mind to new heights.

Bob Danzig—Author of the new eBook *The Hummingbird Effect: A Journey to Confidence*

The Miracle Years is an outstanding, clear compilation of Norma Locker's life work. I have often looked for an encyclopedia of intuition development. This is it! This book covers many amazing life-altering experiences and techniques: her personal story; a deep understanding of life and many strategies to help you awaken your own intuitive skills and healing abilities. Spoken from the voice of experience, *The Miracle Years* is truly profound.

Dawn Lianna, M.A.—Author of *The New Tao Te Ching: The Art of Happiness.*

Honest and compelling, *The Miracle Years* spans four decades of Norma Locker's expansive mystical journey. What touched me most was the quality of her heart. Like every spiritual leader, Dr. Locker embodies what she writes.

Kira Rosner—Author of *The Power of Being Human* and *When Souls Take Flight.*

TABLE OF CONTENTS

Part II: WHAT'S IT ALL ABOUT?

THE *MIRACLE* YEARS

What I Learned about God, Miracles, Life, the Parnormal, and Why We Are Here

IN MEMORIAM

I DEDICATE THIS book with love and blessings to Sophie (*Strick*) Strichartz who valiantly scooped up the pieces when our *sky fell down;* to Charlie Locker who learned humility and patience the hard way and whose indomitable wit prevailed throughout; to my mother-in-law, Goldie, (Mama/*Mamela*/*Bubby*) Locker whose love and inborn wisdom resonate with all of us to this day; to my nephew/Godson Harry Locker whose young life was lovingly devoted to God's beloved creatures and who, I believe, is now tending to them in a higher realm; to Shana Pooh Janice-Locker, my adorable four-legged granddaughter who is now romping with her playmates in the clouds; and to all of those blessed souls who have touched our hearts and imprinted our souls for eternity.

INTRODUCTION

"Humankind has not woven the web of life. We are but one thread
within it. Whatever we do to the web, we do to ourselves. All things
are bound together. All things connect."
Chief Seattle.

WHAT WE PERCEIVE as "miracles" can be the results of the
dynamic currents of our most passionate thoughts, dreams, desires
and prayers or merely natural occurrences relative to a positive
mindset. We call them "miracles" for want of a more appropriate
term because often they seem to appear when we need them mostly.

When miracles appear in the lives of people whose mindsets
have always been pragmatic or agnostic they are frequently not recognized or acknowledged as such. They are usually called coincidences. It is customary for these individuals to allow no room for
enlightenment or transformation, thus they exist in a self-created
vacuum.

Yet, there is hope for everyone. It may take a life-altering
trauma; a near-death experience; the loss of a loved one; an extreme
challenge, to ignite the spark for discovery and change. For me, it was
almost as dramatic as you will see when you read on because I was
one of those closed-minded people. Apparently, the spark was always
here within me, patiently smoldering, waiting to be kindled.

My early years were bittersweet; sometimes joyful, but most frequently littered with drama; insecurity, distress and disillusion. Consequently, I suffered deep emotional scars.

When I first met Charlie Locker in 1946, he was 28 and I was 21. He had recently mustered out of the army following his European stint in World War II. He was glib with an irresistible knack for persuasion. The very first night he convinced me that he could shampoo hair like no one else, and he was right! We were wed on a rainy Sunday, July 4th, 1947 a couple of months after my 22nd birthday.

It was 1965 when my *spark* was kindled. That was the pivotal year in my transformation and enlightenment. It was my introduction to God, the paranormal, and the power of our thoughts. When I asked God to give me the title for Part I of this work I was inspired with "Tapping the *Reservoir*." Later the title for Part II, "What's It All About?" came to me after I had already chosen "Where Do We Go from Here?" Our amazing experiences with spirit communication which began in 1967 are detailed in Part II. While participating in séances which we also called psychic development classes and dark hours, I trained as a medium; Charlie's inherent faculty for clairvoyance emerged, and our children also developed psychically. I taped as many of the phenomenal sessions that were permitted by our spirit guides. I also filled six hefty school tablets with our mystical and paranormal experiences and demonstrations of faith in God and the remarkable versatility and potential of the mind.

When I asked God for the title for Part III I was also inspired with "The Road to *Utopia*: *Paving the Road*" because it deals with wholesome living, healing, managing stress, self-mastery and self-empowerment.

Whenever I announced that I wanted to learn something new, another door would open and I would stroll through it to wondrous and miraculous encounters. An old proverb states, *When the student is ready the teacher appears,* and that is precisely what was happening. I began to feel as though I was living a charmed life.

In 1967 I founded *The New Life Concept,* and designed a course which I taught for many years. It was based on metaphysical principles inspired partially by the *Science of Mind.* When we relocated from New Jersey to Florida in 1985, I reformulated my course to benefit the retirees in Century Village, Deerfield Beach. I've been teaching my course, *From Negative to Positive with Mind Power* here since 1986.

In 1992 I received my Master's Degree and subsequently in 1995, my Doctorate in Metaphysical Science from the International University of Metaphysics. My Master's thesis was entitled, *Reincarnation and the Karmic Connection: Our Divine Heritage,* and I had conducted well-attended seminars on that topic here for four consecutive years since 2003. *The Destructive and Healing Powers of the Mind: Exploring the Mind/Body Connection* was the theme of my Doctoral dissertation.

Metaphysicians know that we are all connected mentally and spiritually in a *Sea of Mind.* This *Sea of Mind* flows through and around everyone and everything in the Universe. Dr. Irving Oyle in *The Healing Mind* calls it the *Sea of Energy.* Pierre Teilhard de Chardin speaks of the *Noosphere,* the mantle of thoughts or ideas which engage humanity. *Noosphere* and *Field of Mind* are products of the same structure. Physicist David Bohm suggests that particles and people alike may influence each other, because everything in the Universe is connected to everything else—past, present and future in what he calls the *Implicate Order.* His theory alludes to the constant flux of atoms and molecules which comprise all matter including living organisms. Because of this interconnection of all matter, telepathic communication is possible between minds which are attuned to one another. Sea of Mind, Sea of Energy, Noosphere, Field of Mind, Implicate Order and Universe are some examples of what we know as God.

I have learned that you never forget, but that time has a way of sprinkling fairy dust on harsh memories. I have learned that forgiveness is the golden magic wand that can heal the deepest of wounds. I have learned that there is such a thing as unconditional love, and that lesson was gifted to me by the warmhearted Locker family. With all of my negativity in the years before metaphysics and meditation, (what I facetiously call *BM*,) they accepted and embraced me, at first perhaps out of loyalty to Charlie. Then, I imagine that they may have perceived a glimmer of hope for this misguided soul.

I have learned to refrain from questioning, from asking why, because I can now observe, understand and view everything which transpires from a Universal perspective. There is a reason behind every occurrence in the Universe because of the inescapable and definitive Law of Cause and Effect or Karma. I have learned that our thoughts generate a powerful energy; that we are co-creators with the Universe, (or God;) that we are masters of our destiny. The choices that we make; what we believe; what we expect; what we fear; these are the implements which activate the immutable and ever-present universal *Law of Attraction*. We are unequivocally drafting the blueprint of our reality and our destiny. If the structure we have delineated has a weak foundation, it will crumble and ultimately can impact our health, welfare and the world around us.

This is not our final journey on this or any other planet. It's all about the evolution of the soul. Most of us still have a long and sometimes tedious and challenging odyssey to achieve the ultimate completion of our cosmic responsibilities. Our souls cry out for deliverance from mortal restraints. They hunger for the ecstasy of being once again assimilated into the limitless love of our Divine Creator.

This book serves as a tribute to the events, the teachers, the people, the spirit guides and our beloved Father/Mother God, who have been so instrumental in our development and enlightenment.

To my blessed readers, if your attitudes and preconceived opinions have been tweaked just a little, and if you can integrate into your life anything that you can glean from this book then my effort is made worthwhile.

"We are not human beings on a spiritual journey.
We are spiritual beings on a human journey."
Pierre Teilhard de Chardin

PART I
TAPPING THE *RESERVOIR*

Chapter I

A LIFE-ALTERING EPIPHANY

"We must not cease from exploration."
T.S. Eliot.

"I DREAMT THAT my father came to me and gave me a number," my mother casually reported to me on more than one occasion. My Zayda, (grandfather,) was deceased and the kicker was that she played those numbers, illegally in those days, and won a bundle every time. She sought out fortune-tellers and even learned how to give readings from ordinary playing cards. All the while, I thought the whole business was a *crock,* until one afternoon in 1967 I had a life-altering epiphany.

While sitting under a hair dryer in my neighborhood beauty salon, I selected a Lady's Home Journal magazine from the available stack. As I ruffled the pages, they fell open to somewhere in the center. The title of an article, *My Psychic Friends,* impudently glared at me, imploring me to take heed. It contained excerpts from a recently published book, *A Search for the Truth,* by Ruth Montgomery, a nationally syndicated columnist out of Washington.

The basis for her book was her interest in spirit survival; (life after death,) and psychic phenomena. After having ventured into the psychic world, she was inspired to try her hand at automatic writing. She began with a pencil and then graduated to the typewriter at the suggestion of her spirit guide. The messages which *came through* changed her life dramatically and she was encouraged to write the book.

As I continued to absorb the article, my entire body tingled with a familiarity which I couldn't understand at that time. I thought, "Oh, my God, Mom isn't bonkers after all!" I couldn't wait to get home and phone her. "Mom, guess what! I apologize for doubting you all this time. I just became a believer in life after death."

My fortieth birthday was coming up in April and I was scheduled to enter the hospital, as I had done in past years, for gastro-intestinal X-rays, (a *G.I.* series.) Since I was to spend my birthday there, I suggested to my kids that if they plan to give me a gift, *A Search for the Truth* was what I most desired.

I hungrily devoured every thrilling word in that book during my three days there, and that convinced me that I, too, could do automatic writing. That is when I embarked on my endless journey into the world of the paranormal. Every day, according to Montgomery's advice, I entered a relaxed, meditative state, affirmed that I was protected and I would accept only good and true communication from the other side. My pen was poised over a page in a school tablet and I asked my guides to use me as an instrument for communication. The three school tablets which I filled with responses to my inquiries contained scrawled messages from deceased family members and relatives of friends, entities claiming to be guides, precognitive messages and spiritual guidance and instruction. Charlie eagerly looked forward to those that were from his father and sister, Marcella, who had long since passed over.

In my thirties I discovered that I could predict the weather but at that time I didn't equate it with a psychic ability. When my old, abdominal surgical scars began to itch I knew it would rain within three days, and that phenomenon faithfully remains with me to this day. When the source of the itch was inaccessible, Charlie promptly sheltered the car in the garage in anticipation of a snowstorm.

I avidly consumed every book I could find on mysticism and the paranormal. The more I read, the more convinced I became that I wanted to do it all.

Chapter II
THAT POWERHOUSE IMAGINATION
"Perceive that which cannot be seen with the eyes."
Musashi Miyamoto.

PRIOR TO THE foregoing, we had been living in a cramped one-family dwelling for six years. Charlie wanted a two-family because he felt that the tenant's rental would help to pay the mortgage. At that time I knew little of the paranormal, except for my Mom's experiences, and I was totally ignorant of metaphysical principles. I did, however, have a creative imagination which I used to envision a large house with spacious rooms on a sizable plot of land. Gardening was a favorite pastime of mine, and I treasured the lavish flower beds I had lovingly cultivated from seed on our small property. So, I delighted in fantasies of a sprawling spectrum of brilliance mellowed by lush green shrubs and trees.

After several months of tedious house hunting, the real estate agent finally located a massive two-family house in our town on an incredible spread, much larger than I had imagined. But it was also being bid upon by a contracting firm. They were outbidding us, yet Charlie resolutely refused to be swayed from his original offer.

The following week he had a business appointment with partners in a contracting firm. He sold them a partnership insurance policy and they were so pleased with his expertise in handling their case that they offered to be of service some day. Charlie quickly seized the opportunity. "Maybe you can help me out right now," he suggested hopefully, recounting our dilemma with the house. "The realtor told me that the competitive bidder isn't interested in the house at all," he said. "He just wants the attached woods to build on." "That's funny," one of the partners observed, "Fred and I are involved in a similar deal. Where is this house, anyway?"

Well, when they heard the address, they both laughed. "Talk about coincidence! That's the one we've been bidding on and we're planning to tear down the old house." "Why can't we get together?" Charlie offered. "Let me buy the house at my price and I'll sell you that parcel of land." And so it was. It sounded great. Actually, we felt that we had triumphed, because now we had the funds to refurbish and modernize what would be our living quarters.

As a metaphysician, I know that there are no coincidences. I'm fully aware that the Universal Law of Cause and Effect or Karma morphs into the Law of Attraction. At that time, I didn't understand that my colorful imagination was actually predicting the outcome. I had painted such a vivid picture on the canvas of my mind that Universal Mind, (God,) was impelled to provide it. This was the first of many miraculous events which manifested in and blessed our lives.

Chapter III

THE REVELATION; DISCOVERING GOD

"Our outlook on life must be transformed
by the renewing of the mind."
Ernest Holmes.

IT TOOK 40 years of pseudo-existence before my life really began in 1965. That overworked proverb, *Life begins at 40*, actually does apply to me. I was one of the confused majority who proclaim a belief in God, but cannot really define who or what God is. The only God I knew of was the one who would punish me if I was a bad girl. I had never thought of praying for anything or anyone. My upbringing was more secular, even though I was born a Jew.

Before I turned 40, I was a hopeless neurotic; a negative, cynical hypochondriac; a self-opinionated, complaining nag with multiple disorders, all of which were psychosomatic; the offshoot of dreadful ingrained memories.

In March of 1964 we hired a contractor after closing on the old two-family house. We had sold our small one-family with the understanding that we would vacate by August. When August arrived, work on our house was at a standstill, because the contractor had absconded with our deposit, and subsequently filed for bankruptcy.

We were forced to vacate the one-family because the buyers had nowhere to go. Well, neither did we. Kind neighbors offered to take our daughter, Layne, our puppy, who was their dog's offspring, and me into their home, temporarily. Charlie and our son, Neal moved in with my sister's family. Incidentally, my sister Bernice is wed to Charlie's younger brother, Irving. (We are so blessed to be a part of the very special, loving Locker family.)

What was supposed to be a couple of weeks stretched into almost four stressful months until the new carpenters completed the renovation.

Charlie stood about five feet eight inches, slim and wiry. I couldn't call him handsome, though he was ruggedly good-looking. His brown eyes under thick, rusty brows were cushioned by soft pouches of flesh which terminated in faint upward creases at the outer corners. Those eyes twinkled with an impish wit which I found captivating. Beginning high on his smooth, ruddy forehead, his dark, tightly rippled hair stiffly framed a small, heart-shaped patch of scalp at the crown. The hilly nose deviated in many directions and eventually culminated in a downward slope. On either side of his broad nostrils, a deep furrow traveled down to greet the faint upturn of his pleasantly shaped lips. His lower jaw protruded slightly causing in dental terms, a malocclusion.

He was an extraordinary man, one of seven children, a product of a struggling childhood with an incomplete education due to family obligations. He was an extravert, always *on stage*, entertaining with his vast repertoire of jokes; a self-sufficient, capable dynamo.

In seventeen years of marriage, Charlie and I had never been separated. He was a mother hen, satisfied only when his brood was safely tucked under his protective wing and his possessive eye. The forced separation plus the myriad problems with the contractors heaped upon pressures and friction at his office began to affect him.

My meticulous demands for detail and relentless nagging and complaining were also stoking the furnace.

When we finally moved in, we had to knuckle down to create
some order out of the chaos. We tried to breathe some life into the
old place so we could call it home at last. Charlie was a capable, energetic man for whom no challenge was ever too great; a perfectionist
who took pride in his skills. He sallied forth with his usual enthusiasm, but soon the fuse on his patience began to fizzle. In one week
he had three encounters with water. The first one occurred while
installing a plywood sub-floor in the kitchen. A nail punctured a main
pipe and a new *Old Faithful* was born. Then after he located the cut-
off valve in the basement, the knob snapped off in his hand and the
floor flooded with enough water to float a boat. Shortly after that, the
washing machine on the floor above us overflowed. *Water, water,
everywhere....* Charlie began to dread picking up a hammer and lost all
confidence in himself and his ability. He insisted that the house was
jinxed and blamed me for every incident. I know now that he was
probably right because of my unreasonable demands and negativity.
Meanwhile, the pressures from his boss reached the boiling point and
he impulsively quit his position as staff manager with John Hancock
which he had proudly held for seven years.

This strong, indomitable personality; this fighter who had overcome many adversities, surmounting a childhood of indigence and
inadequate education; surviving the *big war* overseas; finally gave up.
He had been everybody's knight in shining armor, a champion who
intervened for others in trouble and need. This is the man who one
day retreated to our bed, buried himself under the covers and refused
to move. He could no longer make decisions and considered himself
a total failure.

Watching this dynamo reduced to tears of futility and frustration
was unbearable for me. He refused to see a psychiatrist. "Only weak,
insane people need psychiatrists." I felt helpless as he withdrew into

his own snug and undemanding cocoon. He was convinced that this wonderful house had turned against him as some evil, menacing force. Each night as he turned his back on me with recrimination in his heart, I cried myself to sleep, praying to God for the first time in my life from the depths of my soul to bring this man back to the living.

Soon after, he arose and inspected himself in the mirror. "What am I doing to myself?" he asked, startled at the strange, disheveled image squinting back at him through red-streaked, puffy eyes. "What have I been doing to you and the kids?" he sobbed uncontrollably. As I held him close with a prayer in my heart, I suggested that he at least see our family doctor who prescribed an antidepressant.

Due to Charlie's thirteen years of loyal service to the company, he was able to maneuver a transfer to another local office as a debit agent. He no longer desired the pressures and responsibilities of management which was not protected by the union. Gradually, his self-confidence and enthusiasm were restored and he realized that he had made the right decision.

After Charlie's miraculous recovery, I charged into the completion of the renovation with a fierce determination, helping to sand down all the blackened paneling and woodwork, puttying the holes and refinishing the surfaces. Something had changed. It was a strange, surreal sensation. I felt all-powerful, as though I could conquer any challenge which faced me. A warm, confident glow emanated from within me. A dazzling radiance seemed to follow me wherever I moved. (I now realize that I had unconsciously become aware of my aura.) Petty incidents ceased to annoy me. I smiled more and faced every challenge with calm endurance.

I had discovered that prayers can be answered and it was an enlightening and glorious revelation. There was, after all, a God; some invisible force which became a source of comfort and contentment. A secret door had been unlocked. An unprecedented series of events began to unfold in my life affecting everyone around me.

Chapter IV

AN ENLIGHTENING REVITALIZATION

"Faith is to believe what we do not see;
the reward of this faith is to see what we believe."
St. Augustine.

THE REALIZATION THAT prayers are answered, that there is a God, an invisible force which has the power to implement the solution, inspired me to experiment further. If I could ask for help for someone else and that was provided, why can't I do the same for myself? With my newfound enlightenment I had finally gained insight into my own shortcomings, so one day I naively asked God to help me become a positive thinker, not quite certain what that meant.

Shortly thereafter, Charlie and I attended services at our temple, and at the *Oneg Shabbat*, (fellowship with refreshments,) which followed, I overheard a woman mention the word *metaphysical* to the rabbi. It was an unfamiliar, new word, but something stirred within me. My curiosity was piqued, so I lingered around until she moved on, then I intercepted her. I introduced myself, explaining my ignorance about the word. "Oh," she said, "my husband is the expert on that. He's been into metaphysics for 40 years. Come, I'll introduce you."

This man who towered over me appeared to be in his seventies, and claimed to be a *Science of Mind* practitioner. As we conversed, I became so absorbed in his erudite discourse, it seemed that we had risen above the din of the crowded room, and we were alone in oblivion. I listened wide-eyed and tingly all over. This was the answer to my prayer; I felt it in every fiber of my being. He insisted that there was no need for anyone to be unhappy or to suffer in any way, as he related how *Science of Mind* had changed his life. "We are the cause of all of our problems," he asserted confidently.

Charlie interrupted to remind me that everyone was leaving, and I snapped back to earth reluctantly yielding to obligation. Dave hastily asked me what my problems were. I began to enumerate all of my ailments which obviously seemed endless to him, for he winced and smiled patiently. "Whoa! Let's take one at a time," he advised. "Which one do you want to be rid of first?" That wasn't a difficult choice. I had been suffering painful, ineffective urological treatments for a severe bladder infection for almost a year. I felt that I had no control over the intolerable symptoms. More than anything at that moment, I wished to be rid of it forever. He swiftly scribbled the *mental treatment* for me on a scrap of paper and assured me that he would promptly begin to send me healing. "You do your part, and I guarantee you'll be fine in short order," he promised as we parted. "Keep in touch with me as to your progress."

Two weeks later my bladder was healed and it remained so, because I learned how to treat the cause instead of the symptoms. By then I had bought the *Science of Mind* textbook and was meditating conscientiously every day. What puzzled me was my apparently sudden comprehension of philosophy which I had always avoided because it was too deep for me. Yet, I consumed every word in that illustrious volume with a hunger which hasn't been satiated to this day. I had been primed. I was a rosebud whose petals were opening to the radiant sun. It was as if I always knew those esoteric teachings; as if they were secretly submerged, patiently waiting for a catalyst to crystallize them and bring them forth.

My sinus passages were cleansed for the first time in years. The abdominal pains and digestive disturbances for which I was hospitalized every year for gastro-intestinal X-ray series, disappeared. Chronic tension headaches vanished as I learned to relax and meditate. Serenity and peace of mind had replaced the screaming and frustrations. Doctors, hospitals and pharmacists became strangers to me. I finally understood that all of these ailments were psychosomatic. When doctors had told me that it was my nerves that was what they meant. Two years after my introduction to metaphysics and meditation, my brother-in-law George, Charlie's older brother stopped by for a visit. He embraced me, kissed me and warmly declared, "I love you. You used to be a bitch on wheels!"

Chapter V

WE CAN CREATE MIRACLES!

"What we are today comes from our thoughts of yesterday, and our
present thoughts build our life of tomorrow.
Our life is the creation of our mind."
The Buddha.

I HAD EXPANDED my perspective; becoming aware that my
thoughts, ingrained belief systems and behavior were orchestrating
my reality. The Universal Law of Attraction was accommodating my
every desire, conscious or unconscious; negative or positive. I mar-
veled at the utter simplicity of it. In my meditation and throughout
the day I repeated specifically designed positive affirmations which I
called *Positive Mental Treatment*. The amazing result is a *Positive Mental
Attitude*. Any *treatment* culminates in a *demonstration*. The *treatment* is the
cause and the *demonstration* is the effect. Every thought we entertain is
a *treatment*; a prayer; whether it is negative or positive doesn't matter,
and a *demonstration* must follow. According to Ernest Holmes, this
method of affirming, as opposed to asking or pleading, is called
Scientific Prayer. When we state something as if it is already a fact in
our lives and we say *Thank You*, it becomes a reality sooner or later.
We must invest our total faith in the outcome, the *demonstration*, and

not allow doubt or impatience to cloud the issue. The following stories prove that miracles can occur with the proper incentive and attitude. (See Part III for more.)

The Beetle Dilemma Resolved

"Prayer is so mighty an instrument that no one has ever thoroughly
mastered all its keys. They sweep along the infinite scale of man's
wants and God's goodness."
H. Miller.

With the blessed expanse of our new back yard, I was free to plant all
of the vegetables I desired--tomatoes, peppers, cucumbers, zucchini,
peas, green beans, carrots, radishes, and so many more with which I
experimented. Everything was started from seed.

One morning I went out to assess the situation and water the
plants. I was horrified to find my green beans swarming with
Japanese beetles. Since I was determined to sustain as organic a garden as possible, I refrained from using pesticides. After the watering
was done, I went upstairs and spoke to God about it. *You know I
don't want to hurt those beetles. They need to eat, too. But, I
need to protect my green beans. Those beetles are leaving now
never to return. They are free to find another place to feed. I
bless them and send them on their way. Thank You.*

I repeated that *treatment* several times throughout the day. The
next morning when I checked out my garden, there wasn't a beetle in
sight. I thanked God for the *demonstration,* plucked the damaged beans
and threw them on my compost heap.

The Saga of Neal

Our son, Neal was being inducted into the army in June of 1969. His final high school exams were scheduled for June 12th and 13th. He was supposed to depart for Fort Dix on June 15th a few days prior to the formal high school graduation ceremonies. His diploma would be mailed to him.

Neal loved animals and his passion was to become a veterinarian, so the Veterinary Corps was his first choice. The recruiter for Neal's case, Sergeant H., phoned and informed us that Neal must leave on June 5th instead of the original date of the 15th. He said all the arrangements had been made for that date. I cried incredulously, "No, it can't be! He has to take his final exams. It must be a typographical error." Sergeant H. said he'd look into it further. By now I had learned not to leave anything to chance, so I proceeded to *treat* for the later date, even later than the 15th. My original *treatment* was: ***These words are for Neal Locker. He is leaving for Fort Dix on June 16th. This entire matter is in God's Hands. Thank You.*** (*Thank You* affirms that it is done as we have *treated*.) Two days later Sergeant H. called and told us that it had been an error and the date was the 15th but more likely the 16th. (Voila!)

<u>April 23, 1969</u>: Sergeant H. phoned again after all arrangements had been completed. Neal is due to leave on the 16th, but he had received word that the Veterinary school had been filled in the Baltimore and Washington area. There was no room for Neal. Of course that was unacceptable. This required a change of strategy. Charlie contacted our congressman's office and they promised to work on it. My *treatment* for the Veterinary school: ***There is a place for Neal in the Veterinary school and everything goes according to the original schedule. When the place is made available, no one will be hurt in any way. This entire matter is in God's Hands. Thank You.***

<u>May 9th and 10th</u>: *Demonstration:* We received positive notification from Washington and from most of those concerned with the case, that Neal is taking the place of one boy who really wanted the Food Handler's Corps. The boy was transferred there and Neal and he were both satisfied. (Voila, once again!)

I continued to *treat:* **Neal Locker is stationed in the First Army area for the duration of his military service because they <u>need</u> him here. This entire matter is in God's Hands. Thank You.** On October 2nd I had a vision of the map of the east coast and saw him stationed between New Jersey and Maryland. All I saw were those two states. *Demonstration:* On October 17th Neal phoned with the anxiously awaited news. Eight boys from his class were sent to Viet Nam. Only two were to remain as Walter Reed Army Medical Center personnel and all the rest were shipped to diverse parts of the world. He could scarcely contain himself; "Guess what! I'm staying here and my best friend with me!" The following week he called to tell us that he and his friend were shipping out to Fort Detrick, Maryland as WRAMC personnel. I said, "Remember, I had seen you stationed between New Jersey and Maryland? But I thought that meant Washington, D.C." He explained that Washington was not between the two, but that Maryland is north of Washington. This brought him 40 miles closer to our home in New Jersey. Fort Detrick was the army research center for the Veterinary Corps, the best place to be stationed for practical experience. This was another amazing *demonstration.*

Another *Miracle*

Originally, I began to teach my ten lesson course, *The New Life Concept,* in our home. On November 12th, 1976, I needed to find six more pamphlets entitled *From Here to Greater Happiness* for my class. I was going to send for them to California where they were published but thought that would take too long. Thumbing through the yellow pages of the telephone book, I called six book stores and only one said they could order them but it would take a week or two, so I decided to *treat*. Previously, I had read a book by James Mangan entitled, *The Secret of Perfect Living* in which I was introduced to the use of *Switch Words*. The concept is so simple, yet the results are so miraculous that I have adopted the most essential ones into my courses and into my life. *Treatment:* **We want to find six From Here to Greater Happiness pamphlets now. Reach-Together-Thank You.** *Reach-Together-Thank You* is the *Switch Word* (phrase,) to find or locate something. *We* and *Together* help to bring our conscious and subconscious levels of mind together to perform as one single unit. And we know that when we say *Thank You*, we are affirming that it is done as we have stated. *Demonstration:* I was ready to close the telephone book when I was inspired to turn one more page. My finger rested on the Ws; Walden Book store in a local mall. When I phoned, the clerk said she had the pamphlets. "Now," I asked eagerly, "how many do you have? I need six." She went to look for them and returned laughing. "It just happens I have only six in stock." (Triple voila!)

Faith Reaffirmed

"Trust in the Lord with all thine heart and lean not unto thine own understanding. In all thy ways acknowledge Him and
He shall direct thy paths."
Proverbs; 3:5-6; Bible.

We were planning to tour some of the states for about three weeks, but Charlie didn't want to use our car, so he placed an ad in the classified section of our local newspaper requesting a car which was to be delivered to California, our final destination. I began to *treat* immediately. The very day that the ad appeared an acquaintance of Charlie's, Lou B. called and said he has a 1970 Dodge sedan which he needed to be delivered to California by a prearranged date. The two men made a deal that we would pay for the fuel, but if any repairs were necessary, Lou would be responsible for the cost.

September 4, 1975: We eagerly departed for Minneapolis to visit Charlie's aunt and uncle. From there we stopped to view many of the incredible sights. I resolutely continued to *treat* to insure us a safe and pleasant journey. On our way to the Grand Canyon in Arizona on September 15th, we drove through Navajo country and the Painted Desert. After having traveled a sizable stretch of the desert, we finally encountered a service station where we gassed up. Charlie was concerned that the rear of the car seemed lower than usual, so he asked the attendant to check the air in the tires. The young man, who was also a mechanic, informed us that we didn't need air, but the inside of the right rear wheel was wet with oil or brake fluid. Upon further examination he determined that the rear right axle seal had rotted through and it was leaking transmission fluid.

There we were in the middle of the desert in need of a rear right axle seal and shock absorbers with the discouraging news that it would take three to five days to get the parts. Furthermore, the mechanic warned us that if we continued with the car in that condition there was danger that the fluid would ignite and catch fire, or at the very least, the wheel could lock and we would be stranded somewhere in the open desert. Charlie and I gaped pop-eyed at each other, knowing full well that we couldn't spare five days because we had a deadline to deliver the car. We decided to continue despite the mechanic's foreboding predictions. "Look honey," I reminded him, "God has been with us throughout this entire trip and there's no reason that He won't sustain us for the remainder of it. If we have enough faith we should be assured that we'll make it to the Canyon and to the motel in Williams with no problems." As we drove off, the young man stood there squinting and eyeing us dubiously, scratching his tousled, tawny-haired head with one greasy hand and mopping his sweaty brow with the other.

Not only did we get through the desert, but we totaled over 100 hilly miles viewing the magnificent Grand Canyon. We finally reached the Ponderosa Motel in Williams, Arizona with no more inconvenience than merely reducing our speed. Naturally, I *treated* all the way encircling the car with a psychic *Shield of Protection*. (See Part III, Chapter XL, *The Truth about Accidents*.)

But, the wonder of God's hand in our destiny had yet to become manifest. There just happened to be a service station at the foot of the entrance to the motel which stood above us on a hill. As we drove up the winding driveway to check in, Charlie avowed that he'd have the car checked as soon as we unloaded our luggage.

The attendant informed him that the mechanic had gone home for dinner and might not return for the rest of the evening. I urged Charlie to call the mechanic's home and being the great persuader that he was, he convinced the man to return after dinner. While examining the car, the mechanic discovered that the transmission was out of fluid and he was amazed that it had held up all day without damaging the gears. He further confirmed that we did, indeed, need a rear right axle seal and new shocks. He drawled incredulously, "How fur'd you say you come in this condition?" Charlie repeated the story. "Whew! You shore must live right, Mister. Not only ain't that possible, but jest last week, some dude come in here with a busted left rear axle seal, an' ah hadda order up a whole new set of shocks." The young man waggled his sweaty head in utter disbelief. "Why, with that brake linin' soaked like that, it's a wonder you got as fur as this 'thout burnin' up!"

All the necessary repairs were completed within two hours and we were on our way towards Hoover Dam, murmuring words of gratitude for God's *demonstration*.

We traveled across another glaring, arid stretch of Arizona desert and arrived at Hoover Dam at 1:30 PM. We emerged from the air-cooled car into a dragon's fiery breath. The temperature was a scorching 110 degrees Fahrenheit. After hastily touring the area including Lake Mead, we retreated into the cool haven of the car. As we trundled up the steep hill from the dam, the front end of the car began to spout steam. There wasn't a service station in sight. Charlie parked and gingerly removed the radiator cap to relieve the pressure. He hiked over to a luncheonette for some water for the radiator and the problem was temporarily eased. Meanwhile, the hill ominously loomed ahead of us. Undaunted, I silently encircled the car with the *Shield of Protection* and affirmed: ***Whatever is causing this mishap is temporary; and swiftly and positively dealt with, for we and this car are in God's Hands. Thank You.*** As we reached the crest of the hill, we were delighted to behold a blessed service station, because *Old Faithful* radiator was doing its thing again. The diagnosis was a leak in the radiator hose. The mechanic explained that they didn't usually stock those hoses because of the huge variety of sizes for every car, but he offered to check, anyway. A look of blank astonishment was evident on his grease-smudged face as he ambled towards us with the new hose dangling from his grimy hand!

The Elevator Miracle

Charlie and I vacationed in Mexico in the late 1970s. We were on the beach in Acapulco one afternoon when I needed to use the restroom. Our room was on the fourth floor of the hotel. I didn't want to use the public facility, so I entered the elevator and pressed the number four button. The doors closed and I waited. Nothing happened, so I pressed it again and waited. Then, I pressed the door open button. Still, nothing happened. After trying the fourth floor and door open buttons again with no results, I pressed the alarm button and waited. I tried it again and again but nobody responded. Finally, I calmly took a deep breath, closed my eyes, leaned against the wall with arms spread out in submission and said aloud, "Okay, God, do your stuff." Six syllables. When I opened my eyes, we had somehow miraculously risen to the ninth floor, ten floors above the beach level, with absolutely no vibration. I said, "Thank You, God," as the doors opened and I exited the elevator. A man was washing windows and I asked him if he heard the alarm bell. He shrugged and responded, "No comprendo." The other elevator was awaiting me. I entered it and finally arrived at the fourth floor, again thanking God for a strong bladder.

The Universe Knows All

At age 62, Charlie decided to take an early retirement from John Hancock. A friend offered him a part-time job as a travel agent and we enjoyed many fascinating trips as a result. He had always claimed that while Mama Locker was still with us, we would remain in New Jersey. It was the warm Florida climate that intrigued him, but I had lived in Miami as a teenager and swore I'd never return, so we checked out California. Our friends Alma and Seymour had moved to Century Village, Deerfield Beach, Florida, and we also spent some time with them. The lifestyle offered us a mosaic of amusement and diversity, and that was the deciding factor.

I began to *treat* for a condominium apartment comparable to our friends' on the second or third floor in the same building which was a short walk to the clubhouse. In 1984, before we were ready to relocate, Alma notified us that one was available on her floor, the second floor. We flew down to view it, bought it and furnished it for rental. A year later we moved down in August, earlier than we had anticipated because we were told that the building bylaws prohibited rentals. That was an erroneous judgment by one of the board members who neglected to read the bylaws. As usual, the Universe knew more than we did at that time. Charlie only enjoyed two good years in Florida before he became paralyzed in 1987 from brain tumor surgery and passed on in 1989. If we hadn't been compelled to move when we did, he wouldn't have had that time to indulge in his tropical Paradise.

Ask and It Is Given

In 1993, I was enjoying my regular walks on our catwalk, because I wanted to avoid the harmful tropical sun, when I began to experience pain, predominantly in my right heel. It also occurred sometimes during the night and when I arose from bed. Since I was unable to continue with my walking, I enrolled in a Tai Chi class. However, I was able to walk and dance in high heels comfortably. A podiatrist took X-rays and reported heel spurs. I refused cortisone shots as always. After listening to the other unacceptable options, one of which was surgery as a last resort, I told him I'd deal with it my way.

Of course, I *treated* for healing and also spoke to God about another option, a natural one. The following week, a strange thing occurred. I received a surprise phone call from an acquaintance who I hardly ever see. It seemed that we hadn't seen each other for ages. When she asked me how I was, I replied, "Wonderful!" as I always do. In conversation, she casually mentioned her heel spurs and how she's curing them with a natural remedy her chiropractor recommended. It was called Acid-a-Cal distributed by Enzymatic Therapy. My body prickled sensibly when I heard that. Eureka! The answer to another prayer!

I found it at a local health-food store and followed the directions on the bottle. About a year later, I returned to the podiatrist for X-rays again, because the pain had vanished. (During that time I was also visualizing Pac-Man gobbling up those unwelcome spurs.) The X-rays revealed much smaller formations. When I told the doctor what I had done, he exclaimed, "Boy! If you've found a natural remedy to dissolve heel spurs that would really be something!"

I was able to discontinue Tai Chi classes and resume with my daily walks.

Divine Intervention Again

Before we relocated to Florida, I never carried a shoulder handbag, but it seemed to be the rage down here, so I adapted. However, I foolishly suspended it from my shoulder with nothing supporting it. Women are notorious for cramming more than is necessary into their handbags, and I was no exception. In 1996 I began to experience extreme pain in my left upper arm and shoulder. Raising my arm or lifting anything proved to be an arduous and distressful task. A doctor diagnosed it as bursitis and tendonitis. I refused the offer of cortisone shots, as usual, and proceeded to *treat* for healing, stubbornly continuing with my exercises. When we lived up north my right arm was similarly affected, but I was able to heal it myself, (with God's help, of course.) But, this time I was only able to achieve temporary relief.

One morning, while exercising in my den, I told God that I needed help to heal my arm. "What do you suggest?" I asked. The response was instantaneous. The word acupuncture flashed in my consciousness. "Acupuncture," I thought, "I remember recently reading an article by a local acupuncturist." I hastened to find the magazine, located the article and phoned the doctor. While we

were conversing, he described a form of non-invasive acupuncture administered without needles. It entailed the use of
electro-stimulation on the pressure points of the ears. He
called it auriculotherapy. He explained that there are hundreds of
these points which are directly associated with the meridians in the
body, which in turn are connected to various organs and other vital
parts. That sounded like it was the answer to my query, because the
idea of needles didn't appeal to me.

With the first treatment of auriculotherapy, the relief was
miraculous. I knew that God had again shown me the way. I continued for four months when healing was completed.

The Mystery Is Solved

Since 1995 I have been receiving Chelation Therapy which, in addi-
tion to flushing out heavy metallic deposits from the body, is also
purported to cleanse the excess calcium from the arteries. I thought it
would be helpful to protect my heart because my maternal family
history is heart disease. I'll adopt into my life any alternative to traditional medicine which I deem is sensible and may be viable. One
afternoon in 2004, I prevailed upon Sid, my present love, to drive me
to the clinic so we could have dinner later at a favorite restaurant.
That proved to be a fortuitous plan. While I was sitting with the
intravenous needle in my arm, I began to feel queasy and lightheaded.
This had never occurred before. I asked for help, and as the attendant helped me up, I collapsed on the floor. They revived me, and I
said, "I'm going to throw up!" The doctor practically carried me into
the rest room. It was so embarrassing because he stood there supporting me while I heaved. It took awhile before I was able to leave,
equipped with a large double plastic bag which was a blessing in the
car. If I had driven to the clinic in my car, they would have called an

ambulance to take me to the hospital and my car would have been deserted.

When we arrived at my apartment, I continued to be sick and faint. Finally, at 8:00PM, Sid phoned my doctor who told him, "If Norma is calling me for help at this hour, she must really need me. I'll meet you at the hospital shortly." He kept his promise. When we arrived at the hospital and checked in, I needed to use the rest room. As we were headed in that direction, I collapsed again on the tile floor and injured my knee. That's what spurred everyone to action. The attendants quickly scooped me up into a wheelchair and hustled me upstairs into a bed.

I spent eighteen agonizing hours in that hospital bed with intravenous to curb the nausea and re-hydrate me. Why were they agonizing? Because, I hadn't been hospitalized for 38 years! My proudly sustained record was blemished. While I was there I rummaged in my brain for the source of this sudden affliction. Since I'm no longer used to being sick, I spoke to God about it. "What could have caused it?" I asked.

The following morning as I poured the milk into my breakfast cereal, it curdled in the bowl. I smelled it and it was sour. A bulb flashed in my brain. For some reason the previous morning my sense of smell and taste had taken a holiday. The milk was sour and I didn't perceive it. A gastro-intestinal specialist explained that my symptoms could have been precipitated by any number of things. When I asked him if sour milk could have been the culprit, he agreed that sour milk contains harmful bacteria which could definitely cause food-poisoning.

Again, I thanked God for yet another miracle; for restoring my sense of smell in order to solve the mystery. Since then, I've been using soy milk and dating it. This was another lesson in mindfulness which will serve me for the rest of my life.

The weakness continued sporadically for a few weeks, but I'm a Taurus, and because of my bull-headedness, I refused to submit to illness. I stubbornly marched around the apartment daily, loudly proclaiming, *I am stronger than any negativity. I am in complete control and command of my mind and body. With God's help I am healed now! Thank You.*

Chapter VI

ATTRACTING THE RIGHT PERSON

"If we desire something with every fiber of our being, it must
ultimately evolve into our lives; but we must choose carefully."
Norma Locker.

I HAD BEEN in a relationship with Nat S. for six years before he
passed on from a massive stroke. He came into my life ten months
after Charlie's passing. Throughout those six years I continued to *treat*
for the right man. Nat and I had a fairly compatible relationship, but
we weren't in love with one another. We cared for each other in different ways. It was more of a symbiotic affair. I felt that he fulfilled a
need in my life at that time, but I knew that God would send the
right man into my life at the right time for both of us. Part of what I
specified in my *treatment* was that he, like Nat, lives in our village, that
he is tall like Nat and would also be satisfied to be separately domiciled. After Charlie passed on, I was happy to have my solitude in
order to fulfill my aspirations. We don't know when our time is up
and I was 64 by then with a bagful of goals to achieve; some of which
were working toward my Doctorate and writing this book.

I refused to date, because every time a man was attracted to me he enrolled in my class and then expected me to be a conquest. I sadly had to reject two men in the past and I swore I'd never hurt anyone's feelings again, if I could possibly help it. If instant physical chemistry was lacking, I couldn't be interested. After Nat's demise, I was alone for three years continuing to maintain faithfully that the right man is here in the village and it will seem that God has just dropped him into my life. That was what apparently and miraculously happened.

It was class registration time in the clubhouse ballroom, October 1, 1998. I was floating, distributing my class flyers when I spotted a tall, lone figure of a man in a tee shirt and shorts standing on the opposite end of the room. He appeared to be quite bewildered, unsure of the procedure. I'm nearsighted and we were separated by fifty yards or more. A current of excitement sent shivers through me. I asked God, "Is this the man?" As I approached him I thought, "God, he's a gorgeous hunk!" I greeted him and handed him my flyer. "Have you ever registered for classes before?" He replied, "This is my first time." "This is the class that I teach here," I said, and I thought, "I wonder if he can hear my heart thumping." He scanned the flyer and asked, "Are you Dr. Locker?" I said, "Yes, but you can call me Norma." "I can use a class like this. I lost my wife a year ago and support groups depress me more," he said, offering his hand. "I don't shake hands, I hug. May I?" I asked, hopefully. "I can sure use one," he said. We hugged. It was electric. I knew at that moment that this is the guy for whom I've prayed and anticipated. I was so flustered, I neglected to ask his name. As I departed after I registered for my sculpture class, I saw him conversing with a blonde woman at a table across the room. I brazenly thought, "You can't have him, lady. He's mine!"

A week later I stopped at the class office to check on my registration and I asked the class director if he enrolled. I described him and she immediately recognized who he was. She told me his name was Sid S. and remarked, "Oh, I'm introducing him to my friend. She's looking for a man." I boldly blurted, "No you don't. He's mine!" The following Wednesday I went to the clubhouse to pick up my season show tickets and there he was chatting with a security guard. I said, "Hi! Are you getting show tickets?" He nodded. I sat down after retrieving my number and he came over to sit next to me. We chatted for a bit; then I asked him if he wanted to discuss what happened to his wife. He told me that after 54 years of marriage, she suddenly dropped dead of a heart attack. Because she had refused to see doctors even though she was ailing and apparently suffering cardiac incidents in silence, he went ballistic. He wept openly while relating his tragic tale and I moved in closer to him, placing my hand upon his shoulder. I so wanted to hold him and comfort him. I told him that my friend and I have tickets for that night's show. He said he was getting one and he'd look for me, which he did. After the show, we walked out together and he offered to drive us home. Since I live just down the hill from the clubhouse, I asked if he could drive my friend home. That night I dreamt about him and obsessed about him throughout the following days. After that, when I spotted him in the clubhouse lobby, I followed him and sat beside him. We were getting acquainted.

At the opening session of my course, he entered my classroom and teased, "Do I get double hugs today?" I wondered how he knew that I hug everyone in my class. I knew then that he was a rascal and it warmed my heart. His acceptance of the material in my course was reserved. When I conducted the healing session, he chose to abstain and asked for a hug instead. Much later, I discovered that he is an atheist, or at the least, an agnostic. My philosophy teaches that people are drawn to one another for a reason, so I was able to accept his credo, whatever it was.

After each show we stopped at Denny's for a snack. This was totally opposed to my healthy lifestyle, but I savored every moment with him. We'd come back to my apartment sometimes and smooch. He took me to dinner frequently. We were becoming a couple. He'd look into my eyes and tenderly utter phrases like, "You gladden my heart."

I'm a one man woman and I stressed my desire for commitment. Though he seemed reluctant at first, his feelings for me were obvious. One night when I was changing my clothes after a movie, Charlie was there impressing me with *Fly Me to the Moon*, his favorite song. That's how I recognize his energy. The message was, "I like this guy. Whatever you do, it's okay with me." Charlie probably perceived that Sid would be more financially benevolent than he was. He was right. A limitation consciousness was his major hang-up. Due to his indigent youth, the fear of falling prey to poverty governed and influenced his behavior and emotions. Yet, he was a successful provider. Prior to that, I had no inkling that Sid and I would make love that night. Afterwards, he said, "So much for no commitment." The following morning he phoned at 8:30. I was still asleep. "How about breakfast?" he asked. "I'm still in bed and I don't eat breakfast out. Thanks anyway," I mumbled drowsily. Then he mentioned the previous night and how wonderful it was and he muttered some endearing words. I boldly asked, "Are we in love?" He replied, "I think so."

We have recently celebrated our thirteenth year as a separately domiciled, but loving couple. I recommend it. Every night is like a date, romantic and intimate. We anticipate our evening trysts. He's so good to me; so generous and affectionate. He says he's lucky, but I insist that I'm blessed—don't believe in luck. It's all Karma. He doubts and questions life after death, but I share my incredible experiences with him so when it's his time to go, he'll be prepared and summarily surprised.

So, if you desire to enter into a relationship, it's as simple as knowing that the *right person is in your life now*. Assemble your thoughts; summarize, visualize and rehearse every detail, every quality of this very special individual in your mind. What do you require from this person? If you are harboring an ingrained negative attitude about relationships because of past experience, that is the first thing that must change.

The *treatment: I know that the right man/woman is here in my life now. I deserve all of the good which flows into my life. I deserve to have a man/woman in my life who loves and respects me for who and what I am. I deserve to love and be loved unconditionally. The right man/woman is in my life now. Thank You.*

It's not necessary to go out *hunting* for that person. The Universe gladly provides him/her as long as you believe implicitly. Repeat that *treatment* every day as often as you can, even to other people. My response when someone wanted to fix me up with a friend: *Thanks. But I know that God is dropping the right man into my life at the right time.* Know in your heart and soul that it is done as you have affirmed.

One of my students once asked me, "I thought I married the right man, but after ten years we were divorced. How do you explain that?" "At that time in both of your lives you needed to be together and for that period of time," I said. "If you desire to enter into another relationship, there's another right man waiting for you." It's past life stuff. They either expiated their Karmic debts to one another, or they augmented them through certain ill-advised behaviors toward one another. Every experience provides us with the opportunity to learn and grow spiritually. (More about Karma in Chapter XXXV.)

Chapter VII

LOVE THOUGHTS MAKE IT HAPPEN

"Love and forgiveness work hand-in-hand. We must first resolve to
love and forgive ourselves before we can love
and forgive others; then miracles occur."

Norma Locker.

The Hot Water Boiler

CONDOMINIUM LIVING IS a major change from a private
home, even if it's from a two family house. For me, it would have
been extremely stressful if not for my daily meditative practice which
helps me to accept change with equanimity. It was quite an adjustment to be relegated from eight massive rooms with seven closets,
and a spacious attic and basement to the confinement of six smaller
rooms with two closets. It's similar to apartment dwelling, whereas
you might have a resident above and below you and on either side.

In the spring of 1994 our maintenance service company offered
the owners in our building a special rate to install new hot water boil-
ers in each unit. Since at that time, they were almost fifteen years old,
there had been many which had sprung leaks and wreaked severe

damage to the owner's apartments and those below them. I opted to have one installed, but the man in the unit above me declined for reasons of his own. I felt that was unacceptable, so I decided to implement a *Love Treatment* for him: **I love, respect, forgive, and bless myself and (the man's name) and I give him over to God for Divine Guidance. Thank You.** That was all that was necessary. I continued this every day for two weeks, the length of time it took to complete everyone's installation. One morning I stepped downstairs to mail a letter and I noticed a pickup truck was parked in front of our building. A lone carton was sitting on it with the man's name and apartment number boldly printed across it. I thanked God for the *demonstration*. The next day I met my neighbor by the elevator and thanked him also. When I asked him what made him change his mind, he shrugged and replied, "I don't know." (But, *I* knew!)

The Loan

I've experienced many such *Love Treatment demonstrations*. Another prominent one unfolded when I was explaining them to my class, *From Negative to Positive with Mind Power* in our clubhouse. A timid woman approached me during recess and related her dilemma; "I loaned someone a lot of money many years ago and since then I haven't heard a word from him. What can I do?" I pointed to the *Love Treatment* chart on the wall and suggested she repeat that affirmation every day. Two weeks later she again approached me and said, "You'll never believe what happened. A couple of days ago I received a check in the mail for the full amount of the loan!" I asked her if she had had any verbal contact with the borrower and she said, "No, not for years." "Were you repeating the *Love Treatment*?" I asked. "Oh, yes; every day without fail." "Do you think this resulted from the *Love Treatment?*" She replied, "What else could it have been after all this time? It's a miracle!"

Healing Feelings

In 1967 my Aunt Tillie, my mother's younger sister was evicted from her apartment because the building was being demolished. Since she had nowhere to live, Mom took her in temporarily until another one became available. Aunt Tillie, bless her, was quite neurotic due to a life of hardship and degradation by her mother, my maternal grandmother. When she was in her thirties my grandfather arranged a marriage for her. It survived for a mere few months when it was annulled because of incompatibility. Aunt Tillie worked very hard to support herself after her parents' passing. Throughout her life she had very few friends.

After suffering her sister's constant complaints and harassment, Mom was on the verge of an emotional breakdown. So, Bernice and I thought we'd better find Aunt Tillie an apartment. We moved her out of Mom's place and set her up in her own within a couple of weeks. That was the impetus which prompted her to stop speaking to either of us for eight years! When I phoned her to ask how she was doing, she vehemently blurted, "Don't ever call me again! I don't ever want to speak to you!"

By then I was fully aware why I was suffering from the pain of arthritis. I had been harboring noxious resentment against people whom I felt had done me wrong. An emotional detoxification was essential to promote a physical cleansing. I began to repeat the *Love Treatment* for myself and each of them every day in my meditation. I even included Aunt Tillie's name, though I felt no animosity towards her. It was her resentment towards me that needed to be purged and mellowed.

Not long after that, we received an invitation to a family wedding. The phone rang and it was Aunt Tillie inquiring, as if eight years of silence hadn't elapsed, "Hello, Norma? Are you going to the wedding?" I confess I was momentarily startled, but I replied, "Yes, we are." "Can I have a ride?" she asked sheepishly. In those eight years there had been several family affairs with no request for transportation.

My bonus: the arthritic pain and impairment vanished after a few weeks of *Love Treatments*. Why do the *Love Treatments* work so miraculously? When we say those words, whether or not we believe or feel them doesn't matter. We are letting go; releasing our negative thought patterns and resentment. As soon as we do that, the Universe is free to respond and provide a *demonstration*.

When I was involved with Nat, an older man in our clay class who had suffered a stroke at one time was attracted to me and persisted with his attentions. He even presented me with what he thought was a likeness of me. It was more of a caricature due his trembling hands. I resisted his pleas for a date because I was in a relationship, but Nat felt sorry for him. "Give the guy a break," he said, "let him take you out once." So I relented. Riding in his car was an adventure so I continued to invoke the *Shield of Protection*. One date wasn't enough for Herman. He persisted in begging me for more. That wasn't all; he wanted me to go to bed with him. I reluctantly consented to join him for dinner with his brother and wife to celebrate his birthday. As I mulled over that decision, I knew it was an unacceptable one; so I spoke to God about it. ***You know I don't want to hurt Herman's feelings by rejecting him, but I really don't want to do this. I'm giving him over to You with love and blessings to resolve this matter. Thank You.*** The very next day I received a message on my answering machine from Herman. "I'm sorry to disappoint you, but my brother has other plans for my birthday." The next time I saw Herman a few of us from the clay class visited him in a nursing home where he was pursuing the women there.

Chapter VIII

THE MANY FACES OF PERCEPTION

"Everything is natural, because it springs
from the Almighty Creative Mind of the Universe."
Norma Locker.

WE ARE ALL born with the faculty to mentally receive unsolicited information. For some people it can become a frequent occurrence and welcomed as a Divine gift. Others may choose to ignore those inborn intuitive feelings, hunches, flashes of insight, as nonsense, coincidence, or their religious persuasion precludes them from acknowledging them.

I call any spontaneous spark of information an impression because the source is not always recognized. It might emanate from one's Higher Self or a spirit guide; from the soul, the source of all knowledge, or from a familiar spirit. I try to be mindfully conscious of the message when it arises, though I admit at times I am remiss.

Extra-sensory perception, (ESP,) is an inaccurate term. Extended-sense perception is much more fitting. It isn't another sense, such as a sixth sense. It's a heightened awareness; an extension and expansion of our five senses.

For example: Clairvoyance is the innate ability to see without the use of the physical eyes. The sense of smell and taste are associated with clairsentience. When you feel as if you're being touched, or you have an uncomfortable sensation which has no apparent foundation, that's also clairsentience. When I was 18 in 1943 as I walked to and from work I consistently smelled flesh burning and couldn't identify the source. When I heard about the holocaust atrocities it didn't occur to me at that time that I was experiencing clairsentience. Clairaudience is hearing voices or other sounds without the use of your physical ears, though it may seem so at times. The ability to discern the difference can be developed with attention and practice.

If you have a strong feeling, hunch, about something, try not to ignore it. Act upon it, because it is your intuition and perhaps even your spirit guides either warning you to avoid an act or inspiring you to go for it.

The fact that I'm sharing my personal experiences with you might make me appear egotistical. I'm merely stressing that you, too, can be privy to similar perceptive adventures. Perhaps you already have been host to psychic impressions, but you didn't appreciate the significance at the time. The secret to detection is mindfulness, so open the gates of your senses. Don't do what I did. I'm guilty of neglecting these God-given gifts during the past several years. I became involved with organizing and teaching my classes and pursuing alternative avenues of creativity such as sculpture, writing poetry and moderating a poetry group, and writing articles for our newspaper. Sure, those occasional blips thankfully intrude during my meditation and my daily routine, but I'm no longer intentionally seeking them. I continue to tell myself that I should make the time to concentrate and tune in on people and situations, but I am preoccupied with other matters. I learned long ago that if we don't use it we lose it, and that cliché applies to many other facets of our lives.

If you are seriously interested in developing and expanding these abilities, you can do it; you can create a bridge to your intuition. When you receive unsolicited information, record it in a journal with dates, as I did. Even if it comes in a dream and you intuitively feel it may have some import, don't ignore it. Record it in your journal, and when it becomes a hit, record that, too. If not, just enter no. Maximize your ability by meditating every day for a few moments specifically honing in on friends or relatives. Record what you get, or try your hand at automatic writing as detailed in Chapter I. You might even amass enough material to eventually write a book.

If you receive a warning that some harm will beset someone, process it carefully before you disclose it. That kind of insight should be dealt with tactfully. Mentally encircle the subject with a psychic *Shield of Protection*; (see Lesson IX in How to Conduct a Psychic Development Class which follows;) then mitigate the message by asking if what she is planning is carved in stone, or might she change her mind. An example is the case of Bert's accident. (See "Bert's Story," Chapter XXXIII.) She was warned by a psychic friend to cancel the gem-hunting trip to Virginia because she envisioned an accident. What might have precipitated that tragedy was her belief in, and fear of the potential outcome, plus the informant's confidence in her own premonition. Our thoughts are a powerful source of energy, and the Law of Attraction is immutable unless we cancel and negate the probability, and invoke the *Shield of Protection.*

Telepathy is the most common form of mental communication between two or more entities, and it occurs most frequently between emotionally connected people. (I say entities, because animals, insects and plants are also subject to mental telepathy.)

One January day in 1969, Charlie arrived home at 11:45 expecting lunch. I told him it was much too early and the subject was dropped. About a half hour later he said, "Guess what! I just had an idea." I continued with my laundry folding and casually replied, "You want to take me to Syl's for lunch." "That was exactly what I was going to say, so help me God!" he gasped. "Boy! I'm afraid to think anything anymore!" When I needed to contact him about something important, I would transmit a telepathic message to him to phone me. It was successful about 50% of the time. Obviously, this was before the advent of cell phones.

Chapter IX

HOW TO CONDUCT A PSYCHIC DEVELOPMENT CLASS

IF YOU HAVE experienced perceptive episodes throughout your life and you feel that you may be qualified to teach a Psychic Development Class, following are some suggestions. Decide whatever fee you wish to charge and use a room with a table in your own home as a classroom. After you have registered a viable group of people, introduce them to each other so names are remembered. They must be prepared with notebooks and pens. Caution them against sharing personal information with one another. If you prefer not to organize a class, just two people can test each other with some of the suggested tests.

Lesson I. Sensitivity Tests.

(Scoring: A=Excellent; B=Very good; C=Good; D=Fair; P=Poor.)

(Precise records must be kept for each participant. Prepare one code list for each person as in #6.)

1.) Have objects ready for testing. Before you present the objects, each person is tested individually, blindfolded and out of sight of the other participants. (Some suggestions for the touch and feel test:) Fruit of different sizes and textures; veggies, coins; fabrics such as velour, terry cloth, satin, denim, wool, felt, chiffon. A feather, tools, utensils, sand paper, comb, hair brush. For the smell test: Herbs, spices, vinegar, mustard, flowers, etc. (Do not reveal any of the objects before testing.) (Score.)

2.) Blindfold half the class and have each one identify a pre-selected student through finger-touch, by gently feeling the face, hair, hands, etc. as a blind person would. Then let the other half do the same thing. (Score.)

3.) Ask the group to carefully observe every aspect of the room, then have each person move around the room blindfolded. Stay close by to avoid mishaps. (Only those who wish to participate.) (Score.)

4.) Ask who is better at receiving than sending. Who is better at sending or projecting? Who is better at imagery or visualization? (If they're not sure, it's okay.)

5.) Observe each person's emotional response to the proceedings. Make a note of each one's forte, etc.

**Medical researchers with the Toronto Society for Psychical Research discovered that while a sender, (projector,) and receiver, (percipient,) were monitored via Electro-encephalograph, (EEG,) each of them showed brain responses—energy.

6.) Each person is given the following code list for homework. The numbers and letters are what the sender projects at pre-selected times, but in a different order, of course. (4) Blow your nose. (5) Drink a glass of water. (6) Draw a snake. (7) Write your name,

address and birthday. (8) Sneeze or cough. (S) SOS. (A) Write me a
note. Don't mail it; bring it to class. (Z) Look out the window. (O)
Scratch your head. (W) Hands on hips.

Precise records must be kept by both participants in order to compare at class, even if nothing has been sent or received.

7.) Assign homework partners according to each one's talents;
(sending or receiving.) (**Note: This is not really essential. It only
pertains to those who have had prior psychic experience.) Each pair
sets a specific time which is best for them to meditate. The sender
projects the number or letter at that time for at least five minutes,
while the percipient is opening his or her mind to receive and records
it with day and time received. (If it doesn't come at the time designated, it may suddenly pop in later on. It is also possible to receive
the message before it is sent. That is precognition.) Verbal communication during the week is restricted. Notes are compared at the next
session.

Lesson II

(Before anyone arrives, prepare divining rods for each person by
reshaping wire hangers. Hide one object per person. Make a list of
the objects and where you hid them. Also have color cards ready.
Colors: Glue circles in RED, YELLOW, BRIGHT BLUE AND
GREEN to black or white oak tag cards. Five cards of each color; 25
cards. Be certain that when the cards are inverted, the color doesn't
show through.)

1.) Conduct a *Progressive Relaxation* session. With their eyes closed they
take three slow, deep breaths and you say, **_Relax, relax, relax._**
Traveling through the body beginning with the feet and ending with
the hands, suggest that every muscle and nerve is relaxed. When their

eyes are open partners share their experiences with the homework. Record everything and score.

2.) Blindfold half the class and have each person identify another through finger-touch as in Lesson I. (Score.)

3.) Color Card Test: Five chances for each person. The more these tests are repeated, the better the *psi* ability is enhanced. (Score.)

4.) Distribute *divining rods*. Explain the *Switch Word phrase, Reach-To-gether-Thank You*. They say these words mentally and repeat them as often as necessary: **We want to find (name the article,) Reach-Together-Thank You**. Each person holds the hanger, (*divining rod,*) with the point facing up or down. Inform each one what he or she is seeking. Record that. The *divining rod* will move toward the designated article. They should just relax and follow. When the item is located, they retrieve it and return it to the teacher. (Record the hits and misses.)

5.) Homework: They bring in an object which is not theirs for the next session for *Psychometrizing*. It can be metallic which is preferable, or any item which bears the vibrations of someone with whom they are familiar. It can be a photo of someone about whose life they know, also.

Clairsentient test: Pair off compatible people. The *sender* transmits for five minutes at a specified time to the *percipient*, (receiver.) There is one test for every day of the week. Only the sender knows what is being transmitted. *Sensations:* (a.) Hold a hot cup of something. Feel the heat and send it mentally. (b.) Hold an ice cold glass of water and send. (c.) Pinch the top of your hand until it hurts. Send. (d.) Scratch your scalp. Send. (e.) Hold a heavy object in your hand or hands. Send. (f.) File your nails with an emery board. Send. (g.) Light a match and burn a piece of paper over a sink. Send.

Instructions for the receiver, (*percipient*): Keep records of what you receive, day and time. NO verbal communication during the week. Tell yourself: *"I am now receiving what is being transmitted to me."*

Lesson III

(Teacher, prepare a photo of someone known to you; also an object to be psychometrized. Remember to score each student.)

1.) Conduct the *Progressive Relaxation* exercise. Then, partners share their *clairsentient* experiences from the homework. (Score.)

2.) Pair off partners for *psychometry* readings. The reader holds the object in his/her hand. Each couple should be seated separately from the others for privacy. No personal information; just yes or no. Everything is recorded by both parties.

3.) Partners *psychometrize* each other through touch, hand-holding, holding the head, etc. to receive impressions. As in #2 couples should be seated separately. (Score #2 and #3.)

4.) Teacher, concentrate and project to the class a person known to you, but not known to the class. Write down the name clearly and invert the notation. Do the same with a photo of that person. (Score the hits and misses.) Go into another room and hold your selected object. Transmit it to the class. (Score.)

5.) Homework: Pair off partners for *telepathic* work. *Senders* are now *percipients*. When they have agreed on the time of day the sender is to project TASTE. This is another *clairsentient* test. One test for each day of the week. Send for one or two minutes each time. (1.) Taste salt. (2.) Taste lemon. (3.) Taste bitter coffee. (4.) Taste spicy salsa or cayenne pepper. (5.) Taste sugar or honey. (6.) Taste salt. (7.) Taste lemon or vinegar.

Lesson IV

(Have sandpaper, velvet, toothbrush or hairbrush, and sticky tape ready for projection. Keep them hidden. Also, prepare a photo of a missing person.)

1.) Conduct the *Progressive Relaxation* exercise. Have the class visualize a *Shield of Protection* around them as a bright light.

2.) The partners share their *Taste* homework from the previous week. Score.

3.) The room should be semi-dark. Stand in front of a blank wall. The class focuses on the center of your forehead without shifting their gaze. Chant a loud OM after taking three deep breaths. Record and score those who see your *Aura* and the colors they see. Explain how they can energize their own *Auras* with deep abdominal breathing exercises to use as their *Shield of Protection*. (Chapter XL.)

4.) With the room illuminated again, everyone concentrate on the photo of the missing person and record their impressions.

5.) Take the items you have prepared for the telepathic test into another room. As you project each item to the class, they record their impressions. Announce when you are feeling each item. Feel the sandpaper. (Project.) Feel the brush bristles. (Project.) Feel the sticky tape. (Project.) Feel the velvet. (Project.) Score each person's impressions.

6.) <u>Homework</u>: Pair off different partners for sending and receiving. The time of day is agreed upon by both parties. Senders project

ACTION, one for each day of the week for one to two minutes and record what they send and when. They may use a photo of each action if available. (1.) Someone skating. (2.) Skiing. (3.) Swimming. (4.) Climbing. (5.) Dancing. (6.) Jumping. (7.) Horse galloping. (*Percipients* record what they receive.)

Lesson V

(Prepare a small bowl, toothpicks, ping-pong balls and a lead pencil or crayon for each person.)

1.) *Progressive Relaxation* and *Shield of Protection.*

2.) Partners share *telepathic* impressions from homework assignment. (Score.)

3.) Fill bowls partially with water. Distribute one bowl, one toothpick and one ping-pong ball per person. The bowls should be on a level surface. Hands should be off and away from the table. Each person floats a toothpick on the surface of the water. When it is stationary, each one concentrates on moving the toothpick. Then, the same test for the ping-pong ball. (Score.)

4.) Distribute pencils or crayons. Each person places the pencil or crayon in front of them on the table on a smooth, level surface. They slowly move a hand over the pencil or crayon three to five inches above it and concentrate on making it roll. (In number 3 and 4 blowing or breathing heavily on the objects is disallowed.) (Score.)

5.) Take your notebook and pen with you so you can record the following: Tell the class you are going into another room and you are going to perform the following movements; but you are mixing them up. Call out when you start a new movement. (1.) Take three steps.

(2.) Hold your nose. (3.) Hands on hips. (4.) Cup hands over ears. (5.) Raise left arm. (6.) Squat. (7.) Stretch both arms up as high as you can. (8.) Sit down. (9.) Stand up and shake your shoulders. (Class records impressions and then you compare with them and score.)

6.) Homework: Everyone bring in a plumb-bob attached to a yard of string. Plumb-bobs are sold in hardware stores. Partners pair off before departing. The sender is to project and record an image of him or herself on a pre-selected day performing any task. The recipient records the impression.

Lesson VI

(Have a photo of another missing person ready with a map of the United States.)

1.) *Progressive Relaxation* and *Shield of Protection*.

2.) Partners share the week's homework assignment for hits and misses. (Score.)

3.) Table Tapping: Everyone sits around the bare table. Hands are placed palms down on the table. Bodies and knees should not touch the table. Everyone imagines energy flowing down arms and into hands. Now, everyone commands the table to rise, repeating that many times. Concentrate deeply on the table rising. When it begins to respond ask it to count to three. Then each one asks a question which requires yes, no or maybe. Tell the table two taps for yes, one tap for no and three taps for maybe. (If there is no response try bridge tables with at least four people around each.) This is an experiment in mental impetus.

4.) <u>Missing Persons</u>: Display the map on the table. Everyone except one person is herded into another room to prevent them from witnessing the proceedings. Each person takes turns holding the plumb-bob over the map while focusing on the missing person photo. They say mentally: **We want to locate where this person is now; Reach-Together-Thank You.** They must hold the plumb-bob steadily in one place, relax and obey its guidance as it moves up, down, diagonally or laterally. Record the most popular site. (In the event that there are several similar impressions, you might want to report your findings to law enforcement officials.)

5.) <u>Homework</u>: Partners decide who will send and who will receive and the best time of day for both. The sender smells each of the following and transmits ODORS. (Day 1:) Perfume; especially a floral scent. (Day 2:) Garlic. (Day 3:) Cinnamon. (Day 4:) Onions. SOUNDS: (Day 5:) Make the sound of a siren. (Day 6:) Loud whistle. (Day 7:) Bells tinkling or ring your doorbell. (*Clairsentience* and *clairaudience*.)

Lesson VII

(Have a mat or clean blanket ready for a healing session; also a neck support of some kind. It can be a rolled up towel.)

1.) *Progressive Relaxation* and *Shield of Protection.*

2.) <u>Cold Readings</u>: Pair off couples, and include yourself. Each couple should be sitting apart from the others for privacy. One person *tunes in* to the other and reveals impressions. (Caution *recipients* to respond only with **yes, no, not sure, or don't know**.) Then switch people with other partners so each one has the opportunity to read. *Recipients* record the hits, if any. (Score.)

3.) <u>Healing Session</u>: Place the mat or blanket on the table, a sofa or the floor. Each person gets the opportunity to lie down, and each one individually, after taking a few deep, relaxing breaths, slowly passes his or her hands over the recipient's body into the field of energy; *Aura*. Mentally send healing energy into the subject. (*He/she is healed and restored now. Thank you.*) If a diagnostic impression is received, this should be discreetly discussed later with the subject in private. Teacher records each subject's responses.

4.) <u>Homework</u>: Partners paired off. They decide the best time of day for each of the seven days of the week. The sender transmits for five minutes each time anything which evokes strong emotion. (1.) Hurricane or earthquake. (2.) Tornado. (3.) Blizzard. (4.) Funeral or burial. (5.) Auto accident. (6.) Woman giving birth. (7.) Huge tidal wave. (Senders and recipients must keep precise records.)

Lesson VIII

(Prepare 25 cards, five of each type of geometric shapes: Star, square, cross, circle and three wavy lines. Have a deck of regular playing cards ready. Prepare record charts, one for each participant. Twenty numbered lines; ten columns headed CALL and CARD for five runs.)

1.) *Progressive Relaxation* and *Shield of Protection*.

2.) <u>Geometric Card Test</u>: Test each person with cards inverted. Average is five chance hits. Eighteen hits per run is outstanding. (Score.)

3.) <u>Playing Card Test</u>: (a.) Select 20 playing cards; five of each suit. (b.) Tester and subject sit at table. (c.) Tester shuffle cards. Don't let subject see cards. (d.) Place deck face down. (e.) Remove top card without looking at it. (f.) Subject guesses. (g.) Record the guess on chart under CALL. (h.) Continue with remaining cards. (i.) After all 20 cards have been called, record the order of the cards in the deck from the bottom up under CARD. (j.) Do five runs like this; five series of 20 guesses. (k.) Key: C=Club; D=Diamond; H=Heart; S=Spade. Under the CALL column, record the card that was called. Under the CARD column, record the actual card.

4.) <u>Vibration, Telepathy Test</u>: Tester select nine playing cards. Spread them face down in a straight line after memorizing ONE card and its position. Mentally project the card and its position to the subject who slowly passes a hand over the cards. When the hand dips or feels warm over a particular card, the subject turns that card over. (Five passes for five different cards for each subject.)

5.) Class discusses someone who requires special healing and with eyes closed they mentally project a healing light to that person.

6.) Ask if anyone has any information on the missing person. (This is the final session. Each person is given his/her evaluation.)

Chapter X

IMPRESSIONS AND TELEPATHY

<u>FEBRUARY 25, 1967</u>: At lunch I smelled fire right under my nose. My mother, Charlie and my cleaning lady were there and each one denied smelling anything. We searched the entire house inside and outside. Nothing. At 5:00PM, the first alarm of a fire went off on Fifth Avenue in New York City in a high-rise building. Nine people were killed in that fire. One of them was Dave, a friend of Charlie's from his Knights of Pythias lodge. (This was a *pre-cognitive* impression, and also an example of *clairsentience.*) At a séance, shortly thereafter, our teacher Ben, (name changed,) said, "I'm being impressed with asphyxiation by a Dave." Ben had not been given any information about Dave. He was also positively identified by one of our group who envisioned a drafting board. Dave had been an architect. He had gasped his final breath in an elevator on his way down to the parking garage. I think Dave visited us that night because I had wished him a smooth and easy transition and prayed for the *Divine Progress* of his soul.

<u>January 15, 1969</u>: While meditating I saw my friend Lee's sailor son Bobby flying home in June over water. I called her a week later

and she said he's on his way home from Viet Nam, but not by plane. The following week she told me he phoned from Virginia and he's flying to Florida, *over water,* and won't be home until June.

On March 1, I smelled fire at 10:30AM and then again at 6:00PM. The news reported a small fire at the Montauk Theater on Main Avenue nowhere near our home. (This is another example of *clairsentience.* When we sense something which has not yet transpired, this is *pre-cognition.*)

At my beauty salon, when my hair was being shampooed, I had received many corroborated impressions about the operator's life and family, whomever it happened to be. They are too numerous to recount here, but one of them is quite significant because of symbolism. While *Marie, the proprietor's daughter was shampooing my hair, I said, "I see *Ricky, (her brother,) coming home from Viet Nam and he's riding a *white horse.* He has a friend with carrot-red hair whose name starts with J." (To me, the *white horse* signified heroin.) Marie was astounded. She said, "Ricky came home last night with his friend *Jim who has red hair. They're both spaced out on drugs." (*Names changed.)

If we receive a message or an impression about someone or something, occasionally symbols represent actual facts. This happens in dreams as well, so we must be able to interpret the implication of the symbols as related to the body of the message. When we receive impressions by touch, we are *psychometrizing* as in the *Psychic Development Class.* Every object resonates with its history. Anything fashioned from metal retains and emits the most powerful vibrations. Yet, we can touch someone, or as in my experiences at the beauty salon, someone touches us; thus, we receive flashes of insight.

April 8, 1969: My brother-in-law George who was in the furniture business had been promising for weeks to replace the wheels on our new bed. I had just said his name in my meditation and was impressed to send him a message. I mentally commanded him,

"George, bring the wheels!" That evening the doorbell rang and in strode George with the new wheels.

July 7, 1969: It was the Sunday after Neal had departed for Fort Dix. Charlie awoke at 3:00AM to use the bathroom. When he returned to bed he worried about Neal who was suffering with a bad cold, severe congestion and sore ankles and feet from training. He was due to go on bivouac that morning. As Charlie began to meditate on Neal he thought, "I want to be with him to heal him." He found himself traveling over highways to Fort Dix and up the stairs of the barracks. Neal was asleep and he proceeded to give him healing and massage his body. He felt his head which was warm with fever. As he thought, "I wonder if he knows I'm here," he landed back in his body.

The next morning at breakfast Charlie was discussing his desire to find a job driving a truck since his office was on strike. While he spoke, my brain buzzed with *ice-cream truck*. I tried to shake it off because I couldn't understand why, nor did I know anyone who drove one. Then Charlie said, "You know when Maury R.'s office was on strike, he told me he got a job driving an ice-cream truck." Another example of *mental telepathy*.

Chapter XI

PREMONITIONS

CHARLIE AND I visited our friends Barbara and Conrad in Simi Valley, California on December 9th of 1976. We were to spend the Christmas holidays with them and investigate California for retirement, especially the San Diego area. We spent the first week with them and four beautiful days in San Diego. On Monday the 20th back at our friends' home, Charlie became inconsolably restless and insisted he wanted to go home. "Go home?!" I asked incredulously. "What do you mean? We still have two weeks to go." He spent the day prowling nervously around the house like a caged puma. He tried his best to shake the feeling, but it persisted.

The following morning we heard the phone ring at 8:00. Barbara knocked on our door; "Charlie, phone for you." As he hauled himself out of bed, he said, "When the phone rang, I said to myself, 'That's for me!' I don't know why." As he left to answer the call, I thought in my sleepy stupor, "8:00AM here and 5:00AM at home. God, I hope nothing terrible happened!" It was actually 11:00AM on the east coast.

The call was from Charlie's younger brother, Irv, my sister Bernice's husband. He was phoning from his sister Dotty's house. Her husband Barney had dropped dead at 6:00AM from a massive coronary. Charlie was experiencing a *pre-cognitive* impression; a premonition. On the flight home I told Charlie he got his wish to go home even though he had no clue why.

I knew nothing of George W. Bush in the year 2000 except that he was the eldest son of a former president; a Texas governor and a Republican. My gaze was riveted on his face on the TV screen in November during the disastrous Florida melee of hanging chads and uncertain dominance. I saw something there which terrified me. An icy chill slithered up my spine like a snake. A sickish feeling clutched my stomach. There was a stricken air of desperation in those steely, squinting eyes. His brows were pinched together causing wrinkles of anxiety to squirm across his forehead. I noticed a strained look around his flaring nostrils. The quirk of his firmly set, thin lips; his jaws clamped shut like a vise, revealed a man whose breath was restrained and whose heart was pulsing wildly. I glanced at his hands which were clasped in white-knuckled angst.

I'm a registered Independent voter, so that gives me the freedom to choose the best candidate in my opinion from either side. "If he wins this election, we're in deep shit," I told Sid. "I sense a dark cloud around him. I hope I'm wrong."

It's obvious that he had already hatched his diabolical scheme to eliminate Saddam Hussein regardless of the consequences. He was determined to overshadow his father's erroneous judgment in the Persian Gulf War. The deluded irony is that he believes that this debacle was divinely inspired. *My* God is a God of love and peace, not of violence and war.

Unfortunately, people vote blindly for a candidate out of party loyalty or affiliation without exercising their intuitive skills. But, there is a metaphysical reason behind every occurrence. We have earned whatever transpires in our lives. Those misguided voters who awarded him a second term must rue their decision. Group or mass Karma is responsible for any circumstances which affect nations. If we look back at our history we would better understand that everything is as it should be. (See more in Part II.)

(Addendum; January 20, 2009: Race Consciousness has prevailed. The people have spoken. At last, an African American has been inaugurated as the president of the people; for the people. Our time has come. At present it appears that he can extricate us from this quagmire; that he is our savior. He is faced with challenges that seem insurmountable, but he is determined to overcome and create the changes he has promised. History will be the judge.)

As of 2010 I have changed my political affiliation to Democrat.

Chapter XII
MORE ESP

JANUARY 6, 1977: During the normal course of the day impressions often seeped in when the house was quiet. While I was attending to menial chores, I was impressed that neighborhoods will be banding together as their own crime detectors or deterrents. That same evening, the TV news reported that a group of people in the Midwood section of Brooklyn *banded* together to police their neighborhood.

That month flashes of insight seemed to be paramount in my mind. We had become so immersed in our new inspiring and exciting paranormal adventures that they practically superseded everything else in our lives at that time.

My brother-in-law, Irv had driven home his brand new orange Cadillac on Friday. As I was meditating this Sunday morning, February 13, 1977, I pictured his garage with the doors always open and I mused, "What's he going to do with the car now? He'll have to keep it in the garage." Then I recalled that the door doesn't close, and I thought, "That's negative." Next, I saw a black man, so I *canceled* it and encircled the car with a *Shield of Protection* speculating, "He's going to need it."

Too late. The previous night as Irv was backing out of a parking space after he and Bernice had dined at a restaurant, a black man in a station wagon pulled up behind him, didn't notice him backing out and rammed into the new car.

In 1972 we were planning a trip to Hawaii for our 25th wedding anniversary. We informed the family that if they planned to give us gifts we preferred cash. They regaled us with a surprise party. When we tallied up the gifts, Charlie cheerfully reported that he only needed to withdraw $400.00 from our savings account to finance the trip.

I had previously been introduced to the *Switch Words* and I was experimenting with and silently chanting the master *Switch Word*, **Together**, which was alleged to produce miraculous results. "Don't withdraw any money, yet," I told Charlie. "I have a strong feeling I'm winning $400.00 on the lotto."

That proved to be a blessedly accurate prediction. "Why didn't I opt for a few thousand dollars?" I asked. I suppose it wasn't meant to be at that time.

Chapter XIII

HUMAN/ANIMAL CONNECTIONS

GIGI

JUNE, 1976: Our dear friends Hal and Irene visited us for a weekend from Alexandria, Virginia with Gigi their small poodle of 17 years. Hal had received orders as Field Director with the American Red Cross, to move to Panama in August and they weren't sure when we'd see them again. On the morning of their departure, a phenomenal event occurred. They were already out in the front hallway descending the stairs when Gigi, who was closely hugging their heels, suddenly spun around, scampered to my side, stood up on her hind quarters and leaned against my leg. She gazed up at me with eyes pleading, "Pick me up." If you've ever had a pet dog, you know how uncharacteristic that is. When masters are leaving, they fear being deserted and devotedly cling to them. I picked her up and she wrapped her front paws around my neck, her little body trembling. I knew then that Gigi was bidding me her final, "Goodbye, I love you." I was so moved that I wept.

Before Gigi was permitted access into Panama, she would have to be quarantined in a cage for forty days away from her loved ones.

August 21, 1976: During my meditation while praying for the pets of family and friends, as I said Gigi's name, I saw her descend from above and sit herself down in my lap. My eyes filled with tears and I thought, "Oh, God, she has probably passed on!"

Two days later the first post-card and letter dated August 16th and 17th arrived from Hal and Irene. They were grieving the loss of their beloved Gigi. The quarantine proved to be more than her little aged body was able to tolerate. Ten days after their arrival in Panama, her kidneys failed and she passed on.

I know my experiences are not unique to me; that anyone who has raised a dog can probably relate their own stories. There are documented cases where dogs have instinctively saved a strange person's life without having had any prior training. Being a dog lover I am perhaps biased in their favor, but cats have also exhibited amazing perceptions, and cats are more attuned to the spirit world.

What causes a dog to be attracted to certain people? Is it possible it's the same soul of a previously owned pet which has reincarnated; thus the recognition?

Missy

She was a newborn pup of four weeks when she selected us as her family. Her Mommy was a miniature Shepherd who broke free one day and got nabbed by a neighborhood Chow. This pup was one of a litter of six all of which had Shepherd markings with the shorter snout of a Chow. We visited our friends across the street every day and as we passed the basement window, upon hearing our footfalls, she leaped up on the side of the crate bouncing and yipping gleefully. She was the only one that demanded we pick her up.

Charlie favored a male from the litter. When the day arrived to adopt a pup, we placed both of them on the lawn. Charlie called his choice and Layne and I beckoned the little female. While our pup bounded happily into our arms, the hapless male just sat there obliviously.

We named her Missy. She had an uncanny insight into my thoughts with an understanding that amazed me. But then I also discovered that very often I was able to tune in to her mind. One Sunday after dark when we returned home from an outing in the Paterson Mountains, I was inspired to try an experiment. Before we entered the house I commanded, "Missy *scout!*" She had never heard that word before. She promptly trotted into the house, scoped out each room, and even peered under the beds. When she was satisfied that we could safely enter, she scampered to us with hind quarters proudly and excitedly waggling.

We mated her with a pedigreed Shepherd. One night as we slept, I felt the mattress bouncing on my side of the bed. Missy had done that with her chin to avoid waking Charlie! As I reached down to caress her I felt her body trembling. I intuitively knew she was suffering the throes of false labor. I slid down to the floor and held her close whispering soothing words until they passed.

Charlie had constructed a large crate which stood in a corner of our dining-room. He covered the floor with linoleum and added a shelf to prevent Missy from injuring her pups. I placed an old quilt cover in there and showed it to her every day. "See, Missy? This is where you're going to have your puppies," I said.

It was Sunday afternoon. Mom visited with a friend and we were all at home when Missy became agitated, running from the back door to the front door. I realized that her water was about to break, so I explained to Mom and her friend that she wouldn't give birth with them there. As soon as they left, she leaped into the crate, snatched the quilt cover in her teeth, stood up on hind legs and bore down!

We were all there to witness this phenomenon, but we didn't have the foresight to prepare a camera. The first pup plopped out and the new Mommy performed her instinctive duties. Then it squealed and she bristled, gaped pop-eyed at it and bounded out of the crate escaping to the farthest corner of the house. We found her quaking goggle-eyed in a corner of our bedroom. Charlie lifted her and carried her back to the crate while we soothingly explained that she had more babies to deliver.

Missy presented us with six adorable whelps, all of which were German Shepherds sans a pedigree. The last one was the runt of the litter which required special feeding attention. A dog-breeder friend recommended pumping formula directly into the stomach with a horse-syringe. That puppy flourished.

Missy had selected her very own toilet up on top of a hill at the farthest end of our massive back yard. On freezing winter days as I waited and demanded that she return to me, she took her sweet time, meandering and sniffing every blade of grass. One day I was inspired to reel her in with a mental fishing line from my brain to hers. Her pace quickened as she headed straight for me. It worked every time! No more, "Missy, hurry up! Come now!"

Whenever I meditated in my favorite living-room chair, she would lie down beside me. She probably sensed a serenity which pacified her.

One night when Neal was walking her around the block, she yanked loose from his grip on the leash and dashed into a clump of shrubs. There was a slight scuffle and then out she proudly trotted with a dead rat clutched in her jaws. In her estimation she had heroi-cally saved Neal's life. However, a paradox occurred one evening when I was conducting my class in our dining room. Missy slinked over to my side and sat down staring into the darkened kitchen. She had never done that before. After everyone departed, Charlie arrived home and I mentioned what she did. She balked at entering the kitchen which led us to suspect that something was eerily amiss. We were right. We found boxes of cereal overturned in the pantry and rat droppings. Charlie set traps and the invader was no more. There was road construction along the Passaic River which apparently interloped on the rats' habitat.

At the age of ten, our beloved Missy had throat cancer. She continued to eat without a complaint and we were unaware until I felt a lump on her throat. She underwent surgery in the North Shore Animal Hospital in New York and survived another year thereafter.

Chapter XIV
INTUITION AND IMPRESSIONS GALORE

JUNE, 1974: AFTER having conducted business for two years in my first floral design shop I became almost obsessed with the notion that I must relocate to a larger store. I stubbornly ignored the pleas of my family to hold out for at least another year so I could become better established, and I began to *treat* for a larger store on the same street. About a month later a perfectly suitable store became available across the street from my small shop. In August we moved into the newly decorated, larger facility.

It was the last week in September when the entire building across the street was destroyed by an electrically ignited fire which had started in the wall of my former shop. Not only did the *Shield of Protection,* which I had reinforced every day, prove its value to me, but the amazing bonus was that intuitively I must have been impelled to vacate that shop, though at that time I had no inkling of why. The significance of this event was, since I no longer occupied those premises, the *protective shield* was invalidated. I was concentrating on protecting my new establishment. (See Part III; The Truth About *Accidents.*)

February, 15, 1991: The Persian Gulf War had been raging for months. In my meditation I envisioned our armed forces returning in April. They did.

October 9, 1993: Yesterday as I said my nephew Marco and his wife, Janet's names in my prayers, I was impressed that Janet is pregnant again. (She had previously miscarried.) This morning I called Marco's Mom, my sister-in-law Ione, to confirm. She emphatically declared, "Absolutely not!" She had just spoken to Marco.

November 12, 1993: Ione phoned me and told me "in the strictest confidence," that Janet is pregnant about five weeks or so. They didn't know it when I called in October. When she had suffered the miscarriage the week before, they were devastated, but an ultra-sound revealed another fetus with a strong heartbeat. The doctor said she must have aborted a twin.

Sometime in late October, 1994: My daughter, Layne was visiting her aunt Ione. As she stepped into the bathroom a bright light flashed in front of her. She was impressed that it was her Bubby, my blessed mother-in-law Goldie, who told her that Robbi, Dotty's daughter is pregnant with a little girl, and she will carry her name. Goldie Jane W. entered this world on June 22nd, 1995.

October 19, 1995: I was impressed in my meditation that my friends Myra and Joe's daughter, is pregnant now or will be presenting them with a grandchild before the end of 1996. I got that it's a girl, though I thought that was unlikely because her husband has four brothers. I reported it to Myra's answering machine. When Myra returned my call a few days later, she said they had been away and she also felt that her daughter was pregnant. When she spoke to her, she said she was two months overdue for her period. She had stopped taking the pill, but the doctor said she didn't think she was pregnant.

September 28, 1995: Myra phoned with the news that her daughter is expecting in January, 1996. An amniocentesis revealed a baby girl!

<u>August, 1995</u>: When I attended the funeral service of a friend, Will, I became mesmerized by a cone-shaped pillar of smoke which vibrated with life as it rose from the floor, whirling like a tornado. The spell-binding energy was spinning between the family sitting in the front row of the chapel and the rabbi in the pulpit. I knew it was Will's energy. Usually, I look for spirit hovering around the coffin or the family and rarely see it. This time I wasn't even thinking about it. Later, when I mentioned it to his family, hoping it would comfort them because he had suffered for so long with a debilitating illness; they glared at me as if I had lost my mind.

<u>August 22, 1997</u>: This past week I had received news that a friend and neighbor, Irv L., was critically ill and hospitalized on dialysis. His wife, Pat had requested via a phone conversation with another neighbor Carol that I pray for him. In a case such as this I say: *I place ___?___ in God's hands for whatever is best for him/her. God's will be done. Thank You.* That evening when I returned home from a dinner date with a friend, I stepped into my bathroom when I suddenly exclaimed aloud, "Oh, my God! I'm going to hear that Irv died!" Two minutes later my phone rang. It was Carol informing me that Pat had called her with the news. I'm positive that it was Irv impressing me that he had made his transition since he had been active at some of our séances.

What follows is such a common example of mental telepathy that I'm certain everyone has experienced something similar more than once in their lives.

<u>March 31, 1999</u>: The name of a former student of mine popped into my mind while I was getting washed this morning. I thought, "Gosh, I haven't seen her all season. Hope she's okay." Ruth had made it a practice to repeat my class at least one semester a year. When I went to pick up my mail this evening there was a birthday card from Ruth. On the flap she had written, *Do not open until your birthday*, (which is April 22nd.) On the morning of February 24th, 2002,

I just happened to have read the above entry in my journal. That was the day our art club launched its Art Expo and I was competing and exhibiting my sculptures. I hadn't seen or heard from Ruth for a long time. I thought, "I hope she's okay." That afternoon at the art show, there she was. She said that she had specifically sought me out.

May 6, 2005: While meditating, the message was that my grand-nephew Michael's wife Michele is pregnant. I phoned his parents, and his father, Vic answered and swore they knew nothing. Later I learned that Michele didn't want to air the news until she was safely in her fourth month. On June 21st, my intuition told me it's a boy. A few weeks later Marlene, Michael's Mom, called me to tell me that an ultra-sound had revealed a boy.

In May of 2007, I wrote in my grand-nephew, Steven's birthday card that he will be holding his son by his next birthday. I recently heard from his grandmother, Ione, that his wife, Laurie is carrying a boy. Steven was not able to hold his son by his next birthday because he hadn't been born yet, but he did hold him a month later.

Chapter XV

GOD DELIVERS AGAIN

I HAD HEARD of a family of swans which frequented an area on the west side of our village, but because my condo is on the east side, I had never enjoyed the pleasure of seeing them. One day in my sculpture class the subject was being discussed and someone remarked that the female and her two babies were no longer there. "Something terrible must have happened to them," I said. "Swans mate for life." She replied that the cob was still around, but she felt so sorry for him because now he was all alone. "God, how I'd love to see that swan!" I exclaimed.

The next morning something impelled me to step out on my enclosed patio and look out the window. As I peered to my right, a startling sight greeted my eyes. This magnificent, portly cob was awkwardly lumbering across the lawn headed in my direction. A current of excitement shivered through me and I thanked God and His Angels for this prompt demonstration. Then I thought, "Why are you struggling so on the grass? Why don't you go into the water?" At that he wheeled around and plopped into the canal! Gliding gracefully in regal splendor, he left me almost breathless with glee. Thereafter, I was privileged to see him twice again in my area. He hasn't been seen by anyone since.

Ed, a newcomer, joined us at one of our séances, and afterward someone initiated the topic of hypnosis. I said, "I've always wanted to learn hypnosis because when I was younger I discovered that I'm a good subject." Ed rejoined, "It so happens that a friend of mine is a certified hypnotist and he's been talking about beginning some classes in this area."

Another door had opened for me. Again, all I had to do was express the desire to learn something new. Charlie, Neal and I enrolled in Arthur B.'s hypnosis class. He said he wouldn't commence unless he had at least ten people. So, we notified everyone we knew who we thought might be interested and we were on our way. I was particularly concerned with the therapeutic aspect of hypnotism, while Charlie, the extrovert, was itching to use it for amusement.

It served me well, because I've used it many times in my own life, and I've helped other people to forgo bad habits. I also formulated a program on *ESP and Hypnosis* which we presented at our Country Club, community centers, and hotels. In one phase of it Charlie hypnotized me, stretched me between two chairs, and invited a reluctant volunteer from the audience to sit on my rigid body. I enlightened the audience on the merits and misconceptions of hypnosis and the difference between that and brainwashing. Then I asked for two volunteers who had no connection with one another to come up on the stage. I hypnotized one of them and the other one took the subject on a mental trip to his or her home. No information was revealed except the route to the home. Amazing feats of perception were exhibited in every case. The subjects were able to *see* the residence and often the address, and give descriptions of the exterior and interior. In some cases furniture and other objects which were no longer there were described. Most of the people had no prior experience with perception, so there's hope for everyone.

Chapter XVI

THE STUFF OF DREAMS

FEBRUARY 17, 1968: It was a Saturday evening when Neal borrowed Charlie's car to attend a play at the YM-YWHA in Clifton, our neighboring town. At 11:00PM he phoned us and nervously announced that the car was missing. We reported the theft to the police and Charlie picked him up in my car.

The following morning Neal came downstairs and cheerfully declared, "Mom, I know exactly where to find the car." (Earlier that morning Charlie had driven my car to Mama Locker's house.) "How can you be so sure?" I asked Neal. "I dreamt I was floating around in the air searching for the car," he said. "Then I spotted it parked about a block away from Bubby's house. I'm walking over there because I want to verify it for myself."

About a half hour later Charlie phoned with the welcome news that Neal had, indeed found the car exactly where he had seen it in his dream. There wasn't any vandalism except for empty soda cans and trash left behind by the thieves.

When they arrived home, Charlie told me that while he was having his coffee early that morning, the dining- room door opened.

He thought it was Neal, but he didn't see anyone. When he called Neal's name there was no response. As he closed the door he felt his late father's presence. He said, "Pa, if that's you, come on in." Then he heard Papa say to him, "Go to your Mama, she misses you." Charlie replied, "I'm going soon." Papa urged, "Go now!"

When Charlie entered Mama's house, she cried, "Oy, Charlie, I missed you so much! I've been thinking about you all morning and hoping you would come." The urgency? She just needed someone to read the mail!

Charlie was so devoted to his blessed mother that his visits were an indispensable part of his daily routine. She deserved whatever attention and love we showered upon her. She was an extraordinary woman who exuded love towards everyone.

In August, 1969, Neal had developed some negatives of our June trip to Florida and he believed there were several which had lucrative possibilities. Somehow, they were misplaced and all of his efforts to locate them failed. On January 16th, he dreamed that he took the prints to a New York agent and he bought all of them. During the transaction, he asked Neal where he had found the negatives and Neal wondered how the agent knew they had been missing. He replied, "I found them in a box in my closet." At that, he leaped out of bed, and sitting on a shelf in his closet was the box of negatives which had been missing for five months. So, dreams sometimes help us to locate missing items also. If it's in our subconscious, it can be retrieved. Otherwise, we are being guided by our *Higher Self*, as with the missing car.

March 25, 1969: At 6:00AM I returned to bed from the bathroom and as I began to doze I saw myself in my sister-in-law Ione's kitchen with her firstborn daughter, Diane and her husband, Mike. Their son, Steven was about ten months of age at the time. I was holding Steven in my lap with his little hand in mine and relating his future. Part of the prediction was, at the age of twenty or so he will decide he wants to be a doctor, and he will become one.

In 1991, Steven received a glowing letter of recommendation from the associate dean of student affairs at the University of Texas Southwestern Medical Center. Subsequently, he became a laparoscopic surgeon.

July 10, 1974: I dreamt about Dave, the father of my friend, Lee. I hadn't seen nor heard of him for many months. That dream didn't bode well with me. October 5th, he passed on.

October 17, 1974: In a dream I saw my former employers, Mr. and Mrs. S. whom I adored. My Mom and I were in their store chatting with them when suddenly they were gone.

April 6, 1975: I dreamt about Mr. And Mrs. S. again. I was walking in the road in front of their store carrying a large carton of refuse which overturned. When I entered the store, Mr. and Mrs. S. were standing in the front on the left side by a counter. (That was odd because there was no counter on the left side of the shop.) I kissed them and remarked how wonderful they looked. A crowd of people were lined up waiting to enter into the back room which was partitioned into three sections. They were filing through the doorway very slowly.

The carton of refuse overturning was symbolic of change and freedom from earthly cares. The people lined up and filing slowly symbolized a funeral service. Soon after that, Mr. S. passed on and Mrs. S. joined him less than a year later.

February 23, 1977: It seemed that most of my sleep that night was disturbed by dreams of my two cousins, Melvin and Seymour. I saw them in a bakery where there was a large tub of pickled herring. I knew they were preparing for a funeral. Their mother, my aunt Mae passed on soon after that.

November 20, 1992: I dreamt I was giving birth to a baby boy. Couldn't recall any other details of the dream, but when I awakened I knew that Bernice and Irv's son, my nephew, Jeff's wife, Lois who was due on November 28th, will give birth to another boy. At 11:00AM, on that day, a healthy Matthew Eliot was happily welcomed into this world by his Mom and Dad and his brother Jason.

August 3, 1995: In a dream a huge, bold number five suddenly appeared and I recall thinking maybe I should play that number. I had completely forgotten about it when the following night as I watched TV I saw that the number 500 had been selected in the lottery drawing. You goofed, Norma.

November 23, 2000: I dreamt that I was walking in New York City looking for an Army Outlet store. I found myself on the corner of 70th and 59th streets. As I glanced up at the street sign, the numbers coaxed my attention. There was a grocery store on that corner. When I awoke I knew in my heart that I must play those numbers in the lottery. The four numbers 7059 were selected exactly as I had played them and I won $2600.00!

At a later date, I saw 327 in a dream and played it for one night. It came in at the end of the week. You goofed again, Norma!

Mama Locker's Dreams

("Ven the heart got a zipper to open it up and ve should see vot's inside, then ve vouldn't have to talk." My favorite quote exemplifying Mama Locker's incredible, inborn wisdom.)

Prologue

We exalted this extraordinary woman, my blessed mother-in-law, Goldie Locker, and as I had previously mentioned, she deserved whatever reverence we could shower upon her small supple body.

When you hugged her, you were embracing a soft, cuddly down pillow. She never uttered a harsh word about anyone or anything, and gave of herself unselfishly with a pleasant, humble demeanor. She bore and raised seven exceptional children through a life of indigence, with nary a complaint. Yet, those children survived and flourished due to her resourcefulness. She ruled her clan with an iron hand tempered by a heart brimming with love. She also helped raise her late daughter, Marcella's three young daughters. Her winsome smile, her magnetic, radiant aura lured strangers who hungered to kiss her soft, pudgy cheeks, so we dubbed her the *mezuzah*. (The device which holds the Hebrew interpretation of the Ten Commandments which observant Jews kiss.)

In her sixties Mama Locker was diagnosed with Pemphigus, a serious skin disease which the doctors at the Mayo Clinic and a New York specialist, predicted would be fatal within six months. We never told her of the fateful prognosis. She continued to live her normal life until the age of 93, because she projected herself from year to year to upcoming family weddings and Bar Mitzvahs. When a baby boy arrived in the family, she prevailed upon one of her four sons to drive her to the lower east side of New York City to purchase the prayer shawl and bible for his Bar Mitzvah. We regaled her every year since her 85th birthday with an open-house party in a hired hall. Everyone from town who loved her pleasured her with their presence. After the festivities, Charlie presented her with a dollar bill inscribed with her name and the date of her next birthday celebration which she taped to her bedroom wall.

Our daughter, Layne adored her Bubby, and she enjoyed a special, close relationship with her. The highlight of each week was her visit mainly to listen to the pearls of wisdom which flowed from her Bubby's loving lips. When it was Mama's time to leave us, Layne was in Jamaica on vacation celebrating her birthday with a friend. Mama breathed her final breath on Layne's birthday, November 13th. She tearfully vowed that she would never again be able to celebrate her birthday. I was meditating one day after the funeral, and as I prayed for the *Divine Progress* of Mama's soul, I was impressed that she chose to make her transition on Layne's birthday. That meant that they could celebrate their mutual birthdays together, because the date of the transition is a new birth. Every birthday thereafter, Layne lights a candle for her Bubby and she wishes her a happy birthday.

Her Dreams

Mama Locker was a God-loving believer. After all, she was a product of the *old country*, having emigrated from Russia as a young girl where superstition and mysticism co-existed with common sense as a way of life. She was psychically inspired in her dreams. The following stories were related to my sister-in-law, Ione by Mama Locker.

When Charlie was an infant he was very ill with diphtheria. The entire family had to be quarantined. The night of the crisis, when the doctor predicted that the baby might not make it to the next morning, Mama's vigil was in a rocking chair by the crib. The family's pet dog was asleep under the crib. Mama dozed off and in a dream her father came to her. In Yiddish, he asked her, "Why are you crying, Goldie?" She replied, "My baby is so sick, I don't know if he will live." "Don't cry," he said, "let the little dog be a *kapora* for the baby." (A *kapora* in this case meant a surrogate substitute.) When she awoke the next morning, little Charlie smiled up at her. He was miraculously healed, but the pet dog never awakened. He was found dead under the crib. Days later Mama received a letter from Russia informing her that her father had passed on prior to her dream.

When they lived in St. Paul, Minnesota, Mama had undergone gall bladder surgery. She later became pregnant with Irving, her youngest child. When the time came for the delivery, the doctor discovered that her uterus had adhered to the scar tissue. When the baby was born, they couldn't induce respiration; he was already turning blue. The doctor asked Papa, "Who do you want to save, the baby or your wife?" "I know it's a terrible thing to lose a baby," Papa said, "but I have six other children at home." So, they placed the baby aside in a basket. Mama was very ill. She dreamt that her mother poked her head in the door three times. It appeared to be so real to her that she screamed, "Mama!" The nurses thought she was hallucinating and they summoned the doctor. He asked Mama, "Where is your mother?" "My mother is dead," she said. "Your mother just saved your life," the doctor told her. She had gotten so excited that her circulation was restored.

As a nurse was passing by the basket where little Irving, who was believed to be dead, was lying swathed in a blanket, she heard a whimper. She picked up the baby and discovered that he had miraculously recovered. That baby grew up to become my sister Bernice's husband, Irving.

Ione and her husband Jack operated a bustling hardware store. When she became pregnant with her third child, she didn't tell Mama because it was pre-Christmas and she worked very hard, climbing ladders and lifting heavy items. Her relationship with Mama Locker was particularly intimate, and she knew Mama would worry. One day, Mama phoned, "I had a dream last night. There was a knock on the dining-room door. When I opened it, Papa was there holding a baby. I asked him, 'Harry, whose baby is that?' He said, 'This baby is for Chiala, (Ione,).'" Ione was incredulous. "Why me, Ma? You have other kids." Mama continued, "Papa walked into the living- room, placed the baby on the sofa and said, 'You take care of that baby. That baby is carrying my name.'" Ione's body prickled with icy chills, but she kept her secret until after the holidays had safely passed. When she finally confessed, Mama recalled the dream and almost fainted. Ione's daughter Harriet carries Papa Locker's name.

Divine Companion

You are the product of My love; My own unique creation.
There is no other like you, My precious incarnation.
Never succumb to fear for I always surround you.
I shall be right here, within you and around you.
I comfort you in grief; I am your Guide, your inspiration.
When you are burdened, I support you; I calm your agitation.
When you feel you are alone, I embrace your solitude.
You must sense My loving Presence, for you change your attitude.
You need not despair when you speak to Me in prayer; for I am there;
I am aware; I love you and I care.
I am your close Companion; your Parent; your Friend.
You can place your faith in Me; upon Me you can depend.
Just close your eyes, surrender; I shall never let you fall.
You are the fruit of My vision; My treasure; My all.
I'll enfold you with My Love when you return to Me; then you will
live in peace once more with Me eternally.

Intuition Whispers

Hearken to the whispers that summon you to heed.
They rise within your bosom, to your senses do they plead.
Hearken! Hearken! For the messages are there.
They bring you urgent tidings for your good and your welfare.
Hearken to these urges; never let them vaporize.
When recognition emerges, the thread of knowledge will arise.
They may warn you—approaching peril to beware; or impel you to
*   action on the answer to a prayer.*
You may perceive an image which shouldn't be ignored;
perhaps a view of something which may cause some discord.
Hearken! Hearken! For these whispers are for you.
Be aware when they ascend; seize them and follow through.

PART II

WHAT'S IT ALL ABOUT?

(Note: In October, 2007 I asked God to provide me with the titles for each of Part I and III of this book. Those two titles were given to me immediately. I had already entitled this part, *Where Do We Go From Here?* Months later I was inspired with the above title and wondered where it belonged. When I asked, I was impressed that it was this title which needed to be changed to *What's It All About?*)

Chapter XVII

EXPERIMENTS AND INTRODUCTIONS

"Life is eternal and love is immortal; and death is only a horizon.
A horizon is nothing save the limit of our sight."
Unknown.

WHILE I WAS experimenting with automatic writing in 1967 Charlie became fascinated with the idea that we can receive messages from our loved ones on the other side. He had heard about a popular Spiritualist in Newark who had a sterling reputation. So, it became a Sunday ritual to visit the Reverend Mrs. W.'s church. She was able to *see* Charlie's late sister, Marcella and his father standing behind him on several occasions, and offer messages from them. We knew enough to conceal all personal information from her, even to withholding our own names. She had at least a 90% success rate for accuracy, which is quite remarkable. The upstairs room which she called her church accommodated about 150 people, and sometimes there was only standing room available.

Meanwhile, I had been reading about achieving a trance state because I was passionate about becoming an instrument for spirit to communicate through me. One of the books suggested blindfolding the eyes, and to say a prayer for protection and relax completely. Since I had done automatic writing and had become a meditator, I felt confident enough to try it. My first attempt which turned out to be very prophetic, took place on June 25, 1967 at 11:30AM with Neal transcribing. (More about that session in Chapter XXXII.) We had no tape recorder at that time. The second session was on June 27 at 11:30PM with Charlie transcribing. Charlie's sister, Marcella *came through* and announced that her first born daughter, Carol will give birth to a baby girl the following spring.

Our niece Carol and her husband Alan had been trying to conceive for quite some time with no success. A couple of weeks later, we drove Carol and Alan to Newark to Mrs. W.'s church. Before we entered we instructed them to wait in the outer hall until we had seated ourselves, then they should enter and sit in the back of the room. This session we were able to tape. Mrs. W. spoke for awhile; then she scanned the room and focused on us. Again, she saw Marcella and Papa Locker behind Charlie, and as soon as she identified them, she promptly pointed to Carol and Alan in the rear of the room. "Your sister is going to that young couple," she told Charlie, "and she is telling me that the young lady, her daughter, will be giving birth to a baby girl next spring or summer." That was the confirmation we were hoping for. On July 16, 1968, Michele Faith was born.

By now, I was even more enthused about becoming a trance medium, but I needed proper training. One evening when Dave W., my Science of Mind mentor visited, I mentioned my desire. "Oh, I know just the person who can help you," he said. "Her name is Bert B. and she's been into Spiritualism for years." "Bert B!" I exclaimed. "Is that Bill B.'s widow?" "Yes. Do you know her?" "No," I replied, "but Bill was my father's close buddy. They worked together and I knew him way back when I was a kid! And he and Charlie were also buddies at the Knights of Pythias meetings." I was blown away! I had never had the opportunity in all those years to meet Bill's wife.

Another door was opening for me. "She was in a very serious auto accident," Dave said, "and she doesn't go out much because her face has been reconstructed and it's scarred." "Oh, she'll come out to meet me when she hears who I am," I retorted confidently.

And so it was. On a rainy Friday night, Bert arrived to meet us at our temple. The left side of her face was veiled by a scarf. We became very close friends, though she was 17 years my senior. After that night, she no longer concealed her scars because we convinced her of her intrinsic beauty. Bert related some of her phenomenal experiences with spirit communication and introduced us to the Reverend Dr. Ben, (name changed,) who was a *physical medium*. He ministered a Spiritualistic church, but our encounters with him were predominantly at his modest flat where he conducted metaphysical, psychic development classes and *dark hours*. The dark hours were actually séances which took place in his small, totally dark living-room. Plywood boards covered the windows. In the winter an oil-burning stove heated the room. We met there at least once a week at night, of course.

Ben was a humble, spiritually grounded soul of moderate height in his fifties with a benign demeanor. A debris of mousy hair was scattered over his balding cranium and his chin was thick with short grizzled whiskers. Spectacles poised precariously upon the bridge of his delicate nose caused me to wonder if the prescription had expired, because he frequently peered over them when expounding his erudite metaphysical knowledge. He lived alone since his wife, Tess, (name changed,) had passed on. Apparently, Ben was a man of meager means who had a reputation of existing solely on grilled cheese sandwiches.

It wasn't in Ben's nature to refuse anyone seeking favors, hence people took unfair advantage of his gentle, generous disposition. Because of his phenomenal gift of psychokinesis, his presence was constantly in demand, and he never requested remuneration. The size of the contribution was left to one's discretion.

In May of 1968, prior to our dark hour, Ben explained that most of his metaphysical knowledge was and is transmitted to him through his spirit guides. I was so enthralled and impressed by the vast diversity of information with which this man enlightened us. He was equally erudite in numerology, astrology, the bibles, every traditional religion, reincarnation and life in other dimensions. He frequently favored us with psychic readings and healings. Ben was the consummate metaphysician.

That night in May he also answered questions about past lives which prompted him to furnish us with some of his own background. He said that he "came into" a very wealthy New York family whose name we recognized. "They provided me with all the creature comforts and refinements because I deserved them from my last incarnation. In my last lifetime I was a necromancer priest in Tibet," he continued, "which meant that I was involved with medicine. My grandmother could buy and sell the world with no problem at all." He paused, twinkling. "I became a music lover from infancy. They owned a box at the opera. I learned to appreciate all of the arts. I knew theater people, musicians and many of the doctors in New York. By the age of seven, I was chatting medicine with family friends and handling conversations. In any other family," he quipped, "I would have been hung, drawn and quartered, sent out to pasture or put in a strait-jacket." One of his father's friends showed some of his writings, which most people thought were child's scribbles, to a professor at Fordham University. "My God!" he exclaimed. "This kid's actually writing Aramaic!" "After that everyone respected what I said," Ben added. He humbly mollified that with, "Not that the family revolved around *me*."

The nuclei of our group were earnestly interested in developing psychically and pursuing high teachings from the other side. Our teacher, medium, Ben, Bert B., Ruth B., Myra and Joe R., Helen H., Neal, Charlie and I were the regulars. Occasionally, we would attract or invite transitory seekers, some of whom would become hooked and remain with us at intervals. In her early teens our daughter Layne sat with us on many occasions. Because of our involvement with the spirit world, she feared staying home alone.

At our initial sessions, Charlie and Joe flanked Ben and blocked him with their legs to insure that he couldn't move about to create the phenomena. Even if he could, he always sat in a rocking chair which creaked like an old, rusted bed-spring when he stirred. Ben had three predominant spirit guides who worked with him. One of them was nicknamed *Pottsy*, because he had a long East Indian name. We identified him by the scent of saffron which he wafted under our noses when he appeared. He had been a Buddhist priest in his former lifetime. All of Ben's guides spoke with the accent of their national origin. Dr. James had been a British physician in his past life on earth, and he worked with Ben when he performed healings. He also imparted wisdom and high teachings to our group. Then there was Maria Ouspenskaya, that beloved, diminutive Russian stage and screen actress who made her transition on December 3, 1949 at age 73 from a stroke following a cigarette-ignited fire in her bed. She amused us with her sparkling wit and even eavesdropped on us at home. Maria was the counterpart of Ben's sense of humor.

John was the silent and diffident guide whose duty it was to tend to the animals and bring forth our pets. Ben's late wife Tess, (name changed,) visited us frequently. She was a soft-spoken soul who occasionally conked Ben on the head with a séance trumpet for reasons of her own.

Chapter XVIII

Signs from the *Other Side*

Prologue

"MY GOD, HONEY, look at him!" I exclaimed to Charlie as our son, Neal disembarked from the military plane at Fort McGuire Air Force Base. He had just returned from a year's stint in Viet Nam. He was sallow and emaciated. It appeared that he had lost at least twenty pounds. Leaden patches underscored his lackluster eyes. His aquiline nose had become even more prominent. His cheekbones protruded over ashen hollows. He was spaced out on drugs, but, he was physically uninjured, and that was the answer to my prayers.

Neal became a hippie with long hair and a bushy beard, the custom of that era. He sequestered himself in his room upstairs for about six months only coming down for meals when he felt the need. Meanwhile, unknown to us, he was raising marijuana in his dark room in our basement, and apparently dealing it as well because a steady stream of *friends* tramped up and down the stairs day and night. Our nephew, Gary became a Jew for Jesus, (a Messianic Jew,) and ultimately persuaded Neal to join him and his group. Charlie had mixed emotions about this conversion, but I was content to witness the radical change in our misguided son. He cleaned up his act; stopped smoking everything, and decided he'd rather become a dentist instead of a veterinarian, because vet duty in Viet Nam had repulsed him. When he graduated from Rutger's University, he matriculated and graduated from the New Jersey School of Medicine and Dentistry after which he received his commission as a captain. When he was stationed at Langley Air Force base in Hampton, Virginia, he became involved with a Baptist church and subsequently chose to become a New Testament bible-believer. On too many occasions he tried unsuccessfully to convert us.

Prior to his army induction, he had attended our séances where his amazing psychic gifts became evident. As a result of his newfound beliefs, he forswore his God-given perception and medium-ship and forced himself to forget all of his personal experiences with the paranormal because he truly believes that all of our adventures are the work of a devil. I know there is no such thing as Satan, (evil personified,) but if one believes that there is, one lives in fear and intolerance.

Charlie was 69 in 1987 when he had to undergo brain surgery for a malignant tumor. He became paralyzed on the left side of his body. An ophthalmologist performed minor surgery on the eyelid because his left eye wouldn't close. After 12 bouts of radiation he was rallying so well that he was able to climb the hill to the clubhouse with only a cane to support him, to work out in the exercise room. He courageously bore his disfigurement without a complaint. His scalp became bare except for one lone patch of hair opposite the scar. Wherever he went a chic cap topped his head which he playfully doffed upon meeting someone. The jocular Charlie Locker that I loved was still in there obscured by the distorted face. Six months after the radiation treatments he began to exhibit seizures. The first indication occurred at breakfast one morning when he tried to speak and his words were garbled. We were both aghast. I stood behind him, embracing his head in my arms and we wept together, realizing that something terrible was happening.

The neurologist scanned the new MRI films and announced, "You see where the white shows on the films? That's fluid on the brain which is causing the seizures." "Why? What has caused that? He was doing so well until now," I said. "Well, that's quite common after brain radiation," he replied nonchalantly. "It's radiation cerebritis which can manifest about four to six months later." My stomach churned with a jolt of shock and anger. A hot flush seared my cheeks. "Why weren't we informed about this when they were selling us on the radiation?" I asked incredulously. He shrugged and replied dispassionately, "I'm sorry, but I had nothing to do with that;" and he added, "He may not last much longer than two weeks."

Thereafter, Charlie's condition began to deteriorate quite rapidly. He wandered perilously during the night; experienced memory lapses, loss of balance, falling in a helpless heap on the floor; incontinence and all of the humiliating results which accompanied it.

Sometimes we don't appreciate the magnitude of our strength until a crisis looms in our life. Most of the time when I was faced with the challenge of lifting him from the floor, I didn't think about it. Yet, I confess there were those times when I became frustrated with his dead weight that I lost it and yelled at him, "For Heaven's sake, help me!" though I knew full well that he couldn't. I scrubbed, disinfected and lugged his twin mattress out to the sunny patio to dry. I emptied and sanitized the bedside commode when necessary. Hoisting the wheelchair in and out of the car trunk became less burdensome each time. I did what was required without regret or self-pity. If our roles were reversed Charlie would have done the same for me. Externally, I put on a happy face for the public. But, the time finally arrived when he required professional tending and supervision. In 1988, our daughter Layne and I located a nursing home and we transferred Charlie there. It was one of the worst days of my life. He survived for seven months after that, steadily deteriorating. The only redeeming factor regarding my daily visits to the nursing home was another miracle. My potent sense of smell had suddenly faded. If it hadn't, I wouldn't have been able to enter that building without a feeling of revulsion. After Charlie's departure, it was restored to full blossom! Once again God had come to my rescue.

Each day when I returned to the apartment from the nursing home, deep sluices of grief overcame me. My sobs echoed off the walls as the floodgates which had been tightly secured, burst open and briny tears streamed down my cheeks. An icy hand clutched at my chest. My throat constricted as visions of this mighty dynamo reduced to a helpless, distorted figure, squirmed through my brain.

When the veil of calm finally enfolded me, I flipped on the radio and sang in a resounding voice, after which I marched around the apartment loudly declaring, *I am a survivor, and I am surviving this in good health!* The release of this pent-up emotion became my salvation. My daily meditation ritual was the panacea which healed me and filled me with hope and peace.

Neal flew down to Florida in April of 1989 with the express purpose of convincing his Dad that if he didn't accept Jesus as his savior, he would go to hell. Charlie, in a weakened, vulnerable mental and physical condition began to doubt all of his previous convictions. He had always known where he was going because of our years of experience with the paranormal; with séances and psychic phenomena. He summoned rabbis, ministers and priests and became more confused as a result.

His sister Ione and brother George flew down in February, 1988 to visit him in the nursing home for his 70th birthday. They presented him with a handsome white sport jacket which he had always wanted.

On May 4th, 1989 Charlie had been transferred to the Hospice facility at University hospital in Coral Springs because his condition had seriously declined. When I arrived for my daily visit on Saturday, May 6th, I found him comatose and gurgling; (the *death rattle*.) Watching his precious life ebbing away was agonizing. His flesh was alabaster; his abdomen bloated as his vital signs betrayed him. I stayed with him until 6:00 PM, caressed his flaccid hand, kissed him, told him I loved him and left. A friend of ours, Hy L., was also losing his beloved wife who languished in a Hospice facility in the final stages of multiple sclerosis. We kept in touch commiserating with one another since we had so much in common at the time. He phoned and asked me to join him for dinner. We returned to my apartment, and while we were watching TV, Layne called. "Mom, call the hospital and tell them that if it happens during the night not to wake you until the morning." I thought that was a good idea since our dear friend Seymour was driving me to the hospital. Layne continued, "Also, what are you dressing Daddy in?" I said, "I hadn't thought about it and we had never discussed it. Whatever they do is okay. I guess they wrap them in a shroud, or whatever, and since he was a veteran the coffin will be covered with a flag." The hospital personnel agreed to call me at 6:00AM if Charlie passed on earlier.

At five the next morning I went to the bathroom and when I returned to bed I couldn't fall asleep. So, I lied on my back and with eyes closed proceeded to send Charlie a telepathic message.

"Honey, you know I love you, and I know you love me, but it's okay to let go. God bless you and let go. Mama, Papa and Marcella are waiting for you. Go to them." I had repeated that a few times, when the phone rang. It was a hospice attendant informing me that Charlie had expired ten minutes ago. I breathed a sigh of relief and murmured, "Thank God it's over." Then, I mentally wished him a smooth and easy transition and Divine Progress to his soul.

The piercing needles of grief which had held me captive throughout the ordeal finally withdrew. When a long endured trial is ended the grieving often ends with it. It's different with a sudden or unexpected death. That's usually the introduction to extended bereavement. However, I have known some men, especially, who had made it their life's career to nurse ailing spouses and after the loved ones were gone they were lost. Thankfully, the fragile tissue of time has a way of softening sad memories. For me, knowing Charlie's destination to a Divine realm and a return to a perfect body eased his absence from my life.

<u>Discovery</u>

I called Seymour, after which I went into the bathroom to get washed. His wife Alma came in and while she stood there, Charlie's dynamic energy was buzzing me. My scalp, neck and spine were prickling with electricity. He was excitedly reporting, "It's really me! I'm still here, and I'm perfect again!" He was confirming that he hadn't gone to the hell with which Neal had tried to intimidate him.

After Alma left, I went to the dresser to get my undies when I distinctly heard plastic hangers rattling in our closet. The only space for unused hangers was on Charlie's side of the closet. I always keep the sliding door open to prevent mildew which is quite common in Florida. It was very early and the sun was just beginning to peek above the horizon. All the windows were closed and it was so quiet I could almost hear my heart throbbing. I glanced into the closet and saw nothing unusual, but I knew I had heard the unmistakable clatter of plastic hangers.

Seymour drove me to the hospital and we bade Charlie's waxen body our final farewell. We returned home by 9:30. As I began to undress on the side of the bed facing the closet, Charlie's electrifying energy was buzzing around me again. "Okay, Honey; I know you're trying to tell me something. What is it?" I got, "White jacket, black slacks and black, gray and white printed shirt." Now, I understood. It suddenly gelled and made sense. My dapper husband wanted to be buried in his favorite outfit. He had only worn the new white sport jacket once in the nursing home and I had completed the ensemble with the slacks and shirt which he was never able to wear. He had obviously tuned in as Layne and I discussed it the previous night when she phoned, hence the rattling hangers. Since he was in a coma preparing for his transition, he was able to travel freely in his astral body and eavesdrop on our conversation.

The first night after I returned home from the funeral and *shiva* in Passaic I felt Charlie's body pressing into mine. He was spooning me as he had done so often in the past. I smiled and expressed my love for him.

The Keys

I hadn't heard from Charlie since his passing, so for several months in my meditation I asked him to give me a sign that he was still around.

Saturday, May 4th, 1991: I was preparing my breakfast on the kitchen counter by the sink. Suddenly, I heard a brilliant metallic clink behind me. I swung around and gasped as I gaped wide-eyed at Charlie's cluster of keys lying on the tile floor. My skin prickled with goose bumps. Those keys had been thrust with such force from the top of the wooden radio on the Parson's table in the dining- room, that they landed in the kitchen. What better sign could Charlie have given me? Those were his keys which he deposited on the radio when he came home and retrieved on his way out. I left them there because they are handy when I need keys. I tearfully and joyously cried, "Charl, you're here! Oh, thank you for showing me that you're still around!"

Later, I realized that he had chosen that particular day to manifest because that very evening I was regaling my new beau, Nat, with a surprise birthday party in our clubhouse ballroom. Charlie had always been very possessive of me. I felt that he was vehemently expressing his objection.

More Signs

One day in 1994 I received a call from Layne. She had been installing a smoke-detector in the basement of the home she shared with her partner at that time. She was using Charlie's power drill for the first time and their own metal-handled hammer. Because she was having a problem with the tools, she asked her Dad to help her. After that, she went upstairs to retrieve something and when she descended the stairs she was surprised to find Charlie's wood-handled hammer lying in full view on the landing by the front door.

It was New Year's day, 1996. Layne and her partner were in their kitchen when a windup musical Santa which hadn't been activated suddenly began to play the tune. No one was anywhere near it. Later, the Santa chimed a few more notes. Layne asked her partner if her Mom had given her the Santa, and if she did, could that have been a sign from her. Her partner confessed that indeed, it had been a gift from her Mom as well as the ceramic Christmas tree on the dining-room table, and that she had earlier asked her Mom for a sign that she was still around.

One February evening in 1996, when I was between relationships, I attended a show in our clubhouse theater. The singer, Julie Budd was appearing on stage. After she presented a few songs from her repertoire, she sang a Yiddish tune. Just before she began to sing the next one, I felt a finger poke me in my left upper arm. I thought, *My Yiddishe Mama,* and that's what she sang! After Mama Locker passed on, when Charlie heard that song, he would weep profusely because of his intense love and devotion for his blessed mother. It was Charlie alerting me to that song which meant so much to him. He used to love the shows as I do, so I imagine he had joined me at times to enjoy them with me again.

Fly Me to the Moon was Charlie's favorite song. He would croon it in the morning and all throughout the day. Since he had made his transition, I know he is here when I spontaneously begin to sing *Fly Me to the Moon,* and I feel his powerful energy around me. It was a September afternoon in 1996, when for the second time that month I sang it and immediately succeeded it with, *On a Clear Day.* Both times I felt Charlie's energy. *On a Clear Day* is the theme song from a movie of the same name about reincarnation starring Barbra Streisand and Yves Montagne. When I asked Charlie why, I was impressed that he was telling me that he was reincarnating. "Isn't this too soon?" I asked. "It's only seven years since your transition." Then I thought, "Well, maybe it's possible because I've prayed for the Divine Progress of his soul every day since." I suppose I'll never be able to prove it, but I know his spirit, the energy, personality and memories which comprise the Charlie Locker that I knew and loved will always be and will remain with us.

After a five and a half year hiatus, Layne visited me. We were having breakfast on Saturday morning, October 28, 1996, when she said, "Daddy, look where I am. I'm visiting Mom. Give me a sign that you know I'm here." The day passed with no spectacular occurrence. That night we attended a show in our theater. We were intently absorbed in a male singer who was performing on stage when I felt a finger poke me in my right upper arm. I peered around at my neighbors, as I had done at the Julie Budd show, but they were all focused on the entertainer. Then, I whispered to Layne, "Someone just poked me in my right arm." As soon as I said that, the performer began to sing, *Fly Me to the Moon.* Two songs later he sang *On a Clear Day.*

Layne remarked, "That was so loud. He didn't even need the mike," when the top half of the microphone stand slid clangorously into the lower half, much to the shock and embarrassment of the entertainer. (That had never happened before, nor did it ever happen thereafter.) I whispered to Layne, "There's your sign from Daddy." Apparently, Charlie's clairvoyance was still fully functioning. He knew weeks prior to Layne's visit what that singer would be presenting that night.

Layne was home on Saturday, May 4th, 2008 treating her lumbar back and left hip with Traumeel, a homeopathic ointment, which provided her with temporary relief. She heard a thud from somewhere in her small studio apartment as if something had fallen on the floor. The only logical place would be in her closet. When she opened the door she found her heating pad lying on the floor. It had been in a bag on the top shelf pushed back far enough to prevent it from falling on its own. When she saw it she knew it was a sign from one of her guides so she said, "Okay, I hear you. Not a bad idea." That night she used it and awakened the next morning feeling no more pain.

Aside from the fact that he had lost his father, I know the other reason Neal wept in the limousine on the way to the cemetery. He was certain his father was doomed to an eternity in hell, because he had failed to *save him*.

It was a Monday morning, October 15, 2008 when I received a surprise phone call from Neal. He said he'd been thinking about me and decided to call between seeing patients. "By the way, Mom, I no longer believe in hell. I don't believe that Grandma, Bubby and Dad are in hell. God saves everybody," he said. "I'm not the type of person who refuses to admit I was wrong; but I was wrong. I've changed a lot of my beliefs." "How did this come about?" I asked. "Further study," was his curt response. I said, "We have a lot to discuss. I've had communication from your father all these years." "Let's not get into that, now," he said crisply. "My next patient is here."

Charlie has been gone from earth since 1989. When I'm impressed to sing *Fly Me to the Moon* now, his energy is much more subtle because he has obviously progressed to a higher level of consciousness; a higher plane where the spiritual atmosphere is more rarified. Even though discarnates progress, if they so desire, they can still densify themselves to manifest, as in the case of Lao Tzu in Chapter XXII.

If you wish you may arrange a sign with a loved one or dear friend. If you love to sing as I do, decide upon a favorite song which will be recognizable to both of you. I've done that with Layne and my guy. It doesn't matter who leaves this earthly domain first. I realize that this subject may be disturbing to some people, but it's about life after all, since there is no death. We all continue after we have departed the physical, so why not be prepared to communicate with one another?

Shana

On Saturday, February 9th, 2008, between 11:30AM and 12:00 noon, Layne finally found the fortitude to put her beloved pet, baby and companion of close to 15 years, to rest. Shana, a mini-poodle, had been suffering extreme ill health for a few weeks prior.

Exactly two weeks later on Saturday, February 23rd between the hours of 11:30 PM and 12:00 midnight, an image of Shana appeared in the snow on a small evergreen tree in her front yard.

Normally Layne parks her car across the street in the garage of a kind neighbor. This particular night she was out with her friend Shirley, whose car was parked in her driveway. When she pulled into her driveway to drop her friend off, they sat there for a spell chatting. On the way to her house, Layne had been lamenting how much she missed Shana and how difficult it is awakening in the morning to find that she's no longer there. Shirley had turned her head and was looking out the window. Tears were flowing down her cheeks. She said, "Layne, look over there at the pine trees, what do you see; anything?" "Oh, my God; it's Shana!" They were both blubbering as they exited the car to take a closer look. They proceeded to take photos of the phenomenon. The only patch of snow that remained on that tree was that of Shana's image. It was still there the following morning.

She doesn't do it anymore, but when Layne used to park in the garage across the street, she just walked directly down the path into the entrance to her apartment in the rear of the building. If she had done that on that particular night, she might have missed seeing Shana's image. Layne is convinced that it was one of her guides showing her that Shana was still around her. Everyone who views those photos exclaims how amazing they are.

Marcella and Dotty

I've mentioned Charlie's sister, Marcella previously in these pages. She was the first of his six siblings to have passed on. Her three daughters ranging in age from 13 up became the responsibility of Mama Locker and Dotty who loved and nurtured them. On February 11, 2009 a healthy baby girl was born to Marcella's youngest daughter's, only daughter. Both the delivery nurse and the night nurse were named *Marcella!* Her baby Susan had become a grandma for the first time. There is no doubt that Marcella was instrumental in arranging this sign for her daughter to let her know she was still watching over her and her family.

On December 19, 2008 Charlie's youngest sister, Dotty made her transition at age 86 while taking an afternoon nap. She is survived by her three children, Gary, Roger and Robbi. Dotty and her husband Barney operated *The Dotty Locker School of Dance* for many years in our home town and after Barney's passing, in a neighboring town. She was known to her students as *Miss Dotty*.

It was the morning of March 27, 2009 when Robbi was overcome with the grief of missing her mother, lovingly caressing and sniffing one of her shirts which was decorated with her name and sobbing, "Oh, Mom, I miss you so much!" Later that day she stepped into the pet grooming facility to pick up her Golden Retriever. Several other dogs were awaiting their masters, but Robbi felt oddly drawn to one small white Terrier/Dalmatian mix with black spots on its back. "Oh, how adorable!" she exclaimed to the proprietor. "What do you call her?" "Her name is *Miss Dotty*," was the reply. How about that for a sign?!

Chapter XIX
THE PROCEDURES REQUIRED FOR A
SUCCESSFUL SÉANCE

(WHAT FOLLOWS MAY sound complex and lengthy, but it serves to relax the participants, prime their psychic centers and heighten the spiritual vibrations.)

1.) A bowl of salt water, a jar of sand and the trumpets are placed on a small table or bench in the center of the room. Séance trumpets are cone-shaped. Some of them are constructed of galvanized metal or aluminum in three or five collapsible sections. Back in the sixties, one of our sitters, Ruth B., brought her trumpet which was constructed of black bakelite, a precursor of plastic. You can construct your own trumpet with black or any other color oak tag. Make sure that it can stand balanced, and hang some bells on it so you can tell when it is activated. The salt water and sand represent some of the elements of the earth.

2.) The windows are boarded up, or draped securely with lightproof fabric or vinyl, and all external light is obliterated with towels or scatter rugs around gaps in doors.

3.) Begin with a minimum of six spiritually grounded people sitting comfortably in a circle without touching one another.

4.) Pass the trumpets around before lights are switched off so each of you can charge them by rubbing them. When sitters are in trance, the trumpets might be activated. If questions are asked, spirit may tap once for *no,* twice for *yes* and three times for *maybe.*

5.) A moderator is selected. If he/she is a trance medium, an alternate moderator is chosen who will remain alert and capable of conducting the session.

6.) The following procedures are explained in detail to neophytes: (a.) Do not offer any personal information, even if someone is giving you a reading. Just answer *yes* or *no,* or *I don't recognize that.* (b.) Do not try to grab the trumpet when it becomes activated. Spirit propels the trumpets and it can affect positive vibrations. (c.) If you think you hear, see, feel or smell someone or something, give it out! No matter how outrageous or silly it may seem, it may hold some essential meaning to someone. Don't wait until the lights are on when it may be too late. (Example: Eight of us were sitting in my den one night. Pat and Irv L. brought Irv's brother, Max, (name changed,) who had never sat before. I briefed him on the procedures and the lights were switched off. After we sang our closing hymn and the room was illuminated, he muttered sheepishly, "I saw the weirdest thing. It was a woman's head hanging in the middle of the room. She had long white or blonde hair and whiskers." I cried, "Max! Why didn't you give it out? That had to be my friend Irene. All the years I knew her, she struggled with facial hair. That's how I would identify her. She must have had a message for me.") (d.) When an entity comes through, it is advisable to offer blessings and kindly suggest, "Please do not bring your condition." Sometimes in order to identify themselves, spirit will impress the medium with what caused their demise. If you are not experienced, you may think, for example, that you are having a heart attack. If he/she had been shot or stabbed to death, you might feel a sharp thrust somewhere in your body. Once you have mastered the fundamentals of séance, you might welcome the cause of death as a clue to the identification. (e.) When someone is in trance, do not call out his or her name. Refer to him/her as the speaker.

7.) Lights are switched off. (If someone is using a recording device, use batteries, or if electricity is required, be sure it's not plugged in to an outlet which is connected to the light switch.) It is necessary to have a flashlight available. The person in charge of the flashlight sits it on the floor facing the ceiling and illuminates it before lights are turned on at the close of the session to prevent optical shock.

8.) Everyone says the opening prayer: (*May the Divine Essence of the Cosmic infuse our beings and cleanse us of all impurities of mind and body so that we may commune in Pureness, Worthiness and Love. Amen.*)

9.) The flashlight is illuminated with the beam aimed at the ceiling so the sitters can focus on and read each other's auras; (the electro-magnetic emanation around everyone.)

10.) The moderator conducts the *Consciousness Awareness* exercise. Everyone closes their eyes. Begin by relaxing the muscles of the feet and continue through every muscular group in the body until you arrive at the hands. (Example: *Place your consciousness into your feet. The muscles of the feet are relaxed and the joints are healed. Now think of the ankles. They are healed. Think of the calf muscles. Relax them*.) As you travel through the body the muscles are relaxed and the joints and organs are healed. (The following chakra exercise is optional:) While you are doing that, when you arrive at the pubic area, mention the *root chakra* which is at the *base of the spine*. Suggest, *See a bright red light there*. The *pubic chakra* is bright **orange**. The *spleen, navel or umbilical chakra* just above the solar plexus, is *golden yellow*. (The solar plexus is the center from which the ectoplasm flows, especially when one is in trance. It is identified in the room as grayish clouds floating about. This is what the entities use to materialize and manifest objects.) When you arrive at the *heart center;* that is *bright green*. The *throat chakra* is *silvery blue*. Suggest that they concentrate on the *third eye* which is located at the center of the forehead, the *pineal gland*. They are to imagine a *psychic eye* opening there and they see an *indigo light*, (violet-blue.) The *crown chakra* or *pituitary center* at the top of the head is the ultimate energy center. This is a *vivid violet*. (The seven *chakras* coincide with the seven endocrine glands in those locations.)

When you arrive at the hands, instruct the group to vigorously rub them together to create healing energy. They then aim their hands at the bowl of water and relax. Then each successive person verbally mentions the name or names of family, pets, and/or friends who require special healing. You can also send out Universal peace, love and healing. Next, instruct the group to mentally wish *Divine Progress* to the souls of departed family and/or friends.

11.) When someone sees a green light flashing in the room; that is the signal to commence giving out impressions and/or entering a trance state. (Even if a green light is not evident, begin at your discretion.)

12.) Someone may feel that his or her head is being pulled back. That indicates that spirit guides are initiating a trance state in that person, attempting to *take him or her out*. If this causes discomfort or trepidation, tell the person to bless and thank the guides and firmly refuse at this time. Spirit guides can recognize potentially gifted mediums. Also, these sessions can generate and/or improve one's psychic ability as you will witness when you read on. That is why we call them psychic development classes as well.

13.) In a totally dark room, spirit lights are as clearly visible as stars twinkling in the night sky. Should the room suddenly become really black, the group sings or chants an OM up to three times to restore the high vibrations. Encourage the sitters to be verbally active, and not to merely wait for personal messages. Also, an atmosphere of levity is essential to sustain the high psychic energy and vibrations.

14.) Once you have established a viable and active group, a team of loyal guides on the other side will be conducting a séance with you. Those who sit in on your sessions must believe in God. This guarantees that participants are protected from negative energy. Do not permit anyone who fears the dark to join your group. Again, if anyone should express anxiety or trepidation during a session, try to calm and relax that person and promptly sing a lively tune or chant an OM. Do not invite that person back again. You may notice an umbrella-like formation over the proceedings. That is your spiritual protective shield.

15.) After about one to two hours, spirit will signal with a red light that it's time to conclude the session. If no one notices a red light, use your discretion. Before the room is illuminated, the closing hymn is sung: (***Great Fount of Love and Life and Light; inspire our hearts to do the right. Let us respond to Truth's high call, with Peace on earth, good will to all. Amen.***) Turn on the flashlight with the beam facing the ceiling to spare the sitters optical shock.

I must add a warning here. *DO NOT* under any circumstances dabble in spirit communication on your own. It's essential that you join with people who are spiritually based and seriously interested in developing. Always protect yourselves with the opening prayer and know that you will attract only the highest and purest energies. Another caveat; don't use the Ouija board for spirit communication. If you do work with a Ouija board, you should have a partner and use it solely for answering questions. It's advisable to invite someone who can record the proceedings.

Primarily, the Ouija board merely responds to your own psychic energy and the messages emanate from your subconscious. The same principle is involved with Table Tapping. (See Chapter IX.) When I taught my psychic development class up north, one of the experiments was an exercise in table tapping. My students and I sat around our massive cherry-wood dining-room table. Everyone's hands were placed in full view on the surface. We closed our eyes and concentrated on raising the table. Soon, we felt a vibration; then we all realized that the composition of the table began to feel alive! The wood actually felt like it was turning to gelatin under our hands! The table began to sway from side to side. It never left the floor, but the experiment was a success, nevertheless.

One evening four of us began in our bedroom with a bridge table. We were standing at the time. In seconds that table rose up from the floor and we practically had to chase it as it flew through the foyer.

Chapter XX

WHAT LIFE IS LIKE ON THE OTHER SIDE

WHEN WE FIRST began to sit in the dark hours, my prime, burning curiosity was what life is like on the other side. So, when our teacher's British guide, Dr. James came through for the first time it was a timely opportunity to question him.

(Q.) Can you tell us what kind of life you have? What do you do? (A.) It is a busy, bustling life here. We have Halls of Knowledge where anyone can go to study and learn. There are massive libraries, perhaps not as you know them, but information on any topic in the universe is available in an instant. (Q.) What happens at the time a soul enters your realm? (A.) He or she is brought over by highly evolved entities who are assigned to him or her. Then they are welcomed by loved ones and familiar souls whom they recognize. Their initial mission here is to undergo a life review. This is not done as a judgment by God. It is merely what you might recognize as a holographic depiction which impresses him or her instantaneously. His every thought, deed, attitude, behavior; good and bad is transmitted to him for his edification. His past lives are included in this depiction. All in all, he is being prepared for his eventual destiny. He is informed at the outset as to his Karmic duties and he works from there. (Q.) Is it true that whatever you think of is instantly manifested? (A.) Yes, because we are not encumbered by the physical; by time and space. Some newcomers who realize this prefer to wallow in fantasies of riches and lavish material possessions, for example, which they may have been denied on the earth plane. This does not continue, for they soon weary of it. (Q.) How does one know when it's his or her time to return to the physical; to reincarnate? (A.) If he would prefer to remain in this heavenly realm and it is his time to reincarnate, he is impelled by highly evolved entities whose duty it is to enlighten him. He is shown several options for his next sojourn in the physical, and he chooses the most beneficial vehicle for his evolvement. If needs be, and his choice does not suit his requirements, he is offered alternative suggestions. (Q.) What happens to people who believe in hell? (A.) If one believes that a hellish retribution is deserved, he can create that for himself, since there is no such thing as hell. (Q.) Does he remain in that situation for eternity? (A.) No. That would be counterproductive. He must be rescued from his hellish fantasy and instructed as to his true destiny. (Q.) What about those who don't believe in an afterlife? What happens to them? (A.) Oft'times, they merely sleep, but that is not permitted to continue. There is a council in charge of awakening them and guiding them gently as to their new life.

We then resumed with our regular dark hour.

Chapter XXI
TRAINING AND DEVELOPMENT AND
AN EERIE RESUSCITATION

THE FIRST GUIDE who spoke through me was an Egyptian who called himself Mamat. Because of my inexperience, or perhaps his scanty knowledge of the English language, he spoke very slowly and with an accent. Truthfully, I commend the other sitters for their patience. Their yawns were proof of their boredom, but they persevered with their queries.

Many years passed before I achieved the deepest trance state when I was not aware of any of the proceedings. I preferred the semi-trance because I could feel when an entity entered me and I was aware of what transpired. I would transfigure with their physical features and be privy to what caused their demise. That was one of the most exciting aspects of my trance. It was in the early eighties when Theone came through; (pronounced *Thee-o-knee.)* When asked what her name was, she introduced herself as *The One.* "You may call me Theone," she said; "but what is in a name, after all?" She became what she called my Control. From then on, she relayed all of the messages and disallowed anyone else to speak through me. I guessed that I had probably evolved to a higher level of consciousness by then, but I wasn't thrilled with the gift. I told Theone not to take it personally, that I loved and respected her in spite of it. She said she had lived in ancient Greece.

Most of our sessions were taped and it was our utmost privilege to have been included in those amazing proceedings. Every session was exciting, and the majority of them were inspirational and enlightening. Some of them were mind-blowing as you will see when you read on.

During the time when we were meeting, sometimes at Ben's place, frequently at Myra and Joe's home, and also at Bert's apartment, I expressed the desire to enhance my psychic abilities. Bert introduced me to Nella, (name changed,) a beautiful, gifted soul; a portrait artist and psychic development teacher whose guide was James Abbott McNeill, (Whistler.) It amazed me when this kind of thing occurred. All I had to do was ask to learn something new; another door would open for me and I would stride through it to new and exciting adventures. I knew that God was with me, urging me on to fulfill my metaphysical aspirations and providing me with the resources.

Nella had become involved with the American Society for Psychical Research whose main facility was situated in Illinois at that time. They were conducting research into a machine which was allegedly being developed on the other side by the *Imperator Group*. The machine was to replace the human instrument or medium, for communication with spirit. The *Imperator Group* consists of such notables as William Stanton Moses who apparently heads them; Richard Hodgson, Sir Arthur Conan Doyle, Frederic William Henry Myers, Bishop Samuel Wilberforce, Titus Bull, Sir Oliver Lodge, James A. Hyslop and others who have been involved in and researched the metaphysical and paranormal fields. Some of them identified themselves with a symbol.

In October, 1968, our class began to meditate with the expectation of receiving information from them to implement construction of such a machine on this side. While I was meditating, my pen was poised over my note pad and it began to write. *We have seen you working. You want to know about machines over here. We have been working on many. Just a few perfected. You have experienced sound of one.* (Then it continued with more data and symbols which are irrelevant at this time.)

They were referring to an incident on the night of May 23rd in Myra and Joe's family room. Eight of us were sitting in a circle in the dark as always, with our tape recorder running. Our friends, Barbara and her mother Charlotte had joined us for the last time because they were relocating from New Jersey to California. Barbara was apparently in a depressed state because of it and she should not have attended that night. I was sitting at one end of a Naugahyde sofa with Barbara lying in a semi-prone position at the opposite end. Her guide Selma Cumpayo induced her to sit upright. I could tell, because Barbara was quite heavy and as she moved, the Naugahyde made a swishing sound. There were three séance trumpets on the table in the center of the room with the bowl of salted water and jar of sand. Selma said she was trying to raise a trumpet. Then we heard Barbara slumping back on the sofa, breathing heavily and groaning loudly. Charlie asked, "Is anything wrong with the speaker. Selma?" "We're trying to help, sir. Just relax, please." Charlie: "You want *us* to relax; or are you relaxing the speaker?" Selma: "I'm sorry, sir, but I think I have done a slight bit of damage this evening. Please, I must leave immediately. Please pray." (This was an unusual admission and request by a guide.) Charlie: "What kind of damage could you have done?" (No response. The tape recorder was turned off for a while as we prayed.) Then, it seemed that Selma was still with us, for she spoke again, bringing messages from Harry, Barbara's late father, Charlotte's husband. He was asking his loved ones to give him blessings. Then, Selma said testily, "Why must I be the middle-man?"

(That was highly uncharacteristic of a guide. I can only rationalize that she was a neophyte, lacking in experience.)

Barbara groaned again, and it sounded like she was shifting her position, when she obviously slid off the sofa and landed on the floor with a thump. At this time, I was entering a trance-state. Although I was silent throughout the episode, I was aware of the proceedings. Suddenly, the atmosphere in the room seemed to alter and a strange, new sound was introduced to our perception. It was a barely audible ticking, as of an electric motor, similar to the steady throb of a refrigerator motor. There was a murmured exchange of questions buzzing in the room as this new sound crept into everyone's consciousness.

Charlotte: "Harry, get her out of it." Bert: "Is that water?" Charlotte: "No, it isn't." Harry: "No; it's a machine;" whispered three times. Charlie: "No; it's all right." Bert: "Come on, Barbara." Charlie: "Is that you, Harry?" Harry: (In a hushed voice.) "Yes." (I must interject here that Harry had always regretted not having had the opportunity to become a physician. Due to family circumstances, that wasn't possible in this lifetime.) Charlie: "Well, what is that noise?" Harry: "It's just us working, that's all." Charlie: "Just you working?" Harry: "That's all; the group of us." Charlie: "Huh?" Harry: "The group; the group." Charlie: "The whole group of you?" Harry: "That's right." Charlie: "Are there any problems?" Harry: (In a patient tone;) "We're just putting life back, that's all." Charlie: "Fine. No problems at all, then?" Harry: "Everything's fine, now." Charlotte: "Good." Harry: "She's just waking up, some. Sh; everything will be fine." Charlotte: "That's Harry talking." Harry: "Don't worry. Things are gonna be fine." Charlie: "Keep working hard; we need that girl." Charlotte: "That sounds like a trumpet." Harry: "Yes; we're working." Charlie: "You stay around too, Har. She's coming along just fine? Speak up, Har." Harry: "Just fine. No; I must lose strength so she will gain it. That's my girl." Charlie: "Harry, let go." Harry: "Sh; everything's all right, now. She's just in a little sleep;

just patiently. She will awaken very shortly. I'm leaving." Charlie: "'Bye, Har. Bless you." (Here, Charlie turned off the tape recorder.) Bert, later: "Now, come back, dear. Come back, Barbara. Come back to us. Come back, dear." (We had enjoyed amazing physical phenomena during many of our séances, but nothing quite like that. That's why Charlie was so perplexed.)

Charlie and Bert together urged Barbara to return. When she did, she had no idea what had transpired until we replayed the tape for her. The sound we heard was apparently a spiritual resuscitator to which the *Imperator Group* had referred in my automatic writing.

February 20, 1969: Twelve of us met in Myra and Joe's family room. Nella, my psychic development teacher, and Maude S., (name changed,) from the American Society for Psychical Research, were there to garner information regarding the machines. When Neal was in trance, he transfigured, and Titus Bull spoke through him. Apparently, Titus Bull was a Hitchcock type, for his voice was muffled with a British accent. Nella and Maude questioned him. He said that many all over the world are working on the same project--developing machines with the aid of the *Imperator Group*. "Continue to work together as you do now." Q.: "Do you have the machine on that side?" A.: "For a long time. We are just helping you to help yourselves." They asked for a formula, and he gave it.

All of this technical discourse was affecting vibrations in the room, so Pottsy kindly interjected with an earsplitting OM which resonated through every fiber of our bodies. Then we heard the faint tinkle of bells. Ben said a Hindu Dervish was ringing temple bells.

After several classes with Nella and almost as many sessions in Myra and Joe's family room with representatives from the *ASPR* encouraging our group to focus on the communicating machine, it was finally constructed. They even coerced Neal to cut school one afternoon because he was apparently receiving formulas from the other side. The machine proved to be much too sensitive. It was similar to a telegraph receiver; so if a truck happened to pass the building, it would be activated. So much for that; but it was a unique and worthwhile experience for all of us.

While studying with Nella, we learned a smattering of numerology, palmistry, physiognomy and phrenology. She also acquainted us with the *I Ching;* (pronounced Yee Jing,) the Chinese method of divining via pick-up sticks and hexagrams. This fascinated me and I became addicted to the practice, unaware at the time of the significance, which was revealed to me later on.

Chapter XXII
THE DOG BITE AND LAO TZU

<u>OCTOBER 21, 1969</u>: Our daughter Layne, spotted a dog standing in the middle of the road in front of our house. She bent over and beckoned him to come to her as she saw a car headed towards him. He obeyed but he showed his gratitude by nipping her on the flesh of her inner left calf. We described the dog to the police and the animal control department. The doctor recommended an anti-tetanus shot and briefed us on the unwelcome details and prospects of anti-rabies shots.

For days thereafter, Layne was plagued with panic attacks; trembling and depressed; fearful that the dog may have been rabid. We felt confident that he wasn't because she had seen a license on him and the dog-catcher had also seen him and claimed that he looked okay. He did say that he'd had many complaints about that elusive animal, yet Layne remained inconsolable.

A couple of weeks prior to this incident, we were sitting in our teacher, Ben's living-room and he was in trance. Someone described an old Chinese man with a long, slender beard wearing a skull-cap, when the sweet scent of sandalwood wafted under everyone's nose.

Then, a gentle voice with an Asian accent identified himself as Lao Tzu. This came through as direct voice, with no inflection of our teacher's timbre. He greeted us with blessings, and in response to our queries, he mentioned that he had not reincarnated for approximately 3,000 years our time.

Lao Tzu, who lived between the 6th and 5th centuries BC, was the founder of Taoism and also a co-creator of the hexagrams in the *I Ching*, which I was studying with Nella. *I Ching* is also known as *The Book of Change*. When we use the Chinese fortune-telling sticks, (or pick-up sticks,) we ask a question and flip the sticks to determine which hexagram will provide the answer. I found that interpreting the hexagrams, which are depicted as inscrutable riddles, was proving to be incomprehensible to me most of the time.

This was another propitious and miraculous occurrence which resulted in a *demonstration*. I had been *treating* for help with the *I Ching*, and when I heard Lao Tzu's name, I was equally astounded and ecstatic. I knew this was the answer to my prayer. "Oh, Lao Tzu," I exclaimed, "I'm so thrilled to meet you! You know, I'm learning the *I Ching* and I'm having such a problem deciphering and interpreting the hexagrams. Would you please help me with them?" "Of course, my child," he said in soft, dulcet tones, "I would be honored to do so."

In early November, Layne and I secluded ourselves in my bedroom. I asked the *I Ching*, "Was the dog that bit Layne rabid?" While we sat there quietly and peacefully working, a fragrance passed under our noses. Layne immediately identified it as a perfume and remarked, "Somebody is here." I casually agreed, "Yes, it must be Lao Tzu since he has promised to help me with the *I Ching*; but it's a new incense. He usually brings a sandalwood scent." "Mmmm, that's beautiful," Layne said. "Lay it on me, Lao Tzu," and she received another whiff.

The message from the hexagram was a benign one. In other words, according to my interpretation, it indicated no danger. Soon after, while preparing dinner in the kitchen, I envisioned myself and Layne back in the bedroom and saw myself going into a trance. Lao Tzu spoke through me to Layne; "Have no fear, my child; everything is all right." As soon as my consciousness recovered, Layne ran in and exclaimed, "You know, Mom, I feel much better. When we were in the bedroom working the *I Ching*, I heard a voice say to me, 'Don't worry, my child; everything is all right,' and it sounded like Lao Tzu's voice."

Layne remained more secure for a week or so, and then the half-quenched fears began to burn brightly again because the dog hadn't been caught, nor had we seen him since the incident of October 21st. We tried to convince her that there was no reason for concern because so much time had elapsed and she had no symptoms of hydrophobia, but she was still ambivalent.

So, I began to *treat* to bring him forth. The night of November 8th, Charlie, quite disturbed by Layne's depression also, said a prayer that the dog be seen by us again. The following afternoon he was alone in the kitchen drinking coffee and he smelled saffron under his nose. This was our guide Pottsy identifying himself as he had always done at our classes. Charlie promptly recognized it and said, "Welcome Pottsy, and thank you for visiting, but please come back at class." Then, he was impressed that Pottsy replied, "You asked to see the dog again. Go to your window and look out in your back yard." Charlie obeyed, and there was the same brown dog which had bitten Layne watering our horse-chestnut tree. He appeared to be strong and healthy.

That afternoon, Layne arrived home from school and breathlessly announced that as she waited that morning on the corner for her friends, she saw the dog across the street from her. On Saturday, November 15th, Charlie saw a brown dog with our mailman. He felt that if anyone knew where the dog lived, it would be the mailman, so he asked him. He was told that a mean dog fitting the description lived two blocks away from our house, and he offered the address. Layne joined Charlie to identify the dog and she recognized him as the culprit. We later discovered that the dog belonged to the daughter of a close friend of Charlie's. She adamantly denied that her dog had ever been let loose.

Chapter XXIII
DARK HOURS/(SÉANCES),PHENOMENA

<u>DECEMBER 12, 1968</u>: Seven of us gathered in Ben's living-room. The psychic and spiritual energy was exceptional. Bert's late husband, Bill caressed her with a trumpet, trembling emotionally. Tess, our teacher's late wife explained that he is still new at this and needs to learn to calm down. We all giggled when Bea Z., Bert's late husband's secretary, grabbed a trumpet and exuberantly banged everyone in the room on the lap. Prior to that Bert said she felt Bea's arm which had the consistency of some kind of fuzzy material. According to Bert, Bea had been a hefty, extroverted woman with a rather masculine demeanor. In a stentorian voice she bellowed, "Hey Bert, what plane ya workin' from, now?" This was confirmation of their frequent telephone conversations when she would tease Bert about her paranormal activities.

Helen H., a gentle, unassuming Spiritualistic Minister who stammered when she spoke, often sat with us. She had a Native American guide who also came through thunderously in direct voice. He rumbled, "Me Big Oak. Ugh!" Rabbi Joshua Loth Leibman, the author of *Peace of Mind*, spoke softly and affably, blessing everyone, also in direct voice. Then he rewarded us with a liturgical hymn chanted in sonorous tones.

Maria Ouspenskaya greeted us and we told her we missed hearing from her for some time. "I can't stick mine big nose in all the time," she quipped. This was the day the actress, Tallulah Bankhead made her transition and I mentioned it. She replied, "Yes, and we made her a big party." Then she spoke genially to Joe: "Joseph, we need you," referring to his psychokinetic gift. (Joe denied this, but we were all aware of it because of the activity which besieged him when we sat.) He said sheepishly, "I can't think of anything to say. I'm trying to understand it all." "You don't have to understand; you can just work with us and we'll work with you," Maria said. "Just be like me, stupid and put your nose in. You are such a wonderful circle to work with and we'll see you through. God bless you all."

I saw the Dove of Peace ascending and was impressed that the Vietnamese war will be over soon with no victory, but peace at least.

December 26, 1968: Eight of us met in Ben's living-room. Dr. James came through when Ben went into trance and answered some questions. To give you an idea of how long-winded he was, I am not going to paraphrase his responses. He spoke in his British accent, and while he was expounding, he moved about the room with the trumpet. The tape recorder was situated in the center of the room, so his voice trailed off at times. "I would like you to know that it is not always possible to have physical phenomena, which, in the first place, your sitters bring out the best in each hour for the united phenomena which can be produced in that sitting. There is an inter-audit reaction from each of you to each of you and to us, and we make do with that which you send us. This evening, you have a mental group, and at this specific time in the world there are three planetary conjunctions and those conjunctions are spiritual conjunctions. Therefore, where there are juxtapositions of planets with which we could gather physical strength, we could produce phenomena with your group. But, we must needs work with that which we are given. God bless you and carry on."

Myra: "If spirit feels that one is ready to go into trance, even though one may not feel he or she is ready, should they be willing to go along with spirit's idea?"

Dr. James: "Under protective guidance; yes; which you have about you. And you, my dear girl also have protection when you are ready to come to us. Thank you." (What was implied here is in the trance state one generally leaves the body to allow spirit to enter.)

January 16, 1969: Myra and Joe's family room. Dr. James came through when Ben was in trance. He held forth in his customary verbose manner: "Good evening. As you know we do not sit in judgment. I would like you to know that there are times when you send to us, instead of unitarian feelings, a feeling of controversy; and this there are two of you doing this evening. It is therefore difficult to work with you at times. In the past, whenever we have taken of your time, we have paid you in return for your time. We cannot always do so, because we must needs work with that which you send out. You understand? And when you send out in unitarian language at the séance, it is returned to you. If we have stolen from you, we will multiply and send it back. God bless you. Please do not consider this criticism, but advice. We are all love and budding, and everything is done to you in the name of love, but there must be complete spiritual and mental harmony."

Chapter XXIV
THE TRUTH ABOUT SUICIDE AND MORE

<u>JANUARY 23, 1969</u>: Nine of us met in Myra and Joe's family room. The discussion pre-séance was metaphysical, as usual. Someone questioned suicide and mentioned the suicide of Episcopalian Bishop James Albert Pike's son Jim in 1966, which had caused a sensation in the news and on TV. After he had a homosexual affair he committed suicide experimenting with LSD. Bishop Pike felt inconsolably guilty because he was too busy to notice his son's despair. He wrote the book, *The Other Side*, after consulting with mediums and receiving alleged communication from his son. In the summer of 1969, Bishop Pike fell off a cliff in the Israeli desert. Three days before the discovery of his body, medium Ena Twigg foresaw what had occurred and pinpointed the location of his body. The discussion follows:

Bert: "It's a violent kind of death, and I can't see anybody making contact even within a year, let alone such a short time as ten days, as Bishop Pike's son did." Ben: "Why?" Bert: "If he took his life, this was evidently the time for him to pass over, anyway." Ben: "That's what metaphysics teaches, yes. Otherwise *he would not have been successful*. Is it wrong or right?" Bert and Norma: "It's wrong." Joe: "I don't think it makes any difference in the spirit world whether you take your own life, get run over by a train or die a natural death. You're not supposed to, according to the way we think on earth, but in higher planes, according to what I've read, it doesn't make a difference." Bert: "According to what I have read, it is not a natural death. It's gruesome." Joe: "It's only gruesome to you. They leave the body at the moment of death." Ruth: "I have read that if a soul reincarnates and it finds that once in the physical body, it is not going to be able to accomplish the task it had set for itself before it came into this union, the soul decides that it doesn't want to go on, and it decides to terminate this life. It just stops living. Now, this would be *su-i-cide* also, wouldn't it? If this soul had lived to be 22 like Bishop Pike's son, and then had used a different method like putting his head in the oven, or stabbing himself, or done some other thing, it would still be suicide, here or there. Now, apparently it is perfectly legitimate, according to natural laws to do what the baby does—die without cause; without visible cause. How do you handle that?" Ben: "Now, you brought up a point, Joe, that Bert says it's gruesome to commit suicide. In view of the fact that the person is doing what they want to do; it's not gruesome to them." Bert: "It's gruesome to the one's they left behind." Ben: "Yes." Charlie: "Joe said that it was time for the soul to pass over, whether he was hit by a train, or whatever, that was his time and he went over. If such is the case, then he wouldn't have had to commit suicide. If this is true, then he would have had cause to die differently; or having the body diminished so the soul could be released, if that was his time." Ruth: "But, he was given cause, only it didn't have to come out in the physical. It came out in the mental." Norma: "Besides the conscious act, I can't believe that this conscious act is right." Ben: "If you're having guests that you resent, and you're cooking and fussing and making a salad; your resentment can cause you to end up with a little blood in the salad." Norma: "Yes; I know that." Ben: "Now, this is an accident?" Norma: "No, it's not. There are no accidents." Ben: "That's true. If you walk out in the middle of traffic at high noon, no matter if the day is foggy or clear, and you stop in front of a truck, and you're run over; this is potentially a suicide. But, when you check the (astrological) chart, you'll find that this was the hour you were supposed to go." Norma: "I see; causally." Andy: (name changed,) "The interesting point is that maybe this suicide caused a good thing; like with Bishop Pike; a lot of people are getting aware of it because of his position." Joe: "Does it make any difference to the spirit body?" Ben: "No, it does not. Now, the difference comes in—which makes Bert also partially right; if we have all decided suicide is wrong, and we believe within ourselves that suicide is wrong, when we go over, we are earthbound and we are prevented from progressing." Norma: "Oh, that's what I wanted to get to." Ben: "Now, supposing I was not back-grounded, and we have read that we're all a problem if we commit suicide, and we're here some night and we get gassed because Joe was kind enough to put a hole in the wall and leave the car running in the garage. He gets us all out of our misery, you see. Now, we're not aware of this, but we know that we all die. Now, Joe who knows the one solution and has read and has left the door open on the other side, meets a rabbi that he has known in the past, who he trusts. The rabbi says to him, 'Joseph, what you did was wrong. Now, you have to teach all those friends of yours that you helped come over to this wonderful land of ours, the truth.' So, he comes to us because we trust and love him and he explains one by one and convinces us that we can progress, and he is the only person that we'll listen to. Now, he can't progress until he has straightened all of us out on the other side; then he can reincarnate." Bert: "When we reincarnate, we know with whom we are going to be. We also know the Karmic debts that we may accept here in this earth life, so do we also say, 'I will commit suicide and I accept my suicide?'" Ben: "Certainly. You know your general life plan." Bert: "Then suicide is not such a horrible thing." Ben: "Of course not. That's what we said in the first place." Ruth: "Actually, it's not. It's only what man has believed." Norma: Bishop Pike wears this medallion around his neck and it means 819. Is there another meaning for that symbol?" Ben: "Yes. That also means the extension of God Consciousness, and the Christ Consciousness is symbolic of it through the cross which is formulated with two triangles; two outgoing triangles; complimentary triangles."

(Throughout the years that Bert was in our lives, she attempted suicide three times with an overdose of drugs. Each time, she phoned us at all hours of the night, for help. The fourth attempt, she tried to starve herself to death. One day she looked at her image in the mirror and was so startled, that she proceeded to engorge herself with ice-cream and other fattening foods. She overburdened her gallbladder which then required surgical excision.)

From this discourse on suicide I learned that it isn't wrong; that if it isn't successful, as in Bert's many attempts, it is simply not one's time to go.

Someone asked about the *Etheric Sheath* and what happens to it after physical death. Ben: "The *Etheric Sheath* takes 72 hours to free itself from the physical body; but it does not dissolve until the body dissolves. It hangs around, and that is what is very often seen at funeral homes and cemeteries, etc. The *Astral Body* is gone within 36 hours or so, and it's free within 24 hours of death. Most of the time it starts to free itself three days before the physical death. The *Sheath* has no emotions; no conscious registration of anything. What makes the *Sheath* corrupt in our view is that, for example, when the legs of the body decay, the *Sheath* decays, because it has no protein to sustain strength. So, when all you see is the head and shoulders, if it's a *Sheath*, it means in that case, that from the shoulders down the rest of the body is gone. When the individual is cremated, there is no *Etheric Sheath* left behind, because cremation dissolves the *Sheath* no matter where it is in relation to the body." Bert: "That's why cremation is good. You're not having this *Etheric Sheath* hanging around." Ben: "Right." Neal: "How long does it take the soul to leave, or does it hang around?" Ben: "The soul is usually released an hour or two before physical death. It starts releasing two or three days ahead." Neal: "So, what's the bit when they bring people back to life after they're dead?" Ben: "They only restore life. They do not promise to restore soul, and there's a tremendous difference; right?" Neal: "There have been cases where people die on the operating table or in the ambulance and up to two or three minutes later they can shock them back to life." Ben: "Yes, but how long do they live?" Bert: "Well, some of them do survive, but in those cases the *Astral Body* hasn't been released, so the *silver cord* is still connected." Ben: "Right. Neal, the only people who are restored to life have this coming Karmically. The clinically dead who are brought back usually have an absolutely complete change of personality." (Note: The *silver cord* is the spiritual umbilical cord. Just before a person dies it is released with the *Astral Body*.)

Our dark hour followed this discussion. It was an active night for development and instruction. Ben had a medium friend from Pennsylvania. Her guide was Yellow Rose a Native American Indian princess whom Ben said was an old soul. She preferred to manifest as a young child. Yellow Rose visited us frequently, and she loved to fondle Ben's bushy beard. She would usually join us when we sang *The Yellow Rose of Texas.*

I saw a yellow rosebud and I said Yellow Rose must be here. She tapped twice on the trumpet for acknowledgment. Then she moved around the room and tapped everyone; but she specifically caressed Charlie. Much later, we understood why, because we discovered that in his previous lifetime he had been an Indian prince. (More on that in Chapter XXXV.)

There was much symbolism. Bert saw an umbrella over her: protection. Neal saw a brain: knowledge. He also saw a sunflower: yellow means wisdom and intelligence, and the seeds mean growth, (spiritually.) Neal's Indian guide Red Deer was identified. Bert's Indian guide was Straight Arrow. She saw a pair of moccasins in front of her and she smelled the fresh leather.

When I entered a semi-trance and received a message from Richard Hodgson of the *Imperator Group*, I felt as though I was being bitten by a bug on both of my forearms for quite a while. When the session was over and the lights were on, I examined my arms. There were tiny perforations on the veins on both of them.

Pottsy, Ben's East Indian guide said soothingly, "If you would sustain the vibrations like you have tonight, you would have good results. We are always here to work with you. You are a wonderful group to work with." We thanked him, and he said, "You are very welcome. God bless you." Dr. James, Ben's British doctor repeated a similar message. A hand touched Bert on her left arm, and a voice whispered in her ear, "Take my hand and I'll help you out," encouraging her to go into a trance. Pottsy explained that the hand is only symbolic. Everyone was touched by a hand, and we all felt a breeze passing over us. The room was radiant with light which signified high vibrations and psychic energy.

Our pets came to visit, also. Everyone recognized the particular sound of their pet; Ruth's dog, Beau; Bert's Demitasse, and our fox terrier, Rusty, who bounded in excitedly yapping, and whizzed around the room. He landed in Neal's lap with the trumpet. Neal was a toddler when we had to euthanize Rusty due to a coronary condition.

Charlie saw a bright cone coming down into the room. Pottsy told us that is how spirit enters. He added, "It is up to each individual to make the world a better place." Neal asked "Why haven't I gone into trance since our episodes with Nella?" Pottsy: "No one has the power to control your trance. You should say, 'I *can* go into trance.'" We all discussed how each of us can effect peace on earth. Pottsy offered some spiritual knowledge. Since he spoke with an accent and moved about the room with the trumpet, some of the dialogue came through patchy on the recording tape. He also explained why our teacher, Ben has so many guides working with him. "He is an old and very special soul, and we are privileged to be able to do so."

January 30, 1969: Seven of us met in Ben's home. Andy R., (name changed,) who sat with us occasionally, was a photographer who was involved in UFO research. In the kitchen we listened to a long, technical tape that he brought from a séance in Ohio of what he called *magnetic voice*. It was allegedly direct voice emanating from another galaxy. The voice was very high-pitched and the dialogue quite inaudible because of the extreme velocity of the tape. They tried to slow it down, to no avail.

When we sat in the living-room that night, I asked our guides about the perforations on my arms of the previous week. "Have you done something to cause them?" Two taps on the trumpet meant *yes*. "Did you take something from me, like blood?" One tap meant *no*. "Did you give me something?" *Yes*. "Was it for healing?" Three taps for *maybe*. "For physical and spiritual?" *Yes*. "Thank you."

When Pottsy came through, Charlie told him that he had seen his father high up as if looking in on us. Pottsy said, "Your teacher has mentally built such a beautifully awesome cathedral that your father fears entering." So, when we welcomed Papa Locker, Charlie mentioned that it was 17 years since he had passed over. I was impressed that Charlie's sister, Marcella was also there. We sang *Hava Nagilla*, and they grabbed the trumpets and began to joyously dance around together, banging noisily on the glass water bowl and ending in a grand dervish. Pottsy told us that since it was an anniversary, they helped them come through.

Charlie made a remark which prompted me to respond with, "You can't have your cake and eat it, too, honey," when I felt a sharp slap on my left knee. It was Papa's powerful shoemaker hand, and I could almost hear him retorting exultantly, "You said it, kid!"

Yellow Rose joined us when we sang her theme song, *The Yellow Rose of Texas*. There was a toy xylophone on a chair next to where I was sitting, and it tapped out the melody.

Then, a Captain X, (name concealed,) came through for Andy. Andy explained that he had vanished after his book was published exposing the government's *Blue Book Project* which reported false information regarding UFO sightings and landings. In other words, it appeared that Captain X was conveniently eliminated.

Someone asked if we were imposing upon or interrupting them when we meet like this. Exuding geniality, Pottsy responded: "You cannot interrupt us in our world unless we wish to be interrupted. We consider it a privilege to be with you, those of us who have dedicated themselves to bettering of the world. And, the world is bettered by individuality, not necessarily by group. Because of the differentiation in Karma, you cannot have a group world Karma. No one has anything to do with the development of another. We are our own developers.

"New people have been sending through development groups with thoughts of peace, love and harmony. They would like to reform our world and their world, yet they cannot in their own group achieve peace, love and harmony. Also, you know that your path is individual and must remain so, but you could form a unit of a community which could help your own progression.

"So often many people ask why such a band of guides would work with your medium whom we love and serve for so long. He seems to have nothing in the material. The material is an unnecessary thing; it is unimportant. We love and respect this work with him

because he is a living example of what can be done. He lives his philosophy. We love and bless you. God bless you."

One night when we sat in Ben's living-room, my sister-in-law
Marcella greeted me with, "Hi, Norm!" directly into my left ear.
Charlie was absent for that session otherwise he surely would have
received her greeting.

Marcella adored Layne when she was an infant. She lived
upstairs from us and every morning she visited to play with her. We
were sitting in Ben's living-room one night when Marcella came
through. Because of the love that she felt for Layne, she tried to enter
her. Her head was being pulled back and it disturbed and frightened
her. I said, "Aunt Marcella loves you, sweetheart. She means you no
harm, you know that." In a trembling voice she said, "But, I don't
want it." "Then bless her and tell her you love her, but to please
come back at another time." Layne was fifteen at the time.

Myra's mother, Jeanette, had been involved with the paranormal
for years before her passing. She and Bert were close friends and they
dabbled in it together. One night we were sitting in Myra and Joe's
family room. We were a large group of ten or more people, including
our teacher, Ben. Myra identified her mother's presence and welcomed her. As she did, this being her initial breakthrough, Jeanette
grabbed a trumpet and with amazing energy she flew around the
room repeatedly, whizzing in front of everyone's nose. In that stygian
room, no one was touched or swatted by that trumpet. All we could
feel was the breeze as it whisked past us.

The obvious exhilaration of being able to communicate, in whatever manner they can, is what motivated me at the outset to become
a channel.

May 11, 1969: Eight of us met in Myra and Joe's family room.
Jeanette, Myra's Mom, visited again, and Myra asked her to play the
piano which stood against a remote wall in the room. The lid of the
piano was down. In a dismayed tone Joe said, "I heard that piano."

Myra urged her Mom to play it again. An eerie *bong, bong, bong* echoed in the room. Joe quipped, "This may cause me to change my religion! This is too rich for my blood." When she visited, she would caress him all over his body with the trumpet, which made him very uneasy. Most of the time he sat with his arms folded across his chest and his legs in lotus position, because of the activity which besieged him.

Chapter XXV

MORE DARK HOURS, PHENOMENA AND
EXTRATERRESTRIAL

FEBRUARY 6, 1969: Seven of us gathered in Ben's living-room. Everyone gave out many psychic impressions. Someone made a derogatory remark about a late family member. Ben explained that spirit is always shielded from any unhappiness. "When we think of them they pick it up," he said, "but not the bad things. If you ask them anything about a previous evening when they manifested, to them it's still the same evening. Time means nothing to them."

Charlie identified Pottsy's saffron aroma, and Pottsy spoke: "You can say anything to guides. We are beyond reaction or feeling insulted."

Helen saw a man by Neal with gray hair. Neal thought of Albert Einstein and he was tapped. He asked him if it was he who gave him formulas for the machine the day he cut school, and he was tapped again. Tess, Ben's late wife called his name. Ben said she was coaxing him to *come over.* Charlie smelled a spicy fragrance which Ben identified as Desert Flower, Tess's favorite cologne. The trumpets collapsed on the floor with a clamor. We sang *Hava Nagilla* and they clangorously reassembled with Papa and Marcella dancing rhythmically again, banging on the water bowl.

Ben's Dr. James came through when Neal mentioned that cigarette commercials have been outlawed on TV, and he wondered if smoking affected spirit communication. We listened attentively as Dr. James responded in his customary rhetoric: "We, because of the allergy factor, cannot work with those of you who are tobacco saturated. Please do not take this as a personal criticism. But, you know, for nine years in your physical body, the harmful deposits of tobacco remain in your cellular structure. Since we are working with that cellular structure, we have a reaction to it. There are also other factors. If your instrumentation is imperfect, your materializations, your mental material and your rapport with us is interfered with. You have the right to destroy that which you wish to destroy, that is your prerogative; but you do not have the right to destroy other mentality, spirituality or work. So, therefore, since God is timeless, and since evolvement is timeless, it cannot matter to us really, whether you do it in this lifetime or the next, because it is of your own choosing. And, since we are with God, we cannot become impatient, nor would we wish to. So, the time span is up to you two wonderful people. God bless you." He was referring to Bert and Neal who were smokers.

Charlie asked, "If my father speaks, will it be his voice or our teacher's?" Dr. James: "That depends entirely on those of you who are contributing to the *instrument*, and the *instrument*, itself." (Referring to the medium.) "If an instrument is in very deep trance with no inhibitory factors, the complete, true voice comes through. As, for example, in my case; if you were to make a voice-print of my voice, as opposed to that of your instrument with whom we are working, you would find the two voice-prints completely dissimilar. Newcomers need training and experience. (Referring to those who have recently made their transition.) You cannot compare those of us who have had special training with those very dear friends of yours who are just reaching out in pure, unselfish love.

"Sometimes sitters wonder why they are touched in peculiar places. The reason for that is because that is the most obvious, strongest part of their aura at the time they are touched. It does not predicate anything in the sexual realm. To those spirits who are touching through, they believe they are touching the hand or the head of the individual." Charlie: "Even though they are touching you on the arm or shoulder." Dr. James: "They also have to learn how to modulate their voices."

Neal asked, "Well, how can they do that? They can see us perfectly, can't they?" Dr. James: "No, they cannot. They see your astral body and they go into the light that they see, even if it extends away from your physical body by many feet. They believe it is outer skin." Neal: "Well, how can they miss us so accurately with the trumpet?" Dr. James: "Perhaps you don't realize that many of you have been touched to their credulity and you have not felt anything physical, because your astral bodies are what they can see as your physical bodies. If your astral has extended earth inches; it is perhaps 30 earth inches away from your physical self; they go into the density which they think is your aura, four or five inches. They do not touch you, but they get the satisfaction of having made physical contact." Bert: "That's what our teacher told us. Sometimes he'll say, 'The trumpet just touched you,' and we deny that. But, it has." Ruth: "Yes, it has touched you, *you,* but you don't know it." (Ruth is touched by trumpet for confirmation.) Neal: "May I ask a question? You say that the spirit sees the astral and not the physical. If the astral is projected from the physical, why doesn't the trumpet crash into the physical body sometimes when it goes flying around the room?" Dr. James: "It sometimes does." Charlie: "Is the aura with the astral body and it's the light of the aura that they see?" (Two taps on the trumpet for *yes.*) Dr. James: "There are times when your teacher, for example, removes his astral with him when he comes to visit us, and many of you have seen the radiant light which surrounds him. This is the area that his aura has been in, and any spirit which enters that zone believes that they are in tactile contact with him, and they believe that it is outer skin. You must realize that the reason for raising your vibratory rate is that you, as a group of sitters come up, so to speak, to our vibratory rate and we lower ours to yours. The two worlds become continuous." Charlie: "Like the meeting of the minds." (Two taps on the trumpet for *yes.*)

Something funny was said, and Bert chuckled about something she had done. She said, "I wonder what my Indian and Hindu guides feel about what I did. They must think I'm wacky." Dr. James: "They are attracted to you out of love and they can see nothing but love coming from you to them." Bert: "Thank you." Ruth: "What do they make of all the levity, Dr.?" Dr. James: "My dear, if we didn't have levity, we could not face life." Charlie: "What kind of guide do I have?" Dr. James: "As you are dealing in the commercial world, you attract those of your friends who have gone over who are of like mind. They therefore impress you when not to talk, when the closing is near, and you sometimes respond to this and quietly subside; then the client signs. But, there are times when you have left a client and you know that you have talked too much and have killed your closing. So, you were not attuned to the guidance that was afforded you at that time. We too, are studying and learning spiritual law and spiritual reaction through work with you. Now, on the physical plane, those friends would be called borderland workers or guides, but they are not that spiritually evolved. You attract to you like-minded guides. They guide you as to when you should stop your sales pitch and when to close, etc. As you go forth, and as you sow in our grounds in spirituality, the next guide who is like-minded and is your chemical type, will work with you." (It was evident that Dr. James was aware that Charlie was a life-insurance salesman.)

<u>March 20, 1969</u>: Nine of us gathered in Ben's living-room for a phenomenal evening. We were visited by flying saucers and a spider-like extra-terrestrial being who sat on the ottoman in front of Ben and me. This beautiful soul spoke to us softly and lovingly in direct voice, with no inflection of our teacher's timbre. At the time, I couldn't make out the features of this creature, but later as I sketched him, he had deep, cavernous eyes. He was unlike any of the stereo-typed aliens that have been depicted in films and on TV.

That night I was so stimulated by that event that it disturbed my sleep. I don't know if this was a dream or reality. I pictured him as I had seen him at Ben's place, and proceeded to question him tele-pathically: (Q.) "What is your size? I was impressed that you are about two to three feet in height." (A.) "That is correct. We range from one to three feet in height depending on intelligence and evolu-tion." (Q.) "How do you communicate with each other? You speak such beautiful English to us. Is that how you relate to each other, also?" (A.) "No, we communicate telepathically as we are now doing and through touch. You know, we have eight limbs, and we can touch each other when close enough. We also have antennae which we use if necessary." (Q.) "Where do you live? Am I correct that you live underground?" (A.) "We submerge or descend to protect us from certain natural atmospheric conditions which occur at certain times of the year, (as you know it.) We live on the surface and we must hibernate for some of the time below the surface. We are equally equipped in both places." (Q.) "I saw you with a bee-hive device over you at one time. I was wrong to assume that you carry this with you, wasn't I? I can't imagine how you would do so." (A.) "Yes. We do have shelters which we use in case of emergency when we cannot descend quickly, or on time. We reach one of these shel-ters and with an electric-eye device which we carry, it rises and we lower it over us with this device. We can remain there indefinitely until it is safe to emerge. There is one for each of us on the surface."

(Q.) "Do you live in peace, or are you threatened at any time by violence or enemies? Are all of your race as beautiful as you are?" (A.)
"We are a peaceful race, but at times unexpected visitors arrive and
are sometimes shocked at our appearance, so they feel they must
protect themselves. We are equipped to defend ourselves, and if
needs be, we do so." This was all I remembered from the *(dream)*? I
don't recall if I asked where they came from.

Later, we were informed that what we witnessed at Ben's place
that night was a projection from another galaxy.

Chapter XXVI
METAPHYSICAL DISCUSSION,
EAVESDROPPING AND
TEACHING BY GUIDES

<u>FEBRUARY 27, 1969</u>: Nine of us gathered at Myra and Joe's place. Before lights out, Ben enlightened us with some of his amazing knowledge. Due to chatter in the background from disinterested people, some of it was inaudible on the tape. Ben: "If the **U** is in the first name, you come from an old tribe. **U** in either name designates an old soul. We have named the planets that have **U** in their name from our own perspective. An old soul is one who has lived many, many lifetimes before this one. Most of those with **U** in the name are involved with, and/or imbued with psychic and metaphysical ability and knowledge." Charlie: "Why was Dave C. taken so young with such technical skills?" Ben: "His skills may be needed elsewhere." (Dave was asphyxiated in an elevator due to a fire in a high-rise office building on February 25, 1967. See Chapter X, *Impressions and Telepathy.*)

Someone asked about mediums who become alcoholics. Ben: "They need to drown the loneliness. An alcoholic attracts the lower forces."

<u>March 6, 1969</u>: We met in Myra and Joe's family room. Ben was in trance when Dr. James came through. Charlie asked: "Why haven't we had any high teaching in the past four or five classes?" Dr. James: "You have not been deserted. Your material is better. You are here to grow and to develop and to receive your impressions, and that you have been doing. What you are fundamentally asking is for phenomena. Phenomena consists of interaction from your world through our world and it is bridged on good harmonic background. If you cannot supply that, we cannot do our part. We stand in, and we stand with you; we do not stand for you. God bless you." Ruth: "What can we do to improve the harmonic background?" Dr. James: "One must create peace in one's heart and so in one's mind, and so into your group. I shall return your medium. Thank you for asking, and God bless each of you. Big Oak is trying to reach through to his medium." Helen: "He is welcome." Charlie: "In regard to the spiritual healing powers which I have been told I possess; how do I progress to learn more about it so I can put it to use?" Dr. James: "You must find what your hands find to do, and as you progress your hands will find more to do." Dave: "I have a friend in a far city from here who is sick. Can he be helped? His name is George R. He was in an auto accident some months back and was very badly injured. He made a good recovery, but then something happened which put him in a coma since last June or July. If prayers can help him, we certainly would appreciate this." (We all rubbed our hands together and sent out healing into the bowl of salt water which spirit takes and directs to the recipient.) Dr. James: "Brother David, your friend has a nerve infection in the spinal column and there is a great deal of pressure. One of the gates has remained open. We shall do all we can, and God bless you for asking." Dave: "Do the doctors know this?" (One tap for *no*.) Dave: "Can they be informed in some way?" (One tap for *no*.) Dave explained, "Healing had been sent out to him, originally and extensive damage to the skull was improved as pressure was relieved.

Then, while eating, he choked a little bit and they thought he had a heart attack. He's been in a coma since." Charlie: "Why do I get between the fourth and fifth vertebrae?" (Two taps for *yes.*) Dave: "Counting from the skull? That would be in the neck." Dr. James: "That would be in the axis area." Charlie: "That would be from the shoulder line down." (Two taps for *yes.*) Dr. James: "From the cranium. We find the evidence of the incipient fina is what has given clue to the infected nerve trunk." Dave: "If this is an infection, is it something that is now a disease or just inflammation from the improper pressure?" Dr. James: "It is a body inflammation."

May 8, 1969: Eight of us gathered again in Myra and Joe's home. Most of us were conversing in the kitchen. While Charlie and Dave M. were securing the window panels in the family room before class, the TV suddenly turned on and blasted at full volume and we all heard it. They had to call Myra to turn it off because they couldn't locate the dial. Later, during our session, Captain X came through again and confirmed that it was he who had done it to alert Ben that he was there waiting.

May 15, 1969: Seven of us were present in Ben's living-room. Ben's wife Tess came through and tossed a bag of candy. (When an object is materialized and obviously transported from elsewhere, it is called an *apport.*) Our Rusty bounded in with his excitable yapping and landed in Neal's lap again. Papa Locker touched Charlie, Neal, our nephew Gary and me. Maria Ouspenskaya spoke at length to Gary who is in show business and answered questions about movie stars who were Spiritualists. She offered quite a bit of evidential information.

Charlie asked if she will join us on our trip to California. She said, "You are planning to go in September, are you not?" He responded, "No, I wasn't. We have another trip planned then." Then I interjected, "But, I was thinking of planning to try for September." At that, Maria piped up, "Aha! Don't you communicate with your wife? Or, would you like to punch me in mine big nose, like the man?" We were stunned. I asked incredulously, "Maria, have you been eavesdropping on us?" She replied, "I'm always sticking mine big nose in."

This was relative to May 2nd when Neal cut school and Mr. G., the attendance officer phoned us. The vice-principal, Mr. J. had phoned earlier in the day and informed me of Neal's absence. I told him all I knew was that Neal had departed for school that morning. Mr. G. phoned at 2:30 and Charlie who had recently arrived home, answered the phone. Prior to that, I had discussed most of the details with him. The attendance officer questioned him regarding Neal's condition, and how he should record him. So, Charlie, instead of responding, said, "Here's my wife; I'll let you speak to her;" whereby Mr. G. promptly retorted, *"What's the matter, don't you communicate with your wife?"* That infuriated Charlie, and crimson-faced, he blurted, "Who do you think you're talking to? *If I had you here, I'd punch you in the nose!"*

Chapter XXVII

EARTHBOUND SPIRIT, APPARITION AND CHIEF RED CLOUD

NEAL PROUDLY ANNOUNCED one day that he doesn't have to switch on his bedroom light anymore. "How come?" I asked. "Someone does it for me," he said. "What do you mean?" "When I enter my room, the light suddenly goes on and I know it's a young boy who's doing it." "Oh, really? You know that's not healthy because if it's an earthbound spirit, he is using your energy to manifest." I said. I dropped the subject, but I knew what I had to do. I repeatedly sent this entity telepathic messages to go to the light; that he doesn't belong here; he belongs with his loved ones and with God.

A few days later, I darkened our bedroom at 5:00PM to take a nap. I was lying on my right side with my back to the windows when I felt a hand on my shoulder. I knew immediately who it was. He was feeling threatened, so he thought he might influence me to change my mind. I didn't panic; took a deep breath and mentally and firmly commanded him, "You must look to the light and go with your loved ones and with God! That is where you belong now. God bless you.

Go!" I repeated that several times when suddenly it felt as if a weight had been lifted from the room. He was gone.

<u>February 24, 1969</u>: When Neal arrived home from school, he reported that he had seen a bent old man with a long beard, wearing a long, black dress and a high hat, walking up the stairs to a synagogue, the Tifereth Israel. What startled him was witnessing the man walk right through the closed doors.

<u>July 16, 1969</u>: Frequently, when combing my hair, for some strange reason I would receive impressions and visions. Perhaps it was the friction created by the plastic composite comb. This morning, the name Chief Red Cloud popped into my mind. I closed my eyes and saw a dark-complected Native American decked out in a full head-dress adorned with fox or raccoon tails and brown-tipped white feathers. I asked why he was here. "I am with Neal on bivouac." It had been a rainy week and Neal wasn't feeling well. I thanked him and blessed him for watching over our son. At our next séance, I asked about Chief Red Cloud. I received corroboration of the message and was informed that he was one of Neal's Indian guides. (On March 18, 1972, our local newspaper published excerpts from a book about Native Americans. Chief Red Cloud was mentioned as chief of a Sioux tribe in 1878.)

Chapter XXVIII
MORE VISITATIONS AND PHENOMENA

<u>JULY 17, 1969</u>: Nine of us met in Ben's living-room, including our nephew Marco. This was his first time with us. Papa Locker came through and greeted Marco by caressing him all over his body with the trumpet. For the first time, Bernice and Irv's boxer, Lucky came through, treated us with his husky bark and landed in Marco's lap. (Lucky remembered Marco as a youngster when they lived in the same house.) Big Oak, Helen H.'s Indian guide boomed, "We bring Indian blessing, Helen. She good. Big Oak no medium. Big Oak talk through medium, Helen. Many nations here."

A couple from New York who had apparently sat with Ben in the past, had lost their pet trained horse, Tigress. When they asked for Tigress to come through, John brought her in. That small, crowded room was fully occupied by a horse whose tail swished and fanned those who were sitting at her rear. They commanded Tigress to count to three and four and five, which she did with the trumpet. Then, she nickered, snorted and whinnied.

August 14, 1969: Seven of us met at Ben's place including our daughter, Layne who saw a dove fly into the room. Ben had a bag of sand on his ottoman that night and the dove took a sand bath in it.

Maria came through and Charlie asked her if she would look in on Neal at Fort Dix. She returned and reported that he was sitting on his cot and wrapping his sore ankles with bandages. When we spoke to Neal later on, he confirmed that was exactly what he was doing because they had been on a long bivouac and had hiked several miles. The army regulation boots were unkind to his bony ankles.

In early December, 1969, Ben's guide, Dr. James instructed us to forgo the use of the tape recorder. They reasoned that it distracted us from developing. Each time we gathered at Ben's place, a shrill whistle emanated from my recorder whenever I activated it. I tried it in every room with no luck. Whenever I activated it at home, it worked perfectly. Finally, on January 29th, I took the hint and reluctantly left it home. At that time I had no plan to write this book. If I had, I would have mentioned my intention and I'm sure the guides would have understood why I taped the sessions.

During the month of June, 1970, we met at Bert's apartment. Charlie darkened the living-room with masonite and paneling on the windows, and we plugged up all the light leaks. The conditions were perfect for our séances. Usually, six to eight of us would gather in a circle, as always. On June 23rd, Claire K. brought her niece to sit with us. Bert immediately tuned in to her and saw just the wings of an airplane plunging down toward her. She said she had the strangest feeling in her head and legs, and a terrible pressure causing her hearing to close off. As she gave that out, I saw Air Force wings on the left shoulder of a tall, good-looking, sandy-haired young fellow. Then Charlie proceeded to describe him in more detail. Claire's niece accepted it. Then I saw the Crab sign of Cancer going toward her, and she acknowledged that.

After we concluded our session, the young lady told us that her son was killed in an Air Force jet seven months previously. The wings had flown off first as it plummeted downward. His zodiac sign was Cancer.

(Charlie became extremely clairvoyant resulting from our sessions. He was capable of describing someone's deceased grandmother down to a mole on her behind.)

March 5, 1970: Eight of us met in Ben's living-room. Messages and impressions were offered at the outset. All four trumpets became activated, and when we sang Hava Nagilla, both Papa and Marcella touched me after dancing around the bowl of water. I was giving Mel M. a message about someone who called him Melvin. He said the only one he could think of was his Uncle Sam when he was a boy. I began to describe a stocky man with gray hair and wire-rimmed eyeglasses, when I suddenly realized that I was describing my own Uncle Sam K., my Aunt Dora's late husband. As I verbalized that, I received two taps on my knee. I greeted him and asked him if that was he whose cigar I had smelled in our car two years ago as we were headed for a visit with Aunt Dora. He confirmed, and I asked, "Do you know who we saw in California?" Again, he tapped me. "How is she?" He tapped twice, again, meaning okay. (We had visited his step-daughter-in-law.) Later, I recalled that the first time Uncle Sam came to me it was also March, around the anniversary of his transition.

January 28, 1971: We met at Bert's apartment. Freda F. brought her hairdresser, JoAnn who said she felt a rumble under her chair and a black shadow pass across her. In a deep semi-trance I responded, "It's an earthquake coming somewhere with death." I suggested she watch the news. "This will take place within a week to ten days." (On Tuesday, February 9th, an earthquake struck Los Angeles resulting in many deaths.)

When this young woman, Jo Ann entered Bert's apartment, I said, "I see you as a gypsy incarnation reading cards," and Freda gasped. "What's the matter?" I asked. "That's just what she does," she replied incredulously. "But, I saw her in a past life, not this one," I said. At the close of the session, Jo Ann related how she had first begun to read cards. Her aunt handed her a deck of playing cards one day when she was in her teens, and said, "Here, read my cards." She had never done that before, yet she gave her aunt a perfect reading. From that day forward, she continued doing it so apparently past-life memory was manifesting.

April 27, 1972: Eleven of us gathered in a circle in Bert's living-room. Freda F. claimed that during the Consciousness Exercise, she saw a white-robed figure with a long white beard enter the room. He was walking with a staff. Joe I. saw sheep in a pastoral scene, and I saw a white figure blessing each one of us in the circle.

As the session progressed, Dominick M. went into a trance and began to whisper. Shelly F. and I flanked him, but I was already out, so she interpreted in a louder voice whatever she could understand. Dominick whispered: "The drops of blood from my heart shall satisfy your soul," repeated many times. Then Gina V. said that she got an I-J, and someone declared, "Isaiah!" Freda saw the white-robed figure all evening. Then Dominick exclaimed, "Isaiah, yes; Isaiah. It's Isaiah! Oh, God. Thank God! Isaiah from God shall come. Take me when the time comes."

As this was transpiring, a male figure was sitting in me open-mouthed waiting to speak. He was teary-eyed and smiling as if in recognition. When Dom became too emotional, Charlie gently brought him back, suggesting that someone else is waiting to come through. Then my male spoke, "Walk with me on the path of righteousness." When he departed, a female came in. She began to sob and tears rolled down my cheeks. In a weepy voice she declared, "I'm so overwhelmed!" She began to pat every part of my body and said, "I'm as I was." She repeated that, and when someone asked what that meant, she said, "Arms, legs, face,..."

Epilogue: Freda researched in her *Prophet Book*, and discovered that the second Isaiah is the one quoted in the bible. That Isaiah was "the servant of the Lord," and described himself as a *lamb that is led to the slaughter, and a sheep that is dumb before his shearers.* He was recognized as God's servant in suffering vicariously for the sins of the gentile world; *the suffering servant of the Lord.* This was regarding the quote which Dom muttered, and the biblical quotes under Isaiah constantly referring to *paths of righteousness.* Dom did some more research and wrote a long historical discourse which is too lengthy to enter here.

March 31, 1972: Five of us gathered in our windowless recreation room. When I entered a semi-trance, I realized that a Chinese man was sitting in me. As I transfigured, my upper teeth felt as if they were slightly protruding; my eyes were slanted and I knew that he wore a skull-cap. He kept repeating, "I am your humble servant." When asked what his name was, he said it was Kao Fung or Fong. He said that he came from *Ming,* (meaning the Ming Dynasty.) "There were peaceful fields by the Great Wall and then blood." When questioned further, he continued, "Men with large yellow faces and large helmets came from the north and then there was blood. The grass flowed gently in the breeze, and then there was blood. They came and they left nothing." When Mongols were mentioned, he said, "That is familiar." When asked when this occurred, he said, "I remember a seven and an eight." He said he was a humble merchant of fish brought to him from the sea. He was "of Canton."

When I researched all of this, I discovered that Canton is a large port on the South China Sea. The Ming Dynasty: 1368 to 1644. Mongols attempted to retake China in the 15th century. They had been driven out in the 14th century. In 1644, China was conquered by Mongols known as Manchus. The Great Wall was built along North China to keep them out in 200 BC. I personally had no knowledge of any of this history prior to this session, since I've never been a history buff.

April 20, 1972: Eight of us met in Bert's living-room. As I began
to go out, I clearly saw a large silver mosque dome; then I felt someone sit in me. My arms and hands suddenly went numb. I began to
whisper in a foreign language which progressed into mumbling. As
the voice augmented, it repeated over and over something about
"Allah." The group requested that the visitor please speak English so
they could understand what he was saying. It appeared that this was
an Arab. After awhile, he identified himself as Sheik Mujib. He
blessed the group with "Allah be with you. There is much love here."
I was aware that he wore a head-dress trimmed with black and gold
braid. (Earlier I had seen a bright light moving around the room
touching each of us, and I reported that we were being blessed by a
beautiful soul. Our visitor took credit for that.)

He became quite emotional as tears began to flow down my
cheeks. He said he was so happy to speak again. Suddenly, Freda said
that she must get down on her knees, which she did. She was very
moved by spirit, and she and others in the room began to cry, also.
He told her, "Please rise now," and she obeyed. She claimed that
ordinarily she would have found it terribly difficult to kneel and rise
like that, but it was like nothing to her this time.

Charlie questioned the Sheik who said he is searching for his
daughter. He wants her to forgive him. He had cast her away because
she was only a girl. He had no sons. Apparently, Freda was
entranced, also, and quite emotionally affected by the entire incident.
She seemed to identify with the lost daughter, but I felt that this
wasn't so. However, he made her feel comfortable and responded to
her courteously. He departed with a blessing, "May Allah be with
you, always, and thank you." (The kneeling is indicative of the
Moslem ritual of kneeling when they pray.)

We were sitting in Bert's living room one night when a friend of
Layne's had joined us. I began to transfigure when I was in a semi-
trance state. "Janet, (name changed,) I have an uncle of yours here

who has a hunched back and he wears a watch fob," I said. She accepted him and I began to utter something in Polish which evoked an emotional response from her.

One night we were sitting in Bert's living-room when our friends Alma and Seymour attended for the first time. I entered a semi-trance almost immediately after the opening exercises. Apparently, Seymour and his father had been estranged for many years. I was ignorant of the fact and didn't even know his father was still alive. I make it a practice not to probe into anyone's personal life, because it helps me to receive valid impressions. The first message was for Seymour. "Seymour, I'm seeing an old man who I am impressed is your father. He is standing by his apartment door and holding it open for you. He's welcoming you with open arms." Seymour and Alma both gasped audibly. That's when Alma revealed the story about the estrangement. I told them that I had a feeling they should act on this as soon as possible. After the session was ended they agreed that they would phone Seymour's father and "feel him out as to his attitude." When they visited him, the old man did indeed welcome his son with open arms. A couple of weeks later, he passed on. This proved to be another example of Divine intervention.

A few weeks later we didn't have a suitable place to meet, so my Mom invited us to try her apartment. We were able to darken the living-room somewhat, but not sufficiently for trumpet activity. There were six of us including Dave M. He had met my Mom previously at one of our sessions; and being a proper gentleman, he presented her with a dozen roses. The highlight of the evening occurred when I entered a semi-trance and my feet began to run vigorously. "Dave," I said, "I have a Frank here for you and he's showing me that he is running." "Oh, my God!" Dave cried, "Frank was a coworker at Westinghouse, and before he passed on, both of his legs were amputated. Isn't this wonderful?!"

This is just one of the many evidentials that have occurred. This also helps to confirm the promise that we are whole and perfect again when we depart our physical bodies.

November 7, 1989: Myra and Joe had settled in Florida some time before we did. Charlie had made his transition on May 7th. There hadn't been a session at their place for 29 months. We were a group of nine. As I began to go out, my entire body shuddered spasmodically. This was a first. Theone had been my control for a few years by then. She spoke very softly, "There is some kind of disturbance. We must withdraw. We will be back." An apprehensive flurry of whispered questions swept through the room. When Theone returned, Myra asked what had happened. She replied, "Someone was trying to force his way in and we had to gently put him in his place. He was a very willful individual." "Who was it?" Myra asked. Theone replied, "By the name of Charles." Myra, fully aware of Charlie's often overbearing personality said sarcastically, "That figures!" Theone offered, "He has a lot to learn, but we are working with him."

One morning in late November as I prepared my breakfast, I spontaneously began to sing, The Yellow Rose of Texas. Then, I felt an energy around me which I identified as Ben, our former teacher. If he wanted to identify himself, that song was the best clue that it's his spirit. "You're very welcome, and bless you," I said, "But why are you here?" He said, "If you meet at Myra and Joe's place, I'll come through." I phoned Myra and we arranged a date.

December 5, 1989: Seven of us gathered in Myra and Joe's kitchen. The energy was phenomenal. I went out into a semi-trance almost immediately after the opening exercises. Someone touched my arm, and I said, "Ben is here." Myra quipped, "Ben, if that's really you, tap once on the trumpet for yes, and if it's not you, tap twice, and if you're not sure, tap three times." She was recalling his keen

sense of humor by confusing the order of the taps. We all giggled.
Two minutes later, we heard a tap on my metal trumpet. Then Myra
said, "Do something with the trumpets," and both trumpets flew off
the small bench in the center of the room. Pearl said the oak tag one
hit her foot, and Myra thought the metal one landed by her foot.
While I was out, there was more activity, and a scuffle on the floor.
When the session was over, and the lights were on, the trumpets had
apparently changed places. The oak tag one was by Myra, and my
metal one sat by Pearl's feet. The room resounded with our excitement. We fervently expressed our gratitude to Ben and the powers
that be for this display of PK, even though I was the only one who
was entranced. Joe was there, too, and though he generally sleeps
during our sessions, his PK energy also contributes. (The metal trumpet had belonged to Bert. When she entered a nursing home she gave
it to me.)

A prevailing message from Theone during virtually every session
was a warning about global changes and ultimate destruction if we do
not send love, forgiveness and peace out into the cosmos. She
advised that each of us is responsible for maintaining our planet as a
healthy entity. "We are all connected with one another spiritually.
There should be no animosity towards our brothers and sisters. Treat
everyone and everything as you would be treated."

February 26, 1990: Nine of us gathered in Myra and Joe's
kitchen. I gave Sylvia J. a message about a Charles; then I saw two
big, fat ears. She said he did not have large ears. I added, "I'm
impressed that you are being informed to listen for news about a lot
of money within three months."

June, 10, 1990: Seven of us met in my den. Sylvia's late husband
relayed a message through my control Theone that she should stay
where she is, because the money will come. (She had been considering selling her condo.)

In August, Sylvia told me that a sister-in-law, her brother's widow, had passed on and she knew she was in her will, but had no idea how much. That same month I entered the clay sculpture room in the clubhouse and as I placed my belongings on the counter I saw the number five for Sylvia. I thought, "The amount she's getting has a five in it," when I received instant confirmation; (chills.) I approached Sylvia and asked, "Did you get that money yet?" She coyly replied, "Yes," and smiled. "Does it have a five in it?" She nodded and declared, "It's more than I ever expected." I asked, "Is it $25,000?" She was aghast, because that's what it was.

May 17, 1993: Eleven of us gathered in Myra and Joe's den. The highlight of the evening came when Isabel B., (name changed,) who had never sat with us before, said that her father was standing on her left. I was impressed to tell her, "You must tell him you welcome him and love him." She hesitated; then said with a slight modification in tone, "But, I don't think I can do that." I asked why, and she blurted, "I can never forgive him for treating my mother so lousy, that son of a bitch!" I repeated, "All the more reason why you must tell him you love and forgive him now. He is apologizing for his behavior. That's why he's here."

It took much convincing from all of us. Finally, she acquiesced and said the words. As soon as she did, the trumpet rattled and I said, "Look how excited he is! Now, bless him and wish him Divine Progress."

When I was in trance, Theone came through with her perennial plea to pray for peace on earth. "Send love, blessings and forgiveness out to all who seem to be enemies and evil-doers in order to save the earth from catastrophe." She brought an Alfred with a military bearing for Joan S. He was tall and blond with blue eyes, and very stern looking. Joan said she thought she could accept that. (A couple of days later, she phoned me and admitted she was mistaken, but her boyfriend identified him as his brother who was killed in World War II. She regretted not having asked for a message from Alfred, because obviously that was why he appeared.)

A Mickey, (name changed,) came through for Isabel. She said, "Oh, my God! Could that be Michael?" (name changed.) The message was, "Mommy, I'm perfect. I'm perfect!" By then, Isabel was sobbing hysterically. "Mommy, let it go. Let it go. It's all right. I love you." He repeated that many times. When Isabel had finally calmed down she said, "I love you, Michael," and the trumpet rattled again. After that episode, the group sang a rollicking song to elevate the vibrations.

All of the proceedings when I was entranced were related to me after we closed the session.

The next morning, Isabel phoned me, still in a state of shock. She explained that Michael was seven when he was killed in an auto accident. Isabel was supposed to pick him up somewhere and she didn't show up. The last words he said to her were, "Mommy, you promised." She had lived with that guilt ever since.

Chapter XXIX

PERCEPTIVE AWARENESS

SOMETIMES WHEN I meditate I hear someone calling my name. More often I feel as though a feather is being gently brushed over certain parts of my body. This indicates to me that spirit is responding to my meditative state. This is sometimes quite disconcerting, so I bless whoever it is and ask them to return another time. When my scalp and neck prickle, I know that a spirit's energy is around me. I've heard my mother, Strick's distinctive, shrill voice call, "*Norma!*" My aunt Tillie, Strick's younger sister didn't believe in God, and she vehemently denounced the doctrine of the hereafter and anything concerning mind control. She would sarcastically say, "You and your hypnosis!" A few months after her transition, she called my name and I knew she was apologizing for all of her denials.

When I was writing my memoirs of the first 25 years of my life for my family, I gathered all the old snapshots and included copies of them in the book in their proper places. My former friend Belle and her older sister Yetta, were a prominent part of my life in my early adult years and their photos were scattered throughout my book. One day while I meditated, I heard Yetta's shrill voice call, "*Hi,*

Norm!" That's what she always called me. I had no idea that she had passed on prior to that. The voices are not always familiar or identifiable. (These were examples of *clairsentience* and *clairaudience.*)

My nephew Harry, Bernice and Irv's first-born son and our Godson, suddenly expired at age 52 on Sunday, January 7, 2007. It was such a shock to everyone. I was inconsolable because I was persuaded not to attend the funeral; couldn't play my stereo or sing; wandered around wallowing in a flood of tears. I prayed for a smooth and easy transition and Divine Progress for his soul, and I knew that he was finally free of the pain which had afflicted him for so long. That was my only consolation. By Tuesday, I was still in the doldrums which is so uncharacteristic of me, when I distinctly heard Harry's voice admonishing me; "Aunt Norma! You of all people should know better! I'm out of pain and I'm in a perfect body again."

My friend Rae was languishing at home, dying from cancer in a hospital bed provided by the Hospice organization. In early February, 2007, the prognosis was that she wouldn't last much longer than six weeks. Her nephew left strict instructions that she is not to be disturbed by visitors because, "She needed to do the *work of dying.*" My instincts told me that she needed people who loved her around her in her final days or she might feel deserted. Since I was prohibited from visiting her, I continuously put her in God's hands for whatever was best for her. On April 4ᵗʰ, I sent her telepathic messages throughout the day. "It's okay for you to let go. Your loved ones are waiting to greet you on the other side where there is only love, peace and beauty." I blessed her and told her that I loved her, but it was time to let go. In spite of hearing some of my experiences with life after death, she still professed a disbelief in an afterlife. At 4:05PM, as I was entering my kitchen from the dining-room, I was stopped in my tracks by an unfamiliar energy encompassing my entire body. I prickled all over and knew instantly that it was Rae hugging me. The next day I phoned her nephew and he said that her condition hadn't changed; she was still breathing. Apparently, she was already out of her body preparing for her transition, responding with love to my exhortation. Rae finally passed on May 1st.

In August, I stopped at Rae's apartment when her nephew and his wife were there reorganizing and dispensing with some of her belongings. I selected some of the best artist's supplies for my sculptures and as we chatted, I felt Rae's energy around me again. She was thanking me for being there for her and telling me that she was happy and perfect again. She also asked me to apologize to her nephew and niece for leaving such a mess. I couldn't share any of this with him at that time, because he is an observant Jew and I had the distinct impression that he was a doubter. However, I did grasp at the opportunity much later when I discovered that his wife was a believer.

Chapter XXX
HAROLD

Part I: Beating the Odds

"Courage combined with energy and perseverance
will overcome difficulties apparently insurmountable."
S. Smiles.

GIGI'S *DADDY*, HAROLD, whom we called Hal, had
endured a childhood of abuse and insecurity after his family structure
disintegrated. Because he was tall for his age, he enlisted in the army
at age 15 in 1940. During his European stint in World War II, his
lumbar spine was struck by shrapnel as he parachuted over enemy
territory. The horrifying prognosis was he would never walk again.
The medical staff didn't know with whom they were dealing. Hal
adamantly and blatantly refused to accept that life-altering verdict. He
fussed and squawked, "I feel tingling in my toes, you sons of bitches!
Do something!" The staff finally yielded and humored him by poking
his feet with a sharp instrument. That was the turning point in his
recovery. (I always relate Hal's story to my classes emphasizing--*Do*

**not** accept the **verdict** if it is a negative one. We have the power to overcome if we keep the faith and persevere.)

From that day on, Hal valiantly struggled and persevered until he was able to walk proudly again. When the war ended, he and Irene were stationed in Japan during the occupation. From there, he was deployed for duty in South Korea, and subsequently received his promotion to Lieutenant Colonel in Viet Nam where he summoned Neal to spend a weekend with him.

When Hal was retired from military duty, he became a used-car salesman, which he couldn't tolerate. It wasn't challenging enough for this macho guy, so he applied to the American Red Cross. With his record and status, they inducted him as Field Director when again he traveled far and wide in that capacity. In all the years that I knew him, I persistently urged him to write or record his life story, but he never did. His macho exterior belied the sensitivity which manifested in the paintings he created and his apparently latent psychic ability.

Part II: Trance Revelations

May 30, 1971: Hal and Irene visited us to celebrate his birthday, and to bid us farewell on their way to Germany. Hal was assigned there in his capacity as Red Cross Field Director.

Eleven of us gathered in our windowless recreation room. I taped the proceedings on my reel-to-reel tape recorder. The vibes were perfect for spirit communication because our home was charged with psychic energy. Hal had never sat before, but he was _taken out_ almost immediately, claiming that his head was being pulled back. He saw streaks of light and stars in a dark sky, as if he was flying high into space. We tried to calm him to allay his trepidation. (He claimed later on, that he heard us, but then apparently spirit took over because his last conscious recollection was seeing the stars.) He was obviously in a deep trance state, because several entities came through him. So many were vying for the opportunity to speak which is quite common. I've experienced it myself when I've felt a host of entities around me.

There was a John who had lived in Syracuse as a lock-tender for canals. Several times Hal's body writhed and twisted and because I was sitting next to him, I gently soothed him. He was sweating profusely and dominated the first part of the session for about forty minutes as one after the other came through. Charlie and I who were more experienced, controlled and disallowed all negative conditions, kindly but firmly, so spirit wouldn't impress Hal with the cause of their demise.

Irene's father, Sam, spoke and wept emotionally upon hearing her voice. He brought a baby with him, Irene's first loss. (She had endured many miscarriages and one still-born, so they finally adopted a son.) Then, her sister, Bella spoke in a higher pitched voice. There were messages for Al, one of our psychics, and for Renie, Strick's friend. Hal had never met Al or Renie prior to that night.

When we illuminated the room, Hal adamantly refused to believe any of this and declined hearing the playback of the tape.

Chapter XXXI

CHARLENE: POST-DEATH REBELLION

"Unexpected events often lead to surprising results."

Norma Locker.

OCTOBER 6, 1971: Ten of us met for the first time in Bert's living-room since we departed Ben's class. Freda F. said that she was already going into trance during the Consciousness Awareness Exercise. About a half-hour later, we were both out in semi-trance when the metal trumpet began to quiver on the marble cocktail table. Then Freda began to speak, apparently to her sister-in-law Charlene, (name changed,) who had passed on a couple of months prior. As she spoke, the trumpet responded by vibrating noisily. This continued for about fifteen minutes. Then Charlie told Charlene to tap once for *no*, twice for *yes*, and three times for *maybe;* but she just rattled the trumpet when the answer was *yes*. (Charlie knew Charlene because she was friendly with the Lockers in their early days.)

It was quite an emotional evening for everyone. As power waned, we sang to restore it. After the lights were on, Freda related the following story: Charlene had been ill for a long time with poor circulation and had submitted to what was supposed to be minor surgery. Something went awry on the operating table and she didn't survive. It was a shock to everyone, especially to Charlene. She had battled obesity all her life, but had recently dieted and lost some weight. Also, due to her illness, she had lost even more. A family feud ignited subsequently ending in an 18 year silence between Charlene and her husband and Freda and her husband.

After Charlene's funeral service, the pallbearers wheeled the casket out of the chapel and placed it in the hearse. The limousine was parked behind the hearse and it suddenly lurched forward and slammed into the hearse sending the pallbearers and the funeral director sprawling. Five of them were hospitalized with lacerated arms and legs and some fractures. The hearse doors had not yet been secured, and as the driver tried to pull away from the limousine, the casket lunged out and onto the pavement, flying open and cracking. The shroud slid off the body, and Charlene's husband quickly hastened to restore it.

Freda hurried out of the chapel upon hearing the commotion and immediately assessed the situation. She said that she could almost see and feel Charlene flinging out her arms in rebellion against her unexpected demise. The limousine driver swore that it was parked, and as he turned on the ignition, it lurched forward. He was in shock. Freda said it was horrible because the casket was replaced at a 45 degree angle in the hearse, and she visualized the body crumpling forward. Her dinette table had begun to creak for no apparent reason at certain intervals. The next time we met, we firmly but gently sent Charlene on her way to the light and to her loved ones who awaited her.

Chapter XXXII
LEO: MY MISGUIDED FATHER

Phase I: Memories

SOMETIMES WE BECOME so complacent in a life filled with love, comfort and plenty that we can't imagine the prospect of a dark cloud casting an ominous shadow over it.

My handsome father, who stood about five feet eight inches in a well-built body, was born in 1900. While still a youth he emigrated from the section of Poland which was called White Russia at the time. He was one of thirteen children, ten of whom survived to emigrate to the United States. His English was flawless by the time he and Mom began dating. When they met, Leo bore a wealth of dark brown wavy hair which he wore slicked down and parted in the middle, the fashion of the early twenties. Upturned creases rippled playfully around his soft, hazel eyes when he laughed. The neatly barbered auburn mustache was punctuated on either side by deep-set dimples. His amicable personality and uninhibited wit augmented his charisma. Those who knew him liked him. At the age of 24 when he and Mom were wed, he was apparently sexually unsophisticated.

During the depression years we lived rather comfortably because Leo had a steady job driving a milk delivery truck. Subsequently, he was employed with the Metropolitan Life Insurance Company as a debit agent; two very vulnerable situations for temptation.

For years Mom had secretly suspected that he was being unfaithful. It was confirmed when he tried to coerce her to submit to an abortion when she became pregnant with my sister. (A Catholic friend of his had told him that the *rhythm system* was foolproof and taught him how to use it. Apparently it wasn't as foolproof as promised.) His behavior toward Mom had changed and that gnawed at her. He brought pets home without discussing it with her. One day he defiantly brought bacon into the house and fried it in her best skillet. He knew that she maintained a Kosher home for him and his family from New York whom she entertained frequently with lavish meals and desserts. It appeared that he was wantonly sabotaging their life together. I recall hearing Mom mutter indignantly, "Your father and Bill B. are bumming around together." (This was Bert's husband, Bill.) Bill worked with Leo and they had become close buddies.

My childhood in New Jersey prior to my eleventh year was a fairly happy one except for being subjected to the bitter arguments between my parents. I used to lie in bed at night listening to their malicious exchanges with my hands cupped over my ears, my stomach churning. Briny tears stung my eyes as I swallowed sobs. I feared I might awaken Bernice who shared the bed with me. I was the *boy* Leo always wanted. Because he was a milk-delivery man and later an insurance salesman his free time was mainly during the day. We spent some quality time together especially in the spring and summer months when he took me fishing in the Passaic River and deep sea fishing out of Sheepshead Bay. We went net-skimming with high boots in the New Jersey meadowland swamps for water-lice to feed his tropical fish. One day when I was five or six, we drove up to the Catskill Mountains with a blonde woman, Blanche. We spent the day there at a large wood-framed hotel which I recognized as a popular vacation resort for our family. Leo boldly snapped a photo of that woman with me sitting on her lap. I was too young and naïve then, to realize how wrong that was. However, all of these excursions, made me feel loved and very special.

Mom's suspicions finally led her to contact a former beau, Sam D., a private detective, to tail Leo and photograph him with his "whores." He had been in love with Mom before she met Leo, so he declined remuneration "for old time's sake." She said she had rejected his marriage proposal because she felt that he didn't have a future at the time.

One afternoon, Mom, Bernice and I arrived home from an outing and surprised Leo in his under-shorts with a woman in her underwear. I recognized her immediately as the woman from the mountains. Mom was understandably mortified and promptly banished them from the house. She didn't need any more evidence than that. Was Leo setting the stage for his next move?

Soon after that, in 1935, we arrived home to find a note from him declaring the he had left for Florida to find a job and he would send for us when he was settled. This was an appalling shock, since he had never communicated to Mom that he planned to leave. She had $2.86 in her handbag and no means of income at the time. Later, she discovered that he had actually absconded with his girlfriend to Florida and cash surrendered all of our life-insurance policies, leaving Mom with two young children to support and raise. She cursed both of them repeatedly. Whenever she alluded to Leo it was, "Your father, that son of a bitch." Of course, he was a lying coward who had no intention of sending for us. I was nearing my eleventh birthday, and I felt as if he had deserted and betrayed *me*.

Nancy Reagan said, "A woman is like a teabag; you never know her strength until you drop her in hot water." That is a colorful portrayal of our Mom. Sophie Krug arrived in America from Russia in

1910 at age ten, one of nine siblings. Leo was attracted to her petite, curvaceous figure when she was 22. Her bobbed, brown hair was accented by dark, deep-set eyes which revealed an innate intelligence and ingenuity, even though her education was curtailed in her early teens. An angular, narrow nose was perched on her small wedge of face. She had smooth, creamy skin which was tautly drawn across alpine cheekbones. The sharp, determined chin indicated a strong, willful nature and self-confidence. Her childhood had been one of hard work and servitude to a farming family. This contributed to a deep desire for independence. She was an attractive woman with an inborn magnetism which served her well during the rigorous years.

Many years later, one of her bosses dubbed her, *Strick* which is condensed from Strichartz, my maiden surname. This moniker stuck with her until she took her final breath.

Within the following two years after Leo's departure, we had relocated twice. It was a sad day for us when we were forced to leave our beautiful home and upper-middle-class life which we had shared with Leo. It was as if Mom couldn't bring herself to hit rock-bottom all at once. We discovered that our petite, beloved mother appeared deceptively delicate. She was actually made of tempered steel. Throughout the entire ordeal she remained undaunted, courageously plunging into the support of her two children. Bernice was six at the time. When you're a kid you're so self-involved and naïve you don't appreciate the mettle of a person. Just these past years while writing my memoirs of the first 25 years of my life, I became emotionally stirred recalling how our Mom grabbed the reins and maneuvered us through the darkest days of our lives.

Our final letdown came when Mom could no longer support us on the meager salary she drew as a salesclerk. Her father, my Zayda, owned a waste material business on the edge of town. The brick building which housed my grandparent's downstairs flat and two small apartments on the second floor, stood in front of the rag shed which was a long, stuffy, fetid barn-like structure. My Zayda offered Mom the vacant three-room cold flat rent-free. She was too proud to accept charity and adamantly insisted on paying $5.00 a month. He was unable to acquire a variance for another tenant, since my aunt and cousin occupied the adjoining flat, so we had to cook our meals on a two-burner hot-plate. We laundered, bathed and washed our dishes in a wash-tub in the kitchen. Bernice and I scrunched together in six inches of tepid water for our baths. The toilet was in the hall, and we nearly froze our asses off in the winter. All three rooms depended on an oil burning stove in the kitchen for heat. Obviously, that was the toastiest spot. We battled roaches and mice, our unwelcome guests all year round. An ice-box kept our perishables chilled.

But, we were kids, after all, and we managed to have fun in spite of an abysmal, degrading situation. As unpleasant as our lives had become, Mom was determined to maintain her dignity. Her hair was always neatly coifed; makeup fastidiously applied and wardrobe impeccably coordinated.

It was a lovely, spring-like day in April, a week before my twelfth birthday. On warmer days I enjoyed sitting outdoors in front of the house after school to do my homework and watch Bernice as she romped with neighbors' kids. When Willis M. rode up on his bike to chat, I thought nothing of it because we were friendly with his family, and his younger brother, Bobby was in my class in school. Willis was a burly, pimple-faced 16, with large, thick-lensed, horn-rimmed eye-glasses. Somehow he inveigled the information from me that no one was home upstairs. He asked his five year old sister to watch his bike while I took him upstairs to help him find an alleged baseball mitt he had loaned my cousin.

Upstairs in the hall, he pretended to search for the mitt when, with sudden force he overpowered me and held me aloft in a corner trying to insert a finger into my vagina. I was so paralyzed with fright that my vocal cords froze. All I could do was struggle helplessly and groan. Electric images were whirling in my head in brief kaleido-scopic flashes. At that age I knew enough to be terrified, but I wasn't certain what to expect. Mom had already prepared me for the arrival of my period, but she reserved the sexual details for later.

Indelibly seared in my memory is my molester's red, sweaty, acne-crusted face and the bulging, rheumy eyes behind those thick-lensed horn-rimmed eyeglasses.

Suddenly, a huge, black hand grasped his shoulder, spun him around and shoved him violently into a wall. I slumped to the floor, quaking and sobbing uncontrollably. Neither of us had heard Bob, Zayda's Herculean worker, leap noiselessly up the staircase. He had spotted Willis' sister with his bike and when he heard where we were, his suspicions were aroused. Zayda's two black workers, Sonny and Bob, adored Mom because she treated them as equals, sharing jokes with them and inquiring about their families. They happily acted as guardian watchmen while Mom worked. After Bob determined that I was all right he grabbed Willis by an arm and vaulted him down the stairs three steps at a time. He rescued me before the situation esca-lated into rape, and I remain ever-grateful to him for that.

Willis' father, a brawny powerhouse of a man, beat him viciously, and insisted that he spend the night in jail. The police were willing to comply, but Mom refused to press charges to spare his mother the inevitable humiliation.

At that age I was lank and gangly with dark shoulder-length hair parted in the center and tucked behind my ears. I was rather shy and introspected, a direct effect of the shame and degradation to which Leo had irresponsibly led us. Traumatic incidents can often scar the psyche irrevocably. I had become the victim of many hang-ups. For years after the Willis incident I struggled against being physically restrained in any manner. A feeling of revulsion overcame me when I saw anyone who resembled my recollection of my molester. I became a shameless *cock-teaser*, and like Circe the temptress of

Greek mythology, I would entice the boys until they were aroused and then brashly reject them. (At least I didn't turn them into beasts; or did I?) Apparently, I had an unconscious need for justification and revenge. All of this contributed to the creation of the mean-spirited, neurotic hypochondriac which I became, and which emotionally scarred my children. My salvation was my introduction to and involvement with metaphysics and meditation in 1965.

Apparently Leo couldn't tolerate the heat and humidity of the Florida summers, so he presumptuously came to spend the summer months with us. Considering Mom's bitter resentment, she still must have loved him deeply to have permitted that. She took him into her bed which I normally shared with her, so I had to bunk with Bernice in the living-room on the studio couch. During his stay with us, Leo cunningly promised us the world, and we were all lovey-dovey until fall arrived, when he vanished again. Lucky man; he enjoyed the best of both worlds, though our cramped, cold-water flat with no shower or bathtub was certainly a departure from his comfortable Florida home.

The summer of 1939 was Leo's final visit. Before he left, he promised that we would finally become a family again. He asked Mom to quit her job and sell the furniture. He would take Bernice, who was nine then, down south with him and enroll her in school. Meanwhile, he would locate an apartment that we were to share together. Mom consented, but warily. She took a leave of absence from her job and placed the furniture in storage. I was in my last semester in Junior High school and it troubled me to have to leave before graduation.

Mom and I traveled to Miami by Greyhound bus. When we arrived, we discovered much to our chagrin, that Leo had deceived us again. His girlfriend must have been responsible for that. There was no apartment, and he had rashly boarded his nine year old daughter, Bernice, with strangers in a new environment; with his employer's parents. She was enrolled in an unfamiliar school also. This was a frightful experience for her. We were shocked and furious at this heinous and irresponsible stunt. Mom and I were forced to stay in a guest house while we plodded around town for two weeks apartment hunting. We finally found an efficiency apartment in a run-down wood-frame tenement building. We retrieved Bernice who was thrilled to be back in the fold of her loved ones. We hadn't improved our status much. We had to share a bathroom with next-door neighbors. It was one room with a small, curtained alcove for a kitchen. Palmetto bugs the size of your thumb delighted in nibbling on Mom's nylon hosiery.

Our indomitable mother secured employment immediately at Burdine's Department Store. I was enrolled in a Junior High school, and when I graduated I entered the magnificent, newly constructed Miami High school which was an exciting adventure for me. The one drawback was that Jews and blacks were not welcome in those days. It disturbed me to witness the segregation—the separate lavatories and water fountains; seating in the back of buses, and other degradations for the blacks. To be accepted, I concealed my ethnic background. For me, the Florida experience was a teen-ager's paradise. I matured quite rapidly and gained a newfound sense of self-esteem, plus 18 pounds. This was the first time in years that I was able to gain a substantial weight. I had barely turned 15 when my new boyfriend of 20, a Georgia *Holy Roller,* who hauled potatoes for a living, proposed marriage. That was the catalyst which prompted Mom to declare, "That does it! Back home we go!"

After almost nine months of acrimonious bickering between Mom and Leo, the situation finally reached a climax. He had not once offered to help us financially or otherwise. There was no hope of reconciliation. Upon my urging, Mom agreed to rid us of him and to free herself ultimately of any further anticipation and humiliation.

At her workplace she encountered a former acquaintance from Passaic, a female lawyer, who consented to represent us. The week before our appointed appearance in court for the divorce proceedings, I suffered an appendicitis attack. A doctor, who Leo recommended, diagnosed it as a chronic case and advised complete rest. Leo never bothered to call to inquire about my condition after that.

The day arrived and we taxied to the courthouse which was within walking distance from our building. Since I had been ill all week, Mom decided against walking. The hearing was to be conducted in the judge's chambers.

While we waited in the vestibule, Leo shuffled in following his lawyer. He cast a constrained glance at the floor when he spotted me, then he turned his back to us and purposefully focused on a distant area of the room. His appearance startled me. When he stayed with us, he had changed considerably, but not to this extent. Maybe I was too immature and enamored of him to candidly assess him. His wealth of hair had remarkably receded and dwindled. The deep waves had shriveled into frizzled kinks. His mustache was thicker, ragged and faded to a dingy rust. The tropical sun had toasted his skin to a withered, parched bronze. The slovenly tropical attire and sluggish slouch gave him a shrunken bearing. At 40, he appeared much older; a desiccated figure of the man I once idolized. He was a shadow of his former splendid self.

I looked pale and gaunt with sores on my lips from fever, but my father behaved as if I never existed, and this was our first encounter since we arrived in Florida. The thickly inhabited silence was almost unbearable. Shreds of fog floated sluggishly through my distressed brain. When I finally collected my faculties, I attributed his behavior to his abysmal shame to face me after his indifference to my illness, compounded by the promises which he had so heartlessly breached. He was also aware that my appearance meant that I would testify against him. Then, there was something of which I was ignorant at the moment. He was about to perjure himself. He had falsified his income records in order to avoid supporting his two children. We were awarded a paltry settlement for both of us until we turned 18. In my estimation, my father had dealt me the final demeaning and reprehensible blow—ultimate and absolute rejection.

Phase II: Predictions, Premonitions and Post-Death Appearances

June 28, 1967: My second attempt at trance in our living-room with Charlie transcribing proved to be the prelude to a series of predictions which took place in three successive Junes. This time I foresaw my father's right kidney as *green,* and I shuddered as I related that he was in the hospital and "the kidney is not there." I said that he had a fever; he was very sick and almost died. I hadn't received any communication from or about him for 27 years.

June 10, 1968: This is the dream I had: Mom and I were at a railroad station riding in something which I couldn't identify, behind a wagon or cart. On the cart was a reddish-brown suitcase with *Strichartz,* (my maiden surname,) engraved across it in gold lettering. The suitcase was piled atop others. There were people walking with the cart, flanking it on both sides. I recognized three of Leo's sisters and two of his brothers. Mom and I then passed the cart and we turned to look back at the procession. She asked, "Who could it be? It must be Uncle Otto. There he is. It is him." Then, I looked at him with tears flooding my eyes, ran to him and hugged and kissed him. (Uncle Otto was my favorite of Leo's brothers.) I knew in my heart that this dream was a portent of Leo's impending funeral.

That same month, Charlie, Neal and I traveled to Florida specifically to see Leo. He had suffered the removal of a kidney before we arrived and refused to see us because he was very ill and too weak. (His vanity apparently wanted me to remember him in better condition.) He and Charlie had never met, and he had never seen his grandson, Neal. My last encounter with him was in 1940 at the Miami courthouse when we divorced him.

In May of 1969, Bernice's husband Irv, Charlie's brother, informed us that he had met Uncle Otto who told him that Leo was in the hospital critically ill. I sent him an invitation to Neal's farewell party. He was leaving for the army the following month. Then on May 19th, I wrote him a ten page letter explaining my newfound philosophy, and how I had forgiven him and continue to do so in my prayers every day. I also mentioned our séances and told him that after he made his transition he could visit us and show himself as a lion since his name was Leo.

A letter dated May 22nd arrived from Miami from my cousin Ruth. She described his condition and that he had undergone another surgery. His wife, Blanche had received my letter and the invitation. She read him the card, but said she couldn't read him the letter because he was unresponsive. My letter was returned post-marked Miami, June 16th. It appeared that it had been read because my envelope was missing. (Bernice told me much later that the letter had been discussed by the family in Miami and they thought I must be some kind of a nut-case.)

I wept when I heard that Leo had departed this earth, not because I had lost a father; he had been lost to me a long time ago. My tears were for a misguided man who had recklessly sacrificed his family for satisfying sex. (Years after Leo had left us, Mom confessed that he wanted her to "go down on him," and that repulsed her.) He must have suffered the guilt, misgivings and shame in silence all those years, and that could have wreaked havoc on him physically.

One week after Leo's passing which occurred on June 18, 1969, we gathered in our teacher Ben's living-room when Bert's late husband, Leo's buddy Bill, brought him through. Someone said, "Norma, there's a lion standing in front of you," then the trumpet touched me on my lap.

A few weeks later, we met in Bert's living-room and Freda described a beautiful, proud looking lion walking around in the center of the circle. It stopped by me; then it went over to my Mom and placed its paws upon her lap. Leo was offering his apologies to us for the first time since he deserted us in 1936. Apparently, the idea of manifesting as a lion appealed to his vanity. How did he know the contents of that letter? If he was in a coma, he was out of his body preparing for his transition and aware of everything.

Chapter XXXIII
OUT OF BODY EXPERIENCES

A Surprising Achievement

"When you least expect it, intention, desire and effort reward you."
Norma Locker.

FOR MANY MONTHS I had been trying to project out of my body by lying on my back in bed and imagining my astral body rising out of me. I was only successful in achieving a kind of bouncing up and down. It wasn't really taking off. It seems that my intention was noted by my Higher Self.

The weekend of October 17th through the 19th, 1975, Charlie and I attended a John Hancock convention at the Tamamint Hotel in the Pennsylvania Pocono Mountains. On Saturday afternoon, the 18th, we were chatting with some of the attendees in the lobby, when at 3:00PM I decided to return to our room for a nap. Saturday is a late night at these affairs with many festivities; an early cocktail hour, a long, tedious banquet with speeches and awards, and dancing and entertainment afterward. I asked Charlie to alert the front desk for a 5:00PM wakeup call when he came up to the room.

After drawing the thermal drapes to darken the room, I settled into a deep sleep. I recall hearing Charlie enter the room, make coffee and phone the front desk. (Later, he told me he had phoned about 4:20.) He finally lied down in his bed and apparently drifted off. Sometime afterward, I became semi-consciously aware that something was amiss. I thought, "Why isn't the phone ringing? It's 5:00." Then I heard Charlie snoring and a deafening crinkling sound as if someone was crumpling cellophane just above my head. I felt a smothering sensation; had trouble breathing. My body was frozen in place and my eyes were glued shut. I wanted desperately to see who or what was causing the disturbance. I thought, "How could someone fit between my head and the headboard?" which was flush against the wall.

Then the crescendo rose to a shrill, earsplitting screech, after which I heard a loud pop which was followed by a dizzying sensation. I was actually propelled out of my body from the top of my head and found myself tumbling uncontrollably in space. I thought a ridiculous thought, "This is what happens to somnambulists. Could I be one?" I seemed to be curled up as if in a pre-natal position as I gyrated dizzily. Then I thought indifferently, "Well, I'm not walking in my sleep. Maybe I'm dying."

I decided to take control. I thought, "I must stop this crazy tumbling," so I began to repeat the master *Switch Word, Together,* several times, and I almost leveled out. "I'll open my eyes," which felt as if they were plastered together. I forced them open and found myself looking down into the room from the ceiling. My back was against the joint of the ceiling and the wall opposite my bed, and I was facing the beds. I looked down below me. The room was still almost black. I'm nearsighted and obviously was not wearing my eyeglasses, but I could see with exceptional clarity the top of the TV set below me with the rabbit-ears pointing up; the dresser top next to it with the wrist watches, our eyeglasses and Charlie's wallet perched atop it. I clearly saw my bed with my head poking out of the blanket, and Charlie's bed and his head.

I felt peculiar, but as excited as a child who has taken its first steps, when I realized what was happening. I thought, "My eyes are open and I'm looking down on us! I should try to get back." I thought, "*Together*," and I began to float up between floors, not quite arriving in the room above. In an infinite instant a Stygian blackness engulfed me. I thought, "What if I go into the room above? I'll be eaves-dropping. I'd better get back if I can. I want to get back." I felt myself moving and suddenly, I was aware that I had returned to my body. I thought, "I'll open my eyes again," and I did. This time the perspective had changed. I had reentered my body, but I don't recall exactly how.

This event thrilled me so, that I promptly eased myself out of bed so I wouldn't disturb Charlie. I grabbed my handbag from the chair in the corner of the room and my wrist watch from the dresser and headed for the bathroom. It was a few minutes after five. The operator never did call to awaken us. That entire episode must have transpired in just a few seconds. I always carry a notepad and pen in my handbag. I sat down on the toilet and quickly recorded every detail of that amazing experience, lest I forget one moment of it.

I knew that when I was in a trance state, I was either partially or totally out of my body, but I had rarely been aware of it. This incredible event proved to me conclusively, that we do have an astral or spirit body which behaves exactly like our physical one, but it is perfect in every way. The fact that I was seeing clearly in that dark room from that vantage point against the ceiling, meant that my vision was functioning perfectly. I was thinking and reasoning also in that body. With what was I thinking? My brain was still in that inert body in the bed. This was also confirmation that the mind and brain are two separate, yet interdependent entities. When we are out of the body we are still thinking and reasoning. What are we using?

Certainly not the brain which is the physical organ left behind in the body. Then it must be the mind with which we can function in the astral or spirit body which is capable of independent ability. The mind is what supplies the power for the brain and the nervous system. It is akin to invisible electricity.

I have never forgotten one exciting detail of that event which also proved to me that it wasn't merely a dream. I also learned that we leave our bodies through the crown of our heads. I had a sudden flash of clarity. It was the corroboration of the metaphysical proposition that we are indeed perfect, because God's Perfect Life dwells within, through, and around us; hence there should be no physical or mental disease or impairment. If there is, it's because our thoughts are not pure and positive. We choose how we think and what we believe to be true about ourselves, other people and the Universe. I had been applying these principles to my life since 1965. Why was I so thrilled with my out-of-body-experience? Because, I suppose it provided me with concrete evidence; with the truth of my convictions. Any malfunction of my body can be attributed to a malfunction of my ingrained thought and belief patterns, and my emotional tenor at the time. How the body responds is merely a sliver of the impact our attitudes, behavior and ingrained belief patterns have on the course of our lives. Every aspect of our existence, every living contact, (and that includes our planet and the entire Universe,) is affected by our thoughts and attitudes because of the connectedness to everyone and everything. Toss a pebble into a pond and observe and imagine the ripples expanding outward infinitely. That analogy explains it.

Bert's Story

"In early spring of 1956 I had heard of an old ruby mine in Virginia which was being opened to prospectors. Since I'd been fascinated with stones most of my life, I tried to convince my husband, Bill to drive down there for a weekend. He wasn't anxious to go, but he eventually conceded. After he agreed to go, a psychic friend of mine warned me to drive carefully as she saw an accident. How could I tell Bill that I had changed my mind at the last minute after he had finally acquiesced?

He was a fast, impatient driver and when I suggested that he take it easy because I had been warned about an accident, he just laughed and said, 'I don't believe in all that hogwash, anyway.' Since he was the only driver, I could only pray that we would be safe.

On our way home we were detoured by an officer just as we were about to travel through a mountain route. He advised us against it because of fog. We traveled a few miles when Bill decided to pass a tremendous trailer truck. I remember tensing and gritting my teeth because I knew that this was it. That was the last thing I recall before the accident, as I had apparently left my body in time to avoid the impact. That is probably what saved my life. Some life-saving mechanism within me had preconceived the exact moment. I was never aware that I had projected out of my body until I realized I was up in the air witnessing the soundless head-on collision of our car with what appeared to be a brownish panel truck. I later discovered that it was a telephone truck. In those days they were painted olive-drab.

All I could see were the noses of both vehicles mashed together, and the rooftops, but I knew that Bill and I were inside the car. Somehow, I felt no emotion, perhaps because I felt no pain. I had received the worst of the injuries. My nose and face were practically obliterated. I had a broken kneecap and I lost a kidney. I remained in critical condition for many days. One evening, I had my second out-of-body-experience, (OOBE.) I was told later that the crisis had arrived. I would either survive or die that night. The sense of euphoria remains indelible in my memory as I drifted above the hospital bed feeling relaxed, unburdened and completely free of pain. As I looked down at my body below, my face almost totally swathed in bandages, I felt completely detached from that body and from all worldly cares, almost as if they had never existed for me.

I began to float toward the door. As I did, I felt positive that once I reached it and turned the knob, I would never need to return to that shattered body which I no longer wanted. As I approached the door, there was an elderly man with a shaggy mane of gray waiting for me. What struck me was that he seemed to be such a beautiful soul and he reminded me of pictures I had seen of Albert Einstein. I reached for the doorknob and as I did, this beautiful soul shook his head and pointed in the direction of the bed. I knew he was telling me it was not my time. But, I didn't want to accept that. I heard myself snap impatiently, 'Get out of my way!' But, he continued to shake his head and point.

The next thing I remember is being back in my body with doctors and nurses working feverishly to save my life. Whatever they did must have helped, because I'm here to tell this story."

Bill sustained minor injuries and was discharged from the hospital after three days. Much later in our friendship, Bert shared with me the torture she endured when they had to graft skin from other parts of her body to reconstruct her face.

The first time her late husband, Bill was able to speak at one of our séances, his heartfelt words were, "I'm sorry, Bert."

Chapter XXXIV

THE WONDERS OF OUR UNIVERSE

"When you make the effort to pay attention to the sights, sounds,
smells and sensations around you,
you're engaging yourself to live in the present moment."
Dr. Deepak Chopra.

HAVE YOU GIVEN much thought to the wonders of life and
the universe? After reading the previous chapters in this book, can
you accept that a Superior Intelligence is our creator? It astonishes
me when someone cynically remarks, "I can only believe in what I
can see and touch." We are each entitled to our own personal opinions and beliefs, but let's at least try to open our minds to possibilities.

Have you ever amazed at the thousands of diversely composed
melodies arranged from just eight original musical notes? There
seems to be an endless stream of music emanating from an equally
endless stream of composers. Who is the actual Creator of these
melodic compositions?

Ponder the marvel of mathematics and what can be accomplished with merely ten primary digits! Think of the astounding

significance of numbers in our lives and in the universe. The most enlightened human brain could not possibly fathom the infinite possibilities. The entire universe is miraculously calculated from a base of ten digits, zero through nine. These digits contain the power to multiply and compute to capacities yet unfathomed by humankind. Without math there would be no science, technology, automation or comprehension of the physical universe.

The magic of words---there is another wonder. What mind save an Infinite Omniscience could have devised so many diverse languages and dialects; so many ways to utter one word; one statement? Such lyricism; such poetry; multiple means of verbal communication through eons of time. What strange and unique languages have we yet to encounter? You may say language was conceived by humankind. I contend that we are guided by a Higher Intelligence.

And, the most awesome of all---the phenomenon of life; conception, birth and death; (change,) in all of nature. Have you ever paused long enough in your busy daily routine to observe the world around you? Not just the surface; not merely admiring the trees, the blossoms, the colors, or conversely grousing about the bugs and the rocks in your garden, or the weeds, most of which have therapeutic value. Have you truly attempted to closely inspect them; to admire the essential beauty; to seriously consider the reason for their existence; the synchronicity, connectedness and interdependence of all creatures and every other natural creation?

Yes, there is a blend of beauty, symmetry, magic and mysticism in everything. Pluck a tiny wildflower and scrutinize every facet of it. You will gain a breathtaking insight like never before. Glance about you. Observe the growth, the changes, the activity. Inhale and let your soul soar to the countless fragrances; each one pertinent to its intrinsic self. Hearken to the natural sounds. Identify each one if you can. Drink it all in. Stimulate your imagination.

Anyone who has cultivated a garden; planting new life, has enjoyed such inspiration. Communion with nature can be a meditative experience. It brings us closer to what is known as God, because we intuitively sense a Higher Presence in everything, everywhere. The peacefulness; the natural order and harmonium; the busyness and preoccupation of every living thing instinctively motivated to accomplish its specific purpose on this earth staggers the imagination.

And how do *we* compare with other life forms? We metaphysicians have already determined our fundamental purpose on earth and in creation. It is the urgent compulsion of the soul to evolve and return to its Creator. Our primordial impulses are programmed into the soul, the urge to survive and progress being the primary ones.

Television has brought us closer to understanding the dazzling and complex machinery of life through the ingenuity and patience of modern photographic technicians. Now microscopic photography reveals secrets of life heretofore unknown. Time-lapse photography discloses to our fascination, the development of any biological species, including the most remarkable of all the human species.

Consider the infinite patterns of individuality. It boggles the mind to attempt to comprehend how each of us has been created as a unique, singular entity. There are no two exactly alike. There never was and there never will be, (excluding cloning, of course.) That comprises every soul as well as every form in the universe. Individuality is the key to creation.

Speaking of uniqueness; if you can accept the concept that you are an integral and essential component of the whole of the universe, then your entire philosophy towards life and the world must change. In other words, think of yourself as one of the cells which comprise the universal body which, without *you* might cease to exist in its present state. As each cell within you is a total universe, so are you created as a total universe unto yourself...a universe within a universe within a universe---(ad infinitum.)

The recent discovery that the mind is everywhere in the body, not only in the brain and that the cells communicate with each other has revolutionized past scientific hypotheses. Science has researched the human fingerprint, footprint, ear-print, voiceprint, and now the eye-print. What else lies ahead as evidence of individuality? I hold that every line, every wrinkle, every crease, every blemish in and on each of us also serves as a template for our uniqueness. And it doesn't end with humans. They are discovering that in every facet of nature there exists the fundamental concept of distinction; of uniqueness. Witness the DNA principle which unequivocally confirms the principle of individuality. Each DNA molecule is pre-programmed to sustain and reproduce itself and the organism which contains it. It exists in every form of life. No life can exist without it, but it is not considered to be alive itself. Each molecule contains all the information required to maintain and sustain the particular organism to which it is assigned for its entire lifetime. Science has not yet determined why it works and how it originated. Can it be that DNA is the seat of the soul and that this is the element which connects all of life? When the truth is discovered, will it herald a revolution in scientific thought? Can this mean that science and spirituality will finally merge as a universal philosophy? Wonder of wonders!

Music, mathematics, language, nature, all of life, the structure of the universe; yes even the horrors of natural catastrophe---we take so much for granted without considering the source or the causation. We miss so much and we really comprehend so little unless we investigate, question, probe, contemplate, marvel and appreciate.

Chapter XXXV

WE HAVE LIVED BEFORE

"What the caterpillar thinks is the end of the world
the butterfly knows is only the beginning."
Unknown author.

HAVE YOU EVER had a glimpse of what might have been another lifetime? It appeared that you were someone else in another place, or you felt a familiar twinge of recognition, déjà vu, in a place you've never been before. You have affinities for foreign or ancient artifacts, languages, historical periods, literature. You array yourself in fashions from a bygone era. You were a gifted musician or artist at an early age with no prior training. Have you ever asked, "Why am I in this situation? I've done nothing to deserve this;" or "Why does that innocent child have to suffer like that?" An apparently angelic soul, one whose life has been devoted to serving and helping those in need, suffers a tortuous illness and you ask, "Why is God punishing her? She is so good." Most people ignore the blatant possibility that there's more to these apparent injustices than they care to admit. Some are trammeled by rigid religious convictions which preclude them from further investigation.

Do I believe that we have lived many lifetimes before this one? No. I can declare with rock-solid conviction that I know we have. The theory of reincarnation makes perfect sense when we analyze the significance of it and the impact it imposes upon our lives and our destiny.

Actually, the idea that we have lived before and will again return many times until we get it right, is relatively simple. If we can accept Darwin's theory of the evolution of the species, then why is it so difficult to accept the concept that the soul also evolves toward a higher level of consciousness?

Theosophy postulates that with each successive life we achieve a greater awareness of our purpose for living. In time, we may expect to outgrow the necessity for rebirth and enter the higher levels of existence beyond human bonds. This means that as long as we progress morally and spiritually in each successive lifetime, conquering and learning from the challenges we encounter, there will come a time when we no longer need to be encumbered with the physical and material worlds. In essence, our earthly domain is the school of the soul and we are each the sum-total of all of our past experiences.

However, this cannot be accomplished without the knowledge and comprehension of the Karmic laws. Karma is a Sanskrit term meaning action and its counterpart reaction; cause and its counterpart effect. There can be no reaction or effect unless there has first been an action or cause. The Golden Rule expresses one facet of Karma: *Do unto others as you would have them do unto you.* Furthermore, what goes around comes around; or toss a boomerang and it returns to you; or, *As ye sow, so shall ye reap; Judge not lest ye, too, be judged. An eye for an eye, a tooth for a tooth* is not a directive by God for we mortals to obey. It merely clarifies the ever-present Karmic law which is enforced by the Universe or God as we know It. In other words, if we gouge out someone's eye, we are destined to endure a similar trauma at some time, whether in this life or a future one. Whatever our thoughts, utterances or deeds may be, whether negative or positive, they exercise a profound influence on our emotional, mental, physical and spiritual existence.

The concept that we have lived many lifetimes before, and we are each reaping our Karmic harvests which have been accumulated, not only in this lifetime, but in previous lifetimes, provides a sensible and credible explanation when fully understood. The philosophy of reincarnation and the Karmic connection answers any and all questions concerning life, events, situations or circumstances, and serves to diminish and even banish the present countless fears and doubts existing in our minds and hearts.

If in the past we have abused our spiritual legacy, we must redeem ourselves in the future, perhaps even presently. Conversely, if we behaved in a loving, beneficent manner, accepting equably and placidly what has befallen us, then we may be reaping those benefits. Everything must balance out. This is a mathematical universe. If we didn't have balance and cosmos, we would be in a perpetual state of chaos.

In *Venture Inward* by Hugh Lynn Cayce, the author's father Edgar Cayce, the famous prophet and healer, said while in trance, "Know that in whatever state you find yourself, of mind, body or physical condition....that is what you have built, and is necessary for your unfoldment. That at the moment is best for you."

Gina Cerminara quoted some passages from the Edgar Cayce readings in her book, *The Edgar Cayce Story: Many Mansions*. He admonished that our choices, actions and behavior in past lifetimes are reflected in our present circumstances.

For me personally, since I have embraced the concept of reincarnation with its Karmic connection, I am filled with a sense of calm objectivity; with a deeper cosmic awareness and understanding and love of humankind. I find that I am capable of unconditionally accepting my fellow mortals with their peculiarities and idiosyncrasies;

their social status, education, race, creed or nationality, and I can humbly confess that in spite of all that, I am fully aware that I still have a long journey ahead of me. I'm grateful that I am able to accept everything which transpires on earth from a universal viewpoint, aware that nothing happens without a reason. I no longer feel that inequities exist on earth. When apparent injustices, crimes, holocausts and even natural catastrophes occur, I am no longer deeply disturbed or confused. I know that the ever-present, immutable law of Karma is operating and that neither I, nor anyone else is exempt from retribution. Nature reacts to the violence perpetrated by humankind; hence we have such catastrophes as tsunamis, devastating fires, hurricanes, tornadoes, earthquakes, volcanic eruptions, floods, droughts, famine and pandemic diseases. No one gets away with anything, though it may appear so at times. If the debts are not repaid in this lifetime, I feel confident that the opportunity to learn the penal lessons will again be presented in the future. I am far better equipped now to deal with any challenge which I may encounter as well as what occurs in the lives of my loved ones and the choices they make. It is not our place to sit in judgment of anyone, no matter how distressing or horrible their deed.

Let's discuss capital punishment. Criminals and law enforcement officials believe that death is the ultimate punishment, when in fact, life imprisonment without the prospect of parole really is. Since there is no death, the criminals are merely being transitioned to a better life. What each of us must face on the other side is an immediate life review which enlightens us as to our expiation in future lifetimes. The real hell is right here on earth. However, if one believes that he or she is deserving of a hellish fate on the other side; that is exactly what is experienced, because we create our own reality there as well as here. What we expect and fear is precisely what we get! Since we aren't restricted by time and space on the other side, the results are instantaneous!! (This was all explained in Chapter XX by our teacher's guide Dr. James.)

A clearer understanding of phobias, disharmonious relationships, loneliness, homosexuality, and countless emotional disorders as well as birth defects and debilitating diseases can be derived from the acceptance of the reincarnation philosophy. People who battle obesity throughout their lives may have mocked others in past lifetimes. We must "walk in everyone's shoes." Homosexuality, for example: If a male has feminine characteristics and favors masculine relationships, he may have been a female in too many previous lifetimes which he enjoyed, therefore adhering to that proclivity; likewise for a lesbian who may have experienced many favorable lifetimes as a male. Eventually, they must each relent in future lifetimes and experience what they have been avoiding. (Their Karma may be why homophobia exists in our society.) Another reason for being compelled to choose a homosexual existence may be the result of having mocked, abased or abused them in past lifetimes; likewise for racial prejudices and chauvinistic behavior. There are many documented cases of children rebelling against and resisting the gender to which they were born. These transgender children are doomed to a life of pain, humiliation and abuse. These are not accidents or aberrations.

This is a reminder: When there is irresistible chemistry between two people, that's past life stuff. There was a close emotional connection in one or more past lifetimes. It could have emanated from a romance, marriage, parental, sibling, or familial relationship.

Dr. Ian Stevenson former professor of medicine at the University of Virginia and his investigative staff researched 2,000 international cases of children recalling their previous life. His book, "Children Who Remember Previous Lives; a Question of Reincarnation" describes the details of 12 of the most evidential cases. As soon as these children begin to speak they insist that they are someone else and they describe every aspect of the immediate past life and even how they died which was positively confirmed by those families. There were birthmarks or defects of some sort on most of the children's bodies which the previous families recognized as the exact location of a serious or fatal injury of the family member described by the child.

Little children are naïve and ignorant about deceased persons or death so their declarations are deemed more credible.

If you were born with prominent birthmarks or defects, it's possible that was the area where you had serious surgery or a critical injury in a previous life. I have a grand-nephew who from his first encounter with solid food as an infant refused to eat meat and used to toddle around munching on raw veggies. Could he have been a Buddhist or 7th Day Adventist in his immediate past life? Jay Greenberg at age two sketched a violin and cello and wrote scales and musical notes, things he had never seen. At age 12 he was composing symphonies and other classical works. He claims that music is constantly playing in his mind, creating all sorts of compositions. At that young age he was accepted on scholarship at the Julliard Academy of Music. We've all heard about Mozart composing at a very young age also.

If you are really curious you can probably speculate on some of your past lifetimes consistent with your own particular affinities and talents.

Charlie was a Native American in his lifetime prior to this. His behavior and affinities substantiated that. (More about this later.)

In *Lighting the Light Within*, Dick Sutphen writes: "Reincarnation was taught by the Essenes with whom Jesus had considerable contact. The historian Josephus refers to reincarnation as a common belief among Jews at the time of Jesus. The fact that reincarnation had at one time been in the bible is indisputable, for in AD 533, during the 2nd Council of Constantinople, the church adopted a decree stating, 'Whomsoever shall support the mythical doctrine of the pre-existence of the soul and the wonderful opinion of its return, let him be anathema.'" Sutphen asserts that nothing can be concealed by official decree unless its existence is being acknowledged in the first place.

Yet, it seems that there are still some biblical references in the old and new testaments which are open to re-interpretation depending on your point of view. In Job, 14:14: *If a man die, shall he live again? All the days of my appointed time will I wait, till my change come.* In Matthew, 17:9-13; 16:13-14: *....and his disciples asked him; 'Why then say the Scribes that Elijah must first come?' Jesus answered, 'Elijah is come already and they knew him not.' Then the disciples understood that he spake unto them of John the Baptist.* In Mark, 6:15 and Luke, 9:8: *....Who do men say that I am? Some say that thou art John the Baptist; some Elijah, and others Jeremiah, or one of the prophets.* In John, 10:17-18: *Therefore doth my father love me because I lay down my life, that I may take it again...I have the power to lay it down, and...the power to take it again.* In John 1:21-25, 3:7, *Marvel not that I said unto thee, ye must be born again.* Jesus also said to the Scribes and Pharisees, *Before Abraham was, I am.*

The literature is replete with biblical references, also with philosophers, poets, statesmen, industrialists, writers, scientists and scholars who espoused the theory of reincarnation. Benjamin Franklin's epitaph reads: *The body of Benjamin Franklin, the printer, (like the cover of an old book, its contents worn out and stript of its lettering and gilding,) lies here, food for the worms. Yet, the work itself shall not be lost, for it shall, as he believes, appear once more in a new and beautiful edition; corrected and amended by the AUTHOR.*

Masefield wrote: *I hold that when a person dies, his soul returns to earth. Arrayed in some new flesh disguise, another mother gives him birth. With sturdier limbs and brighter brain, the old soul takes the road again.*

I'm sure we all know people who appear to come from origins other than their present one. I've had many such encounters. When a person is one race, nationality or creed, yet resembles an entirely different one, this suggests a carryover from a favorite incarnation. This is confirmed when that individual has strong affinities for artifacts, décor, history, attire or language from that particular origin.

Layne was born with distinct Asian features. My Aunt Dora adored her and lovingly called her "My little China doll." As she matured those features changed. Could she have carried over the memory of a favorite past lifetime in the Orient?

When I was in the floral design business, a petite Chinese lady entered my shop one day. Upon closer inspection, I realized she wasn't Chinese, but an Occidental Jew. Her round face was framed with dark, straight bobbed hair and bangs over dark almond-shaped eyes. She handed me a lovely porcelain bowl which was crafted with Chinese art. When I delivered her arrangement I wasn't surprised to find her home abounding in Chinese art and décor. I knew two Occidental gentlemen who looked like East Indian incarnations, even to the color of their skin. They were both steeped in Hindu history and culture. One of them taught it in college. If you look at Richard Gere's eyes you'll understand why he is so immersed in Buddhism and Tibetan culture. I can cite many other examples of carryovers from favorite incarnations.

Regressions and Past-Life Memories

The most common method used today to determine past lives is hypnotic regression performed by a trained specialist, an amateur hypnotist, or by oneself with self-hypnosis. There are many others including astrological charting, meditation, psychic readings and dreams.

Looking back in retrospect to my earlier years, my own affinities and talents, fears and aversions, have helped me to determine some of my past habitations. I have regressed myself a few times in the past on occasions when I felt the urge. The information I received provided me with the insight into my present life, situations and relationships. It has answered many Karmic questions for me, and as I previously stated, it has enabled me to better understand and deal with my lot in this life.

February 1, 1969: As I began to awaken this morning, I was impressed to regress myself to a lifetime or lifetimes which parallel my first forty-four years here. I needed to know what it was that designed and shaped the challenges and circumstances of this life.

The method I used: With my eyes still closed, I remained in a hypnoidal state. (Before we awaken completely, that is where we are.) I suggested to myself : *"I am counting back from 50 to 1, and when I reach #1 I will experience a past lifetime or lifetimes which parallel this one. When I am ready to return, I will count from 1 to 50, return and awaken slowly and recall every detail clearly. I will not be affected in any way by the results."*

It was instantaneous. As I reached the #1, I envisioned a battle. There was no fighting, but I knew it was about to occur. Atop a cliff there were soldiers dressed in tunics wearing metal mesh helmets with armor made of mesh. Their chests were protected by a metal plate of some kind. They wore skirts which appeared to be fashioned with leather strips. Their leather boots rose up in front to cover their knees. I was impressed that this was a Roman army and it was in the Holy Land.

A soldier, (whom I thought was Neal,) stood with a whip in his hand. I felt that he had used it on me, though I wasn't in that scene. He appeared to be quite an imposing figure. The other soldiers were straining to push a huge boulder over the edge of the cliff. I felt that Philistines in the valley below were the enemy.

Then, I found myself as a dancer in a gypsy camp. It seemed that my father was the gypsy king. (I perceived him as my father, Leo, in this lifetime.) I was no angel! I danced and entertained all of the troops from both forces. (I knew one of the officers was Charlie.) He offered to buy me from my father who refused to sell me. I was very flattered that someone of such stature would want me. I disobeyed my father and ran off to join the officer in their encampment. He treated me badly, more as a slave than a wife, which I imagined myself to be. Next, I saw another scene with the gypsy girl carrying a young girl about two or three under her left arm. All I saw was her back. She was running as if attempting to hide from some danger or pursuers. The child was very slim and frail with a lame foot, like a club foot. We vanished into a cave, and that concluded the action. I felt we never came out of that cave alive. (The child was my friend Bert in this life.)

This entire scenario whizzed through my inner vision like a fast-paced movie. It couldn't have lasted longer than a few seconds, though it seemed longer.

When I awakened, I immediately recorded every detail in my journal and sketched the type of costume which the soldiers wore. This regression illuminated much about this lifetime. I had deserted my father, the gypsy king, so in this lifetime he retaliated. When I was a kid, I always opted to wear a gypsy costume on Halloween. In the early years of my marriage to Charlie, I was sexually frigid. Was I unconsciously punishing him for his mistreatment of me in this past lifetime? (Part of it, I'm sure, was the result of Leo's desertion and the ingrained memory of being molested.) I was always fascinated by Mid-eastern belly dancing and the music that accompanied it. Bert was crippled in this lifetime with a broken kneecap from the accident. She would say, "Yes Mommy" when I chided her about something.

I never revealed any of this regression to Charlie, and he had no idea that I kept journals. The automatic writing journals were the only ones I shared with him. I hoped that some day he would regress himself and provide corroboration. For years he begged me to regress him; but I refused because he knew how to do it himself. But, on February 2$^{\underline{nd}}$, 1987, fortuitously, six months before he began to experience loss of balance from the brain tumor, I agreed to regress him. This is the section of the taped session which blew me away: "The gypsies have taken a little girl from me and I'm searching for her. I think I'm a young male riding a horse towards the gypsy camp looking for a little girl. My clothes seem to be a chest plate—mesh, a head of mesh. There is no armor. I'm wearing something that looks like a skirt—like tatters—but not torn. The skirt is made like that. I'm on the edge of the woods. I know there are gypsies in there—wagons and gypsies." This was the confirmation for which I'd waited all these years!

April 23, 1969: I regressed myself once more, suggesting that I want to go back to the lifetime prior to this one. That didn't happen, because I got the year 525BC. I saw myself in ancient Greece as a tall, bald-headed priest or monk. My features resembled my own features of today, but I was more fairly complected. I wore a long white or grayish robe with a gold or yellowish rope around the waist. The fabric of the robe seemed to be quite heavy, but sleeveless, with a large hood which I was impressed covers the head during rites or rituals. I saw myself strolling down a paved road surrounded by people who bowed to me. I was laying my hands on each of them, and they kissed my right hand. There were white marble or granite-like structures all around. The environment was cold, stark and barren; no visible, natural growth of any kind. The next scene: I was sitting at a granite-like table on a broad stone chair or bench reading; surrounded by large tomes. The leather-like pages of the one I was reading were difficult to turn because of the size and weight.

Then, I saw Charlie as a physician wearing black. (Of course, he appeared as a different person.) The black attire made me frown, because it seemed incongruous. This doctor was antagonistic towards me and my methods of healing. He opposed me publicly, and was determined to get rid of me, because I may have been a threat to his profession. Charlie, as this doctor, found a way to disgrace me and had me executed. He gave me some kind of an injection; (which I also questioned in my mind;) and had me placed alive in a stone tomb. It was a very confined space, about the size of a coffin. Sand was poured over my body and I was smothered to death.

This scenario also lasted for seconds as a rapidly scrolling movie. The jealousy of Charlie as the doctor didn't really make sense to me until much later after I had been teaching my course for a few years in Florida in the 1980s. He never verbally expressed his feelings, but there were vague signs of resentment in his attitude. Dozens of students approached me with their success stories resulting from what they gleaned from my course and integrated into their lives. Charlie was insecure about his lack of education, even though he did eventually receive his General Education Development diploma; (GED.) I knew that he feared I might become smarter than he. I frequently tried to convince him that he was capable of doing things that I couldn't do; that he had an innate intelligence that helped him to excel in anything he attempted. With sports, if he had never played or competed before, it was as if he had been professionally trained. He was in the life-insurance business which involves complex, intricate legalese and mathematical expertise. His skills as a handy-man weren't taught, either. He succeeded in anything he attempted to do with electricity, plumbing, painting, wall-papering and carpentry. That is why I waited to work towards, and receive my doctorate in metaphysics until after he had passed on.

Common sense is a blend of creative intelligence, inspiration, intuition, experience and mental dexterity. I think that those who lack it are merely functioning at half of their mental efficiency. Book learning is not everything. Common sense is one of the main ingredients which carries us over and through life's hurdles. Charlie's capabilities were spawned from this incredible faculty.

Another facet of my regression to a Greek life: Charlie's lifelong ambition was to be in the medical field. Because he was deprived of a formal education, this also created a feeling of inadequacy. In the army he enlisted in the medical corps and performed as a medic in World War II. Apparently, the method of my death in this past lifetime in Greece left me with a revulsion of being held closely by Charlie in bed. I always felt as though I was being smothered. I also need ventilation wherever I am. The sensation of being air-restricted creates an uneasy feeling.

Often, tuning in on past lifetimes can be therapeutic. This one in Greece revealed the reasons for some of my behavior. It was a relief to finally understand those peculiarities. When Charlie and I visited Greece in the late 1970s, it was on Cape Sounion where I tingled with déjà vu. I knew I had been there before. I wasn't the only one. The poet Lord Byron had etched his name on one of the ancient pillars. He, too, was convinced that he'd lived there in a past life.

One night when we had gathered in our teacher, Ben's living-room, he told us that the mirror hanging on the wall over the sofa was a *Rosicrucian* mirror and if we stared into it we could tune in on our past lives. It was a cloudy, weird sort of mirror because our own image wasn't reflected in it. The lights were dimmed and each of us took turns focusing on the mirror in a hypnotic gaze. Everyone was successful. I immediately envisioned myself as a diminutive, old Japanese woman hunched over an antiquated wood-burning stove. I knew that I was totally blind, and I lived alone in a simple one-room cabin with a thatched roof. It was in a valley surrounded by snow-capped mountains, isolated from any visible civilization. In the front yard stood a goat tethered to a post with a rope around its neck. I was impressed that I had lived like that for a very long time.

This was also a revelation to me. I had vision weakness at a young age and needed eyeglasses at age 13. (Because of teenage vanity, I only wore them when necessary.) I was always able to maneuver skillfully in the dark, even in an unfamiliar setting, and I am perfectly content to live and be alone.

When we toured Schoenbrun Palace in Vienna, where Marie Antoinette grew up, I knew I had been there before. I saw myself as a handmaiden to her. If I was awarded a free trip to London, I would reject it. I know I had spent some time in the Tower of London, and it was a horrible experience. There were past lives in Argentina or Spain; India, Africa, ancient Egypt, and this may sound even more bizarre—Atlantis. I know there was such a place, and I was a *weather-witch* there. The fact that I can predict the weather in this life originates from that lifetime.

When I met Nat, my first romantic relationship after Charlie's passing, I was 64. There was a strong physical chemistry even though he appeared older than I, with a thick plume of wavy, snowy hair. It was October, class registration time in our clubhouse and at that time we had to line up outdoors very early in the morning to insure acceptance into our preferred classes. He was a long-shanked man and as he leaned against a column, he towered over me. When I handed him my flyer advertising my class, he scanned me appraisingly and flirted with an impish gleam in his eyes. He registered for my class and then I discovered that he was also in my clay sculpture class. When I announced that I was flying up north for the Christmas holidays, he finally asked me to dinner. After I returned home, we became an item.

I've said this before; when there is chemistry between two people that's past life stuff, meaning soul memory and recognition. You were together one or more times in a very close relationship. It could have been a romance, a marriage, or a parental, sibling or familial connection.

It was Nat's birthday on Saturday, May 4th, 1990. He had told me when we began to date that he was 69, four years my senior, so I assumed that this was to be his 70th birthday. The surprise party I had planned was to be held in our ballroom that Saturday evening, and I had the cake decorated with the number 70. His daughter lived in Pennsylvania. The Thursday night before the party, we were in my den when he casually said, "Diane, (name changed,) wants us to fly up next week for my birthday. She's probably planning a party." I thought that would be nice. "I remember when I was a kid there were horse-drawn fire engines," he continued. I mulled over that for a moment. "I was born in 1925. I don't remember horse-drawn fire engines when I was a kid. We had a fire when I was four and they were motor-driven," I said. "You must be thinking of a past life-time." He smiled coyly and confessed, "I lied to you about my age. I'm really going to be 80. I thought you wouldn't have anything to do with me if you knew the truth." I was stunned. He was really 14 years my senior! I ruminated about it for a few moments. Due to my meta-physical background there was no way that I would overreact. "Well," I said, "you're still the same person you were a few minutes ago; but you should have been honest with me at the outset."

The party was a complete surprise; so we celebrated Nat's 70th birthday, anyway. It was that Saturday morning, May 4th, when Charlie flung his keys off the radio in the dining-room. (See Chapter XVIII, *Signs from the Other Side.)*

On January 10th, 1990, I was walking the perimeter of our retirement community. When I walk, I usually enter an alpha level of consciousness and mentally travel through my body for healing. I had just completed the meditation and because I was still in alpha, I decided to ask some questions. "What am I doing with this old man? Why are we together? What happened? Where, when, who were we?" An overwhelming surge of despondency and apprehension crept up from the deepest recesses of my bowels. It slithered up like an

uncoiling cobra to the core of my heart and tears began to flow down
my cheeks. I have never experienced anything like it. I asked why,
and the response was immediate. We were together in France in
1811. He was 23 and I was 18. We were to be wed and he was killed
in a war. We had been childhood sweethearts. "Why did we meet
now so late in our lives?" Our love was never consummated. (Even
at that age, Nat was built for intimacy. So, we made up for the time
we lost in that past lifetime.)

I realized that had to be the lifetime just prior to this one when I
was a social worker in Indian public relations in the mid-west. So I
asked, "How could I have been in France and in this country at the
same time?" I got that after the tragedy I was inconsolable so my parents sent me to New York to school; then I went to work with the
Native Americans. This is how I became acquainted with Charlie in
an Indian lifetime.

When I researched a war in France in 1811, I learned that
Napoleon was defeated in that year. That was likely the army in
which Nat, (as someone else,) was involved.

Nat suffered from painful, numbing peripheral neuropathy in his
feet and legs. I was impressed that just prior to his death in that lifetime, they were amputated from the knees down. This is known as
residual memory.

August 14, 1971: Five of us met in Bert's living-room. After the
opening prayer and exercises, Strick, my Mom saw an American
Indian in full feathered headdress over Charlie's head. As I began to
go out, I said, "Crazy Horse" who was apparently one of his guides.
Then Charlie said, "Well, as long as you are in that condition, perhaps
you can see into past lives, and tell us what we were in our last life."
A few moments elapsed and then I saw an Indian funeral pyre with a
young chief or prince laid out on it. He was wearing a light feathered
headdress and he was covered with a heavy blanket which was woven
with thick strips of something which appeared to be felt, not leather

hide. I was able to discern his physique underneath the blanket. He was well-built, lean; perhaps in his 30s and bare-bodied except for a loin cloth and moccasins.

I said, (or whoever it was that was speaking;) "I see a young chief or prince on a slab." Charlie: "Where is he?" Ans.: "Near the sky." Charlie: "Who is that? Is it me?" Ans.: "Yes." Charlie: "What is my name and what do I look like?" Ans.: "Little Deer." (Then I continued with the above description.) Charlie: "How did I die so young?" (There was a pause, then I felt a thump in my mid-chest.) Ans.: "You were stabbed in the chest." Charlie: "By whom and why?" Ans.: "By a princess because you were unfaithful. She was promised to you." Charlie: "Who was the princess? Is she here?" Ans.: "Yes. But that is not for you to ask." Charlie: "When was all this; and what tribe?" Ans.: "In 1870. You belonged to the Sioux tribe. That is why you were born again in Minnesota." (Charlie's family first settled in St. Paul before relocating to New Jersey.) Charlie: "Who was the speaker in that life? What was she to me?" Ans.: "She was a friend; a white social worker." Charlie: "Oh? Not an Indian princess?" Ans.: "A white social worker." Charlie: "What was the relationship?" Ans.: "Very close friends; an understanding of friends. She tried to help." Charlie: "Could you tell us who the others were?" Ans.: "That is for them—each one to ask." (At that, Charlie gave the questioning over to the group.) Bert: "Was I involved at this time?" Ans.: "Yes. You were a school teacher." Bert: "A school teacher? Hmm; I was white too, evidently." Ans.: "Yes." Bert: "Was I related in any way to the speaker?" Ans.: "Yes; her sister." Strick; my Mom: "Who was I?" Ans.: "An Indian princess." (A whispered buzz rippled around the circle, and someone murmured, "Uh, oh; she must have been the one.") Strick: "Was I related to Charlie in any way?" Ans.: "Yes; betrothed." Strick: "Was I the one who stabbed him?" Ans.: "Yes; he betrayed you."

The significance of this session: When Charlie was a teenager, he was employed as a gofer and sweeper at the local department store where Strick worked. His initial impression of her was negative; didn't like her at first encounter. The feeling must have been mutual, because according to Charlie she bossed him around. There was a definite personality clash. Throughout our marriage there prevailed an underlying air of friction and hostility between them, though they tried to be cordial and occasionally affectionate toward one another.

Later, when I researched the Sioux tribe, I discovered that they moved to Minnesota in the mid-1800s. They were the only tribe whose chiefs wore full headdresses. (We have always attracted Indian guides to our sessions with full headdresses.)

Charlie favored the smell of wood and leaves burning; Western movies; horses and horse-back riding. When we toured this country, he insisted on visiting Indian reservations and curiously intruded himself into the sweat lodges. He was addicted to the steam baths in our town which he attended once a week.

A Past Life Memory Experiment

When my grand-niece Michele was an infant, I tried an experiment with her. I held her in front of a window on a summer day and mentally gave her suggestions. She followed every one of my directions with her eyes, even turning her head when necessary. "Michele, look at the trees. Look at the bird. Look at the squirrel. Look at the flowers. Look at the sky." When a child is so young that is the best time for such an experiment. If you have an infant or at least access to one, try it.

More Karmic Consequences

As long as humanity exists on earth, there will be Karma, and new diseases will continue to appear and plague us. Some of the more recent ones are: Aids, Sars, Nepa, E-Bola, The Bird Flu, Malaria, methicillin-resistant staphylococcus aureus or *MRSA*, Swine Flu, and the resurgence of diseases that have allegedly been abolished, such as tuberculosis. Watch the news for more of them as we increasingly incur additional Karma. I've mentioned a few of these previously.

A popular question from people in my audience when I present my program on *Reincarnation and the Karmic Connection* is "What about the Holocaust?" I questioned God about that, and the reply I received may be difficult to accept, especially for those survivors who experienced the horrors, and who lost loved ones in it. But, it's the only one relative to the complexities of Karmic laws. Hitler was a necessary figure at that time in history because the Holocaust victims needed someone like him to fulfill their Karmic debts. This doesn't necessarily indicate that those people earned their fate in this lifetime. Their souls are the keepers of their past-life Karma. This is known as Group, Mass or Collective Karma. Catastrophes such as hurricanes, tsunamis, earthquakes, floods, draughts, famine, devastating conflagrations, and other genocides, and wars where masses of people are affected, are included in Group Karma. Those who are gone are in a better place, and it was their time to go, whatever the circumstance. The survivors are the ones who suffer. It is their Karma, and if they respond with understanding, acceptance, forgiveness and equanimity, it is expiated. When countless lives are sacrificed, it contributes to the balance of the population. Also, violence begets violence, and I'll repeat, nature reacts to violence. Every natural disaster is the result of humanity's violent and abusive actions, because we are co-creators with Universal Mind or God. Our thoughts and actions have Karmic consequences, good or bad. Therefore, we shouldn't blame God for our misfortunes. Another example is how we are abusing our planet; decimating our precious wildlife and all of nature's creations. Observe now the threat of climate change and global warming.

Because of the unprovoked assault on Iraq, we are witnessing the horrific Karmic results; and that includes some of the current responses from nature, as well. Hate begets hate. The choices that politicians made and are still making are perpetrating more national and global Karma.

A common misconception about the theory of reincarnation: As long as we have so many lives to live, why bother to behave ourselves in this one? On the contrary; the idea is to reduce the need for future mortal lifetimes by living as peace-loving and virtuous a life as possible. Our major mission on this earthly journey is to be of service to our fellow human beings and to the creatures that inhabit this planet. That is how we decrease our Karma and expedite our soul's ultimate return to the Godhead from whence we originated.

Let's discuss the transmigration of the soul. Ancient Egyptians, Pythagoras, Empedocles and Porphyry believed that humans may reincarnate into lower life forms. The Brihadaranyaka Upanishad also states that, and also that the number of incarnations are limitless. That is why animal life is so sacred to Hindus. Kabala suggests that early Jews believed in Gilgul, or transmigration. Even some Kabalists thought that humans could transmigrate into animals, plants or rocks; some Native Americans also. I must stress that this is absolutely not possible! Our mission is to progress; evolve to the highest possible level of consciousness; Cosmic or Christ consciousness. (My guy jokes that when he comes back he wants to be a woman's bicycle seat!)

There are eight principles of which I am certain: (1.) Nothing ever dies or vanishes. Everything is subject to change. (2.) There is a loving Father/Mother God; an invisible Higher Power which permeates within, through and around us and all that exists, which will always be; which is ever-present; omniscient, omnipotent and eternal. (3.) We are immortal. This body is merely a glove from which our spirit slips when we take our final breath. That spirit which embodies our personality and memories from this life, passes on to another dimension; the astral plane, and continues to exist eternally; graduating, progressing to higher levels of consciousness, planes or dimensions. (4.) We are each imbued with a soul which is a compo-nent of the Godhead. That soul contains the sum-total of the embodiment of all of our past lifetimes as well as our future ones. It continues to reincarnate until it has become as perfect as a flawless diamond, pure enough to again reunite with the Godhead; never again to need the earthly experience. (5.) An old soul is one who has experienced many lifetimes; who is fascinated by, and has a deep interest and comprehension of spiritual, paranormal and metaphysical concepts; one who is profoundly spiritual and practices and lives uni-versal love and acceptance. (6.) We are always being guided, not only by our own intuition, which is innate soul guidance, but by guides, teachers, masters and angels on the other side. Whatever we endeavor to do, be it something creative, mechanical, or technical, if we ask for guidance there is help for us if we just relax and tune in. (7.) Everything is as it should be in relation to Karmic Law. There are no mistakes, coincidences or accidents in the universe. Because of the existence of Karma, there is no such thing as luck. (8.) Our primary missions on this earthly journey are to be of service to our fellow human beings, and to respect the creatures that inhabit this planet for the ultimate evolvement of our souls.

I must clarify a very important fact: Before a soul prepares to reincarnate; enter a new vehicle, it chooses the life, the family, the experience, the Karma which it needs to fulfill its debts and requisites and therefore to progress. The Karma of the new family is also con-sidered. If the soul does not make the right choices for the succeeding lifetime, there are those highly evolved souls on the other side who offer suggestions and provide guidance into the necessary one.

Also, as an example, when a fetus is aborted, whether through miscarriage or abortion, that is because the soul has decided *that* particular vehicle, (life choice,) was the wrong one at that time. So the matter of a pregnant girl or woman choosing to abort a fetus is as it should be. Interference from religious extremists, heads of government or otherwise, merely augments *their* Karma.

May 11, 1968: Ten of us met in Myra and Joe's family room. Before lights out, our teacher, Ben answered some questions regarding a discussion about a young child's demise. Someone asked, "Why did a six year old child have to die?" Ben: "Its Karma was to finish out the six years in complete creature comfort and love because it has earned it." Q.: "What about the parents of that child?" Ben: "It was their Karma because they had abused in the past, most likely that child, who might have been an adult at that time."

Ben went on to explain the astrological chart. He said that each person goes through many incarnations in each of the twelve houses. (Referring to the soul, of course.) "Before an infant is born, the name has already been selected, " he said, "and every letter in that name has Karmic significance."

Ironically, scientists are involved today with genetic research on aging. They are endeavoring to find the components which will extend human life way beyond the age of 100. Stem-cell research is replacing body parts which will also impact the extension of life. What this implies is that we are incurring even more Karmic debts, because where do we experience Karma? Right here on earth! In other words, the longer we live here, the more Karma we must expiate. It's interesting how science becomes an instrument for the disposition of Karma.

If you could at least adopt an understanding and acceptance of Karma as a Universal Law and realize that it is here to stay until we have evolved above and beyond the need for it, then together we can be instrumental in improving and changing our world as we know it. Because one doesn't believe in something, doesn't mean it doesn't exist. Universal love and forgiveness are the solution.

Oliver Wendell Holmes said, "Man's mind stretched by a new idea never goes back to its original dimensions."

Remember, every physicist adheres to the fact that where there is an effect, there must first be a cause.

This verse by Edwin Markham concisely affirms the significance of Karma: *There is a destiny which makes us brothers. None goes his way alone. All that we send into the lives of others comes back into our own.*

If you have never read anything convincing about Reincarnation and the Karmic Connection, the best primer is, *The Story of Edgar Cayce: There is a River*, by Thomas Sugrue. From there, you can explore the many publications which are available on those topics.

(I was walking my catwalk one day when I was inspired with the following poem.)

Immortality

O' secret soul, where do you dwell 'neath these folds of faded flesh?
Are you the nucleus of each cell; are you me, or am I you?
How are we related?
Is that you I glimpse in Rover's trusting eyes and innocent infant's
    gaze?

Or do you don a clever disguise to hide this rare, elusive gift that our
    loving God created?
What mysteries do you hold about my past and future?
Are there tales still untold that you can help me to unfold?
What destinies for me are fated?
Hush! A whisper beckoned me, "Do right!" In my dreams it filtered
through; and as I woke at dawn's first light.
Oft'times it warned, "Take heed!" And visions rose as I meditated.
Was that you, o' soul of mine? Are you my conscience, guardian, seer?
Do you embody God's great design; do you possess all lore?
Is it you who keeps me animated?
Do you swell my heart to overflowing with love for all around me?
Yea, I am content in knowing that heaven and earth surround me;
that this rhythm pulsing in me is finely orchestrated.
That I am you and you are me; I've known it all the while.
These queries are a ruse, you see, to trifle and beguile.
I know that we are one and I'm exhilarated.
I know you'll slip away some day and this shell will turn to dust.
There'll come a time, somewhere, some way when you'll appear as
someone else with mem'ries of me sublimated.
But I shall linger in a place where eternity reigns supreme; not
marred by time, nor touched by space, my essence shall
fore'er exist in glory long anticipated.

A Karmic Connection

September 11, 2001

A major law of physics suggests that we are ruled by anything but chance, so let us not be fooled.
Whenever an event occurs there first must be a cause.
Reactions don't just happen without an action as the source.
Karma is the Sanskrit term; it should be understood.
Each occurrence has a reason; it can spring from bad or good.
This may help us to accept, resolve and end the mystery.
Examine some examples from our past history.
It takes one act of aggression to spawn the atmosphere of war.
Forgiveness, love and brotherhood help even out the score.
The disasters in September of the year 2001 were reactions to offenses which had long ago begun.
Let's reconstruct the causes:
Our lives have been controlled by big business and their powers.
The result is classic Karma; the demise of the Trade Towers.
The Pentagon was attacked; the hub of strategies and wars.
Never before in our history has such devastation breached our shores.
Will they recognize the impact of these disastrous events?
It is my fervent prayer that they comprehend the evidence.
These governing bodies hold our survival in their hands.
Their greed and arrogance have spawned this circumstance.
Great changes must take place; we need a spiritual revolution.
Our dominating powers must yield to dissolution.

PART III
THE ROAD TO UTOPIA
(Paving the Road.)

"When we *level the bumps in the Road and pave
and smooth over the depressions,*
our soul is rewarded and God smiles with us."
Norma Locker

Chapter XXXVI
ABOUT RELATIONSHIPS

IN OUR WORLD we are surrounded by people of diverse per-
sonalities, characteristics, belief systems, races and backgrounds. How
we relate and respond to them and how they behave towards us can
determine our social, familial and Karmic fate.

If we present ourselves to the world with a loving, peaceful,
cheerful demeanor and a philosophical outlook on life, the world will
most certainly be more attracted to us. On the other hand, if we are
distrustful, judgmental, controlling, demanding, self-righteous and
argumentative, we are setting the stage for disharmony wherever we
are, and probably wondering why people tend to shun us. Our
behavior reflects in every area of our lives, including family relationships.

If I'm aware that I have thought or verbalized anything negative
or judgmental about anyone, I promptly bless him or her in the same
breath; then I forgive myself for entertaining such thoughts. It's a
worthwhile practice to adopt into our lives. As I've mentioned
before, whatever we put out returns to us and I've seen and experienced so much evidence of that.

In any relationship one of the most essential elements is open
and honest communication. It makes no difference whether your
association is with a partner, children, other relatives or friends. If
you cannot express your true feelings and opinions calmly and

rationally about a certain matter, a person's behavior toward you, or how he or she acts in public which may often embarrass you, then there exists a barrier in the relationship. If *you* cannot accept constructive criticism with equanimity and gratitude, then bricks are added and cemented to the barrier. Suppressing our true feelings about unresolved issues can be detrimental to our health. Not everyone is capable of accepting criticism. No one likes to be belittled. When you find it necessary to criticize, explain that you wish to discuss something, or just say, "We have to talk." Express how his or her behavior makes you feel, as calmly and seriously as you can in order to deflect a negative reaction. Censuring and casting blame typically generates a defensive response. Keep the discussion just between the two of you in order to avoid embarrassment. When you enter into a serious new relationship, express your feelings about open and honest communication and commitment.

If the other party is not a communicator and generally bottles up his feelings and internalizes, convey your displeasure with that behavior as well. Be forthright when you explain that without an open line of candid communication between you, you will ultimately drift apart because it disturbs you and creates an unhealthy atmosphere.

(Sadly, many men fit this description. It may be due to childhood upbringing.)

Compatibility is the sugar that sweetens a relationship. It would be wonderful if every couple was completely compatible, but that's a rarity. However, all it takes is merely a few salient points of agreement on activities and philosophies to fuse the bond between two people. A solid love foundation can bridge any gap which may exist. My current love and I are on opposite poles philosophically. You can see how my life is suffused with my spirituality. He's a non-believer; more atheistic than agnostic. If he can't see it; if it isn't tangible, it doesn't exist. He worries and torments himself over every adversity, every setback; refuses to accept the powerful potential of faith and positive thought. He's a sports enthusiast; I think it's a waste of time, and I don't like to watch athletes maiming themselves. He devours the news of the day, and empathizes with unfavorable reports with a morbid Weltschmerz. I feel that is an unhealthy occupation. I love to dance; he can't dance. But, he compensates for our differences with his love and generosity, and we groove in other ways. We enjoy movies; nature videos, dance shows, musicals, talented comedians, and each other's company. Our mutual love and trust is the glue that bonds us and we can openly communicate our feelings to one another, whatever they may be. That's what works for us.

If flexibility and respect for one another's space and personal preferences is lacking, we can feel shackled and dominated. We should be free to express ourselves and to venture out on our own without fear of jealous condemnation. True love yields and understands.

There is dissension in every relationship regardless of the mutual love and respect. Two people often from different walks of life; different religions or races, who have likely had disparate experiences and opportunities, are united in a common household. Every so often it's a good practice for each partner to create a "Gripe" list. One side of the paper can be headed "Gripes" and the opposite column can be titled, "I love how you…" Gradually every complaint is added to the "Gripe" column. The "Love" column can say for example: "I love how you…" Express your love for me every day. Take out the garbage without being reminded. Walk the dog when necessary. As long as there are two columns counter-balancing each other, resentment should be at a minimum.

After you have exhausted every attempt to reconcile in a marriage, including counseling and a trial separation, it might seem that divorce is the only recourse. If that is the next step in the relationship, whether or not there are children involved, maintaining calm and congenial behavior benefits all parties. If you can possibly bring yourself to invoke the *Love Treatments* at this time you will discover that they can produce a miraculous change in everybody's spirit, attitudes and behavior. It matters not what circumstances generated the split, I know they work! You don't have to believe the words, just think or say them. Include your attorney's name also, because you are probably receiving negative suggestions from him or her, and add your spouse's attorney's name. If in-laws are involved, include their names. You'll notice a remarkable change in your own attitudes as well. *I love, respect, forgive, and bless* ____? ____; name the names here;) *and I give each of them over to God for Divine guidance. I love, respect and forgive myself. I am free of all negative emotions and feelings. This entire situation results in the best possible outcome for all concerned. Thank You.*

Try to avoid and detach yourself from controversial and argumentative people and those with mercurial changes of mood. If you live with such a person, inform her that you will not entertain her need to bicker and debate. Don't respond when she tries to push your buttons. If you are the one who relishes verbal conflict, consider the physical consequences of emotional agitation. In any case, your health is being compromised. Politics, religion, infamous televised courtroom trials and financial matters seem to be the most common topics for discord and controversy. If you respect and care for yourself, you can refrain from being snared into or provoking these discussions. Awhile back I was impressed with a practical method to deflect controversy. Two friends of mine who were in a relationship were having distressful and apparently irreconcilable differences of opinion which nearly severed their union. When they shared their dilemma with me I suggested that when either of them begins to lose it, the other should interject with *Red Light* which is the symbol for Stop. This reminds the contentious one to step on the brake and to carefully reconsider the situation. Whatever has caused the disagreement, once the brakes are applied a calm and rational discussion can then, perhaps clear the air. *Red Light* can be used in just about any situation. If you have a nagging, carping wife or an irascible mate who constantly demeans you, instead of retaliating which may trigger an argument, just say *Red Light*, excuse yourself and walk away. Try it. It might alleviate much distress and dissension.

I have detached myself from friends who were habitual complainers. I still love them, treat for them and keep in touch occasionally, but for the sake of my health it was necessary.

There are people with whom you just can't win, no matter what you do to keep the peace. A close friend of mine despised Nat, the man in my life after Charlie passed on. Whenever we were together at a social affair, she would harshly and blatantly reject his company. Of course, it included me, though she didn't seem to consider my feelings. It was all about her. During the six years that Nat and I were seeing each other, I carefully avoided discussing it, because if I had she would explode and imperiously deny, as she had often done in the past when I dared to mention her irrational behavior. In all the years that I knew her, she was *never wrong* so I sloughed off any anger I may have been harboring and continued to send her love, forgiveness and blessings. When she heard of Nat's passing, she scurried over to my apartment. "Oh, Norma; I'm so sorry!" she wailed. "I never meant him any harm!" With tears flooding my eyes, I wrapped my arms around her and hugged her tightly without uttering a word. At that moment I felt sorry for her. What would I have accomplished if I reminded her of past mistakes?

If you realize that you've been wrong in a discussion, have the courage and humility to admit it and apologize.

When Nat revealed his true age to me the week that I was planning a surprise party for him, my response was, "Well, you're still the same person you were a moment ago. But, you should have been honest with me at the outset." Thank God for meditation, because without that my response might have been quite different.

You've heard the expression, *you can choose your friends but you're stuck with your relatives.* That's true to a certain extent. You can choose the relatives with whom you can enjoy a meaningful and harmonious friendship, because it's really about friendship isn't it? I feel that maintaining close family relationships is sacrosanct, but if there is someone in your family who persists in being contentious, you have a choice to avoid and detach from him or her. My treatment for such a person is: *I love, respect, forgive, and bless myself and ____?____, and I give (him/her or them) over to God for Divine guidance. Thank You.*

This is an excellent example: When visiting a cousin of mine, I noticed an unusual clock arrangement hanging on his kitchen wall. He proudly announced that he had been inspired to create it with materials that were readily available, and that he had been giving them as gifts. I asked him if he would make one for me portraying an undersea scene and in my decor colors. I offered to pay for it, but he declined. When I called him to thank him, I said, "I love it and I always wanted a clock in my bathroom." (That's why I chose an undersea scene.) "You're hanging it in your toilet!?" he shouted. "I didn't make it for you to hang in your toilet! I want it back!" I was so shocked at that outburst and no matter what I said to appease him he continued to bluster until I had to disconnect. I spoke to his wife the following day and her reply was, "Well, he worked very hard on it." Since I wasn't receiving sympathy from her or an apology from him, I ruefully packed up the clock and mailed it back with a note which terminated our friendship. In it I said I love and bless them both and wish them happiness and good health. How can you sincerely social-ize when the atmosphere would always be strained? They're both in my prayers every day for healing and the *Love Treatments.* Since then,

I've designed and fashioned an Angel fish shaped clock out of clay which graces my bathroom wall.

Some parents try to influence their children to become what they wish them to be. They want to mold them into something which the offspring often rejects. They believe they can extract pleasure from vicarious intervention in their children's accomplishments, or it may merely be a matter of exerting control over their lives. I've known several young people who were so dominated by their parents' ambitions for them that they were miserable and in some cases became mentally or physically ill. And what about those parents who have destroyed a child's love affair because they didn't approve of the choice? Many a young person entered a marriage condoned by their parents just to please them, which subsequently ended in divorce.

Too many parents after discovering that a child is homosexual have either tried to cure his or her sexual preference (?) through forced psychotherapy, or banished him or her from the family unit.

I've also personally known of a few of these cases, as well as of children who had been rejected because they wed out of the family religion or race. Does this create peace and harmony? Is the cast of these situations happy or do they harbor a burden of resentment and guilt for the duration of the separation? What about the suicide rate resulting from these tragic mistakes? A decidedly unhealthy scenario.

By no means am I claiming that these adjustments are easy. I know how difficult they can be from personal experience. I've learned that if we love our children and grandchildren whatever their personal choices, faults, omissions or lifestyle, they must be overlooked, understood and forgiven. We have a moral obligation to fuse and maintain a close and harmonious relationship with them. The best recourse is to keep in touch with them, even if sometimes it seems to be a one-sided affair. No matter which direction they choose to take, or whatever is their destiny, it is their lives to live and we should be tolerant and loving and remain there for them.

Everyone has the right to follow whatever may be their personal path in life. Each of us has our own special destiny and we must learn through our own life experiences. If you can accept that concept and learn to love and respect whatever lifestyle your children are destined to experience, you and they will be able to enjoy one another unconditionally and harmoniously and remain healthier as a result. Love and acceptance is always the answer.

We shouldn't demand more from our children than they are willing or able to give. Some parents expect repayment from them for the privilege of having given them life and raising them. I witnessed a woman in a public place cursing her absent daughter relentlessly and viciously, to the astonishment and embarrassment of onlookers. This woman was quite heavy and partially disabled, and it's no wonder, because bitterness, rage and obesity can create multiple physiological complications. I felt sorry for her, because she obviously had alienated her daughter, and probably everyone else in her life with her offensive attitude.

One of our major missions in life is to be kind, generous and helpful to others. It's more beneficial to you if you are deriving pleasure and inner fulfillment from your good deeds, but if you feel the recipients are taking unfair advantage of you and you are resenting the impositions; reconsider your situation. No one can take advantage of you unless you permit it. Also, many do-gooders are disappointed and resentful when the recipients don't reciprocate. They feel they should somehow be repaid for their efforts. Resentment is emotional agitation and it breeds ill health. Remember, what you put out always returns to you; so if you are patient and understand that Karmic laws never fail, you will ultimately be compensated from other sources when you need it. This has been proven to me countless times in my life.

As long as you are a good, loyal and trustworthy friend, and not demeaning yourself by entering into a position of servitude in order to receive approbation, you will be victorious. If you feel that some-one who is physically capable is demanding more of you than he or she is willing to give, calmly explain your true feelings. Tell him or her that you value your friendship, but you feel that a true friend is one who tries to share equally with the other in deeds as well as in communication. Friendship and love are primary in any relationship, especially in the family unit.

It's a statistical fact that a solid love foundation in a relationship can add quality years to one's life. We often neglect to show our appreciation to loved ones. One of the reasons for that may be that we lack the ability to respect and appreciate ourselves. Until we can do that, we may find it difficult to express those feelings towards others. Another factor may be that because our loved ones are ours, we take them for granted. A caress, a hug, an expression of gratitude can be so meaningful in any relationship, even with friends. Why wait until it's too late and then suffer the agony of regret or guilt? Christopher Morley wrote, "If we all discovered that we only had five minutes to say all that we wanted to say, every telephone booth would be occupied by people calling other people to tell them that they loved them." Nowadays the cell phone circuits would be over-taxed.

In a marriage or any close partnership, re-avow your love to one another throughout the day. Just before going to sleep at night, regardless of previous unresolved disagreements or dissensions, reaffirm your love. Don't allow resentment to smolder. Fondle each other; capriciously grab one another by intimate body parts. It can weld the closeness and stimulate the libido. After having discussed the subject of love one day with a widower friend of mine he tearfully and regretfully confessed that he never told his late wife that he loved her. When I asked him why, he replied ruefully, "Well, I showed her by my actions. I gave her everything I thought would make her happy." Everything but those three little words, "I love you." He continued, "I never told my kids or my grandchildren that I love them, either." That changed after I discussed it with him. His loved ones were startled when he phoned them with love and apologies, but it subsequently gave rise to a closer relationship between them. He later explained that he had never heard those words from his own parents, so it was a matter of upbringing.

If you enter into any relationship and you discover that you are the only one sharing your life history willingly and candidly, and the other party is merely an interrogator and listener, then you'd best air your observation immediately. "It seems I'm always talking about myself, and when I ask you about your life I feel that you are being evasive and noncommittal." The response you receive from the other party should be the clue to either continue to pursue the relationship or terminate it before you become too involved. This includes any new acquaintance.

In any conversation, listen attentively. Try not to interrupt if a thought flashes in your mind. Some people have the habit of interjecting their own ideas before the other person completes his or hers.

To summarize: Be an open and honest communicator, a good friend; non-judgmental, unprejudiced, accepting and un-controlling. Try to avoid relationships that are one-sided. Never expect the recipients of your generosity to repay you. Make an effort to repair any rift in a relationship, especially with children, grandchildren or any family member whose friendship is worthwhile saving. First forgive yourself and then convey your forgiveness and love to them without blame or limitation. If a friendship or partnership is beyond repair, after you have made every effort to preserve it; let it go; escape it rather than allow it to be destructive to you. Avoid reacting and entering into contentious discussions to preserve your health and well-being. Appreciate the benefits you are deriving from your relationships and avoid dwelling on the negative aspects. Infuse your being with an inner sense of serenity and peace whatever the situation may be. One final thought---love is the most powerful force in the universe. If you convey it sincerely from the heart, you can heal just about anything, and the rewards you receive in return are immeasurable.

Chapter XXXVII
ABOUT HEALING

"Healing may occur when curing is not possible.
Curing is when the physical disease gets better.
Healing is the process of becoming whole."
Dr. Dean Ornish

The *Healing Hands*

I'VE PREVIOUSLY MENTIONED my floral design business when I related the story about the fire in my first shop. All of the floral arrangements were my own designs and creations, but I stocked boutique items for the bathroom and bedroom as well. Friday nights were the late nights when we remained open until 9:00 PM. One evening a customer requested an item which she spotted in the front of my display window. It was out of stock, so I leaned over the partition which stood about 15 inches high to retrieve it. As I did, I heard a *snap* and felt a sharp stab of pain which made me think I had cracked a rib. The pain was excruciating, so when I closed the shop I drove to the hospital. In the emergency room the X-ray showed no fracture, but I was informed that I had injured the inter-costal nerve which is situated around the mid-to- lower rib cage area. I refused the offer of a muscle relaxant, since I had discontinued all medication in the mid 1960s.

I knew how to control pain and administer self-healing, but it seemed that whatever I attempted merely provided me with tempo-rary relief. One Friday night, a couple of weeks later, by the end of the evening I could barely breathe without feeling pain because my bra was aggravating the area. When I returned home, I stripped and sat down on the toilet; (I facetiously declare I do my best work there.) I closed my eyes, held my face in my hands and said mentally, "Dear God, I've tried everything I know but I'm not healing as I should be. What else can I do to heal myself?"

In an infinitesimal moment a pair of hands appeared in my inner vision. I instinctively knew that they were *Healing Hands*. I was impressed to imagine them encompassing my rib cage, one large hand on my back and the other across the front. Then, I intuitively received the mantra, *Hummmm,* which I knew I needed to chant mentally so that the healing vibration could penetrate the area. I duti-fully obeyed the guidance and sat there for about five minutes men-tally chanting and visualizing. Suddenly, I realized that I was breathing without pain. I stood up, stretched, wiggled and twisted my upper torso. The pain had vanished and it has never recurred. I was miraculously healed in that brief interval on the toilet.

Since then, I have continued to imagine the *Healing Hands* sur-rounding every part of my body and mentally chanting the mantra *Hummmm* in my meditation. You, too, can use the *Healing Hands* method just as I do.

When our friends Hal and Irene visited one weekend, Irene hobbled into the house with a sprained ankle. They were running late to make their flight and on the way down the stairs from their apartment, she twisted it. She had applied some ice on the plane, but it remained quite distressed. I quickly sat her down, elevated her leg and applied an ice pack. While I did that, I explained the *Healing Hands* method to her. They both retired to their room for the night. The next morning when I stepped into the kitchen I found Hal reading the newspaper. "How did you sleep?" I asked him. "I would have slept a lot better if Irene hadn't moaned all night. She must have been in terrible pain," he said. A few minutes later Irene strode out of their room. I gaped at her. "Look at you, you're walking!" "Thanks to you," she said. "Boy! Those *Healing Hands* really do work. Look, it's all better!" Then a flicker of recognition flashed in my brain. "Did you chant the *Hum* aloud?" "Yes, why?" "I'm sorry, Hal," I said, "I forgot to remind Irene to chant the mantra mentally."

So, it seems that the *Hummmm* is just as effective when chanted aloud. Do whatever works for you.

When you are visualizing the *Healing Hands,* they can be as tiny as necessary to encompass a gland, for example, or massive enough to surround the entire body for general healing.

If you want to send healing to someone at a distance, fuse a coherent picture in your mind of that person and imagine that you are directing the *Healing Hands* toward the recipient and mentally chant the *Hummmm.* Both components work in concert with one another. For treatment of specific areas of the body, visualize the *Healing Hands* surrounding the afflicted parts and chant the mantra. Healing should be repeated until the desired results are achieved.

<u>Magnetic (Energy) Healing</u>

In order to qualify to administer healing to someone else we must first feel invincible. A sound, wholesome lifestyle is the keystone to preventing serious illness from besetting us. Physical, mental and emotional fitness take precedence over just about everything else.

One of the most empowering elements is a deep, enduring faith in a Higher Power. Your life will assume an aura of self-actualization.

Our teacher, Ben, taught us to take deep breaths while we simultaneously rub our hands together to produce heat and friction. He called it *Magnetic Healing*. This is one of the healing methods that Charlie, Layne and I have been using for years and also what I teach my students. Anyone can successfully perform a healing as long as the incentive, faith and intention are present. When the spirit moves you, take the initiative, but always ask permission first. "Would you mind if I give you a healing?" Not, "I can heal you," or "Let me heal you."

People who are involved with natural healing utilize whatever works for them. Some of the terms are: psychic, faith, metaphysical, spiritual and energy healing. They are basically related because the mind and spirit are intrinsically involved. *Magnetic Healing* can also be called the laying on of hands, though it's not always necessary to touch the subject. We can penetrate the electro-magnetic field of energy, (the Aura,) and the healing energy is automatically dispatched to the area or areas in need of healing. We become a conduit for Divine Healing Energy to flow through us.

Magnetic Healing is usually directed towards another person, plants or animals, or yourself if necessary with touch. Infants, children and animals are not encumbered by negative thoughts of doubt, fear, skepticism or disbelief. They are so ingenuously open to healing that they become the most receptive subjects. Children essentially operate in a meditative state, an alpha brain-wave level of consciousness. In other words, they are in a perpetual suggestible state of mind. When a child falls and bruises a knee, he/she runs to Mommy blubbering in fear and pain. All Mommy has to say is, "Oh, it's really not that bad. Here, let me kiss the boo-boo and make it all better." Cover it with a Sponge-Bob Bandaid and that child is flaunting a badge of courage! The child is instantly appeased and runs off to play again forgetting the initial anguish. What a blessing trust and innocence can be!

When administering *Magnetic Healing* or any type of healing, try to remember that it is not we who are the healers. We are creating an alignment between our intention and the healing energy provided by a Higher Power. We are not exhausting our own resources. If we believe that we are, we may feel drained and depleted thereafter. An open, accessible mind on everyone's part is generally essential. *Magnetic Healing*, as with any type of healing, may be applied repetitively until results are achieved.

How to:

*Take several deep, slow, full breaths with eyes closed, simultaneously and vigorously rubbing palms together to build up the psychic energy.

*When you feel the heat and tingling in your hands, place them within the energy field, (the Aura,) of the recipient. You may touch the body with infinite precaution where designated only if you have permission to do so.

*You do not have to move to the distressed area or areas as long as you are within the energy field. As I previously mentioned, the energy is automatically dispatched to its essential destination, as well as effecting general healing.

*While you are directing healing, you are rendering a mental treatment, such as: ***This is a pure and perfect spiritual being. God's healing energy, love, peace and harmony flows through me into him/her. He/she is healed and restored now. Thank You.***

*Visualize healing energy as a white or brightly colored light flowing into you through your hands and into the subject.

*After the heat and tingling have subsided and you feel satisfied that you have done your part, you proceed to make washing motions with your hands. This is a psychological cleansing. In severe cases, if you feel that you might have unconsciously absorbed the subject's negative energy, excuse yourself and wash your hands with soap and water. (This should not happen if you maintain the proper, positive attitude.)

*Healing can be administered as often as necessary until success is achieved.

*When you discover that a healing has been achieved, wear your mantle of success gracefully and humbly, always keeping in mind from whence the healing comes.

*You can also teach the subject how to use *Magnetic Healing* on him or herself by touching those affected parts of the body which can be easily accessed.

It's your faith in the Power flowing through you which is the catalyst that creates the final result. The degree of the subject's faith and desire can also play an important role in his/her ultimate healing.

You may also apply *Magnetic Healing* to your own body as long as you can reach the area or areas in need of attention.

On April 6th, 1969 I visited my niece Carol whose baby, Michele was nine months of age. She was very irritable; congested with a bad cold and croup. I tried to hold her, but she insisted on reaching for her Mommy. I asked Carol if I could give her a healing and she agreed. She laid Michele down on the changing table and I administered a *Magnetic Healing* treatment with my right hand above her chest and left hand above her forehead. I imagine the reason she cried was because of the intensity of the heat.

The following day Carol reported that the baby was much better. On April 9th Carol brought Michele to our home. She was in perfect condition and in high spirits. No more congestion.

Distraction

Charlie discovered that he was successfully able to affect healing on other people, but he doubted his ability to heal himself as well. On April 19th, 1969 he noticed a large, unsightly lump on the top of his right hand. It seemed as though it had suddenly appeared. I suggested that he apply healing to it, but he insisted that I do it. I administered *Magnetic Healing* and it receded. For several months thereafter, when he would think negatively, look for it, or become upset over something, it would reappear augmented in size. "Do you think someone is trying to tell you something?" I asked him. Apparently, he had become preoccupied with business and other matters and had completely forgotten about it. It never recurred after that.

Layne had become a product of my negativity in my crazy days, (BM,) before metaphysics. One day in 1967 at age 13, she complained incessantly about a severe headache. When she was on the toilet, I handed her the hefty *Science of Mind* textbook opened to the page for the treatment of headaches. A few minutes later, I heard her bawling, "My foot! My foot!" "What happened?" I asked when I reached the bathroom. "The book fell on my foot and it hurts!" she sobbed. "I'm sure it's not too bad. I'll get an ice pack," I soothed. "How's your head?" She paused and piped incredulously, "My headache is gone!"

So, if you have a tendency to dwell negatively on an injury or any other affliction, chances are you are retarding the body's natural healing process. Treatment: ***My body heals itself and God's Perfect***

Life within me makes it so. I am healed and restored now. Thank You. Become involved with anything which can distract you from your preoccupation with it and allow the body to perform its intrinsic duty. You don't have to drop a book on your foot. Meanwhile, you can utilize some of the healing techniques described herein. You'll be cooperating in the healing process and helping to prove conclusively to yourself that embarking on a new endeavor has incredible possibilities.

About Pain

Most of the causes of disease are obviously the causes of pain, because pain is one of the symptoms of most illnesses. Fear and tension are most commonly the catalysts which cause and increase pain. Even if you have experienced a severe physical trauma, there are natural modalities which you can learn and adapt to relieve the pain which accompanies it. We are not concerned here with medication/drugs, anesthesia, surgery or brain implants; merely with harmless, natural pain control methods. Pain control clinics and physical therapy facilities utilize many of these modalities:

*Complete relaxation techniques, including proper deep breathing. *Meditation and *Positive Mental Treatment.* *Hypnosis and self-hypnosis. *Guided imagery/Visualization. *Acupuncture. *Acupressure. *Auriculotherapy: electrical stimulation of pressure points on ears. *All types of body-work such as massage therapy. *Hydrotherapy, including warm baths, whirlpool, warm pulsating shower massage, hot/cold applications. *Certain herbs; topical ointments: Arnica, Traumeel, Zeel; (homeopathic applications and pills;) capsaicin, (cayenne pepper preparation.) *Chiropractic vertebral adjustment. *Placebos. *Switch Words. *Exercises:Yoga postures, Tai Chi and other martial arts and body workouts. *Electrical stimulation: *TENS:*

Transcutaneous Electrical Nerve Stimulation; Ultra-sound or vibration. *Biofeedback. *Physical Therapy. *Homeopathic remedies. *Weight control. *Magnetic Field Therapy. *Vitamin/Mineral/Herbal supplementation. *Psychological therapy for the pain dependent person.

We've all heard of endorphins, the natural chemicals which originate in the brain as pain-killers and mood-elevators. Endorphin is derived from a Latin word meaning the morphine within. They attach themselves to the nervous system and block the pain messages it sends out to the rest of the body. Acupuncture works by releasing enkephalins, a type of endorphin which relieves pain in the same manner. Endorphins are 200 times more powerful than morphine, and they are produced in our own bodies! Smiling, laughter, complete relaxation, meditation, hypnosis, all kinds of exercise including brisk walking and dancing, singing and chanting a mantra silently or aloud, all influence the release of endorphins. One of the reasons joggers and runners feel no pain after running a long distance is the high sensation they experience when endorphins are secreted. (If you are a jogger, I suggest that you moderate to a rapid stride to preserve your joints. Living in a retirement community, I have witnessed the damage former joggers, macho men and athletes have inflicted on their spinal columns, knees and hips.)

When we are under stress, the body pumps out chemicals, some of which are called norepinephrine and ACTH, (Adrenocorticotrophic Hormone.) They decrease and inhibit the action of endorphins. This is why we feel pain more acutely under stress.

At the top of our list is Complete Relaxation Techniques. That is the very first method to which we resort when pain threatens or strikes, as well as to relieve many other problems such as anxiety or panic attacks. As previously discussed, when we relax completely, our natural pain killers are discharged and provided with a clear path to accomplish their essential mission.

We are primarily concerned here with the natural treatment of chronic, symptomatic or psychosomatic pain; that which has already been analyzed or diagnosed. If there is functional, inoperable spinal damage which creates acute, distressful pain, you may achieve some relief by trying some of the following methods. Any new or unexplained pain which recurs or persists should be referred to a health care practitioner before attempting to alleviate it on your own, because often pain acts as the body's alarm system.

Some people acquire a morbid attachment to pain. It becomes an integral part of them and their lives; something to which they can cling, which they can harbor as their own. It becomes a conversation piece, a means of attracting fancied love and attention. They often feel more accepted among their peers, (who may also be in pain,) giving them a common ground upon which to communicate. They also learn to use their pain and misery as a method to exercise control over those who are close to them. (This describes me before my involvement with metaphysics.) Are you one of these pain dependent people? We have the power to create our pain, discomfort and disease. For example: Kids' tummy aches before school. For the most part, they are not imagined or contrived. A parent should attempt to wheedle out of a child if it is fear that is causing the distress.

When you are in pain, you are apt to focus most of your energies on it, becoming totally consumed by *it* and how *it* is affecting you and your life. The more you obsess on a negative aspect, the worse it becomes. Force yourself to detach from your self-involvement and preoccupy yourself with a diversion; anything which will distract you. (See *Distraction*.) Use your ingenuity to engage yourself in something creative or constructive. Exercise, walk, or stretch if you can; get involved socially. Use the techniques mentioned here to help alleviate the pain and what has caused it. Don't give in to pain. Fight it with every ounce of strength and knowledge you have. If you don't, you may be victimized for the rest of your life by the pain which you have allowed to immobilize and control you.

Consider your attitudes, your emotional state at the time the pain intensified. Try to analyze why it occurred. Keep a journal if necessary. What could have caused the onslaught of pain? Were you emotionally agitated or did you do something to strain yourself? Were you tensing for some reason? Were you recalling a distressful event in your life?

A survey of 3,000 employees at the Boeing Company found that those who strongly disliked their jobs were much more apt to hurt their backs than people who were happy in their workplace. So, if you have back ailments, ask yourself why you are dissatisfied. Who is constantly *getting on your back?* Do you feel that people take advantage of you; that you are overburdened? Ask yourself how you may be contributing to these situations. When you discover the answers, proceed to make changes in your circumstances and behavior. Analyze your posture. Do you slump when you sit; cross one leg over the other; sit in awkward, distorted positions? When you stand, are you resting on one side of your body? Are you toting a cumbersome handbag or backpack?

Americans take over two tons of aspirins every hour in the effort to relieve pain. 80% of our visits to doctors are for pain, and about one in every three people suffer from continuous or recurring pain. This is a shameful commentary on our submission to helplessness and the dependency upon medicine to relieve and heal us.

Instant Pain Control Methods

1.) *Positive Mental Treatment:* With eyes closed, take one to three slow, deep breaths. Tell yourself to relax. Feel your body responding. Place your mind, your consciousness into the distressed area. Command the pain to leave: *Stop now! Get out! I don't want this. I won't allow it to be a part of me. I am in complete control of my mind and body. Stop now! Get out; out; out now! I refuse to accept this!*

2.) After you have relaxed as above, with eyes closed, place your consciousness into the painful area and with your mind push the pain out. (I use this one frequently when during my meditation my body tries to attract my attention with slight twinges.)

3.) After you have relaxed, with eyes closed, place your consciousness into the painful area and inhale deeply into it and as you exhale very slowly, draw the pain out with the breath and imagine it exiting through your parted lips. Repeat if necessary.

4.) *Healing Hands Method:* (This was discussed previously.)

5.) After you have relaxed with eyes closed, visualize a bright, white ball or beam of light. See it penetrating into the area relieving it with its warm glow. This white light, like the *Healing Hands* can also be used to heal any part of your body. (You can visualize any color light which suits you.)

6.) *Switch Word phrase:* (With infinite gratitude to James Mangan.) *Change, Together, Thank You:* (For instant temporary control over pain and other afflictions:) Place your consciousness into the area and say mentally: *We want this pain; (or headache,) to leave now, and whatever is causing it to be healed and eliminated. Change, Together, Thank You.* (*We* and *Together* help to consolidate the conscious and subconscious levels of mind, so they perform in unison.)

You may also use this *Switch Word phrase* to control and/or eliminate what follows: *Ringing in ears; tinnitus. *Foreign object in eye; (no need to touch the eye.) *Palpitations. *Tremors; (use along with

Stop now!) *Muscle spasm. *Dizziness. *Circulatory problem; (limbs asleep, etc.) Think, **We want circulation restored now, Change, Together, Thank You.** *Nosebleed. *Coughing. *Choking. *Hiccups. *Congestion; (excess fluid in tissues, mucous membranes; puffiness under eyes; nasal/sinus congestion.)

Once you have treated, as with all other treatments, let it go. Forget it and go about your business. You must believe implicitly in the forthcoming results, the *demonstration*. You may repeat the *treatment* as often as necessary, but each time, let it go! Maintain a positive attitude and don't dwell on it. Your subconscious has received the message and has no choice but to act upon it. As with any *treatment*, if we allow doubt to mask our intentions, we are inhibiting it and even canceling it out.

Chapter XXXVIII
MENTAL POTENTIAL

"...that mind is the master weaver, both of the inner garment of
character and the outer garment of circumstance, and that, as they
have hitherto woven in ignorance and pain they may now weave in
enlightenment and happiness."
James Allen.

TOO MANY PEOPLE are not aware of their inborn mental
potential. They shuffle along in a mediocre existence ignorant of
what could be if they would forgo their fear of exploration and challenge. They huddle in their safe, snug nests wary of change and discovery. Meanwhile, despite their precautions, changes are
surreptitiously stealing into their bodies and they spend hours in
doctor's offices hoping for a miracle. Can they learn to modify and
even eliminate some of these changes on their own? Previously, I
shared with you some of my own personal experiences with self-
healing. As long as you have a mind with which you can think clearly,
you have the amazing potential to surmount many of life's hurdles;
mental, emotional and physical plights. If you care enough about
yourself, endeavoring to improve your life would be a pleasure not a

chore. All it requires is a slight alteration of your normal, daily routine and habitual insecurities. You will at last be unleashing your inner power.

It's essential that your body knows that you are the boss, otherwise it will continue to challenge you with the old, customary afflictions. When you adopt a dog, you must show him at the outset that you are the alpha influence in his life. If you don't, he will be confused, disobedient and difficult to train. Your body is no different. These effective affirmations can nullify the intrusion and secure a cohesion of your faith and confidence: *I am in complete control* *and command of my nerves, emotions, thoughts, words, deeds,* *mind, body and habits. Thank You. *My body heals itself and* *God's perfect Life within me makes it so. I am healed; I am* *restored, now. Thank You. *There is no room within, through,* *around, on or about me for anything else but for God's perfect* *Life and Love and Light and Being. Thank You.* Adopt a daily, revitalizing habit of relaxing completely and meditating; thus your quest for self-empowerment is guaranteed. It's a cost-efficient investment in the preservation and/or improvement of your over-all health.

Life presents us with challenges; that is one of the reasons we are here on earth. How we respond to those challenges; how we weather them makes all the difference in our development and progress. If we can respect, acknowledge and appreciate that every challenge spawns lessons to be learned and imprinted in our souls, we can move from there to higher consciousness. Something good results from every life experience. We've all made boo-boos in the past, but if we've learned from them then we've chiseled another notch in our growth and progress. When we recall past adversities and crises, some of which may have carved a jagged chink in our lives, and we evaluate them with honesty, we invariably recognize the intricacies of the pattern and how the fabric was woven for our ultimate edification.

We are gifted with a powerful tool, the ability to think. Every thought we have is a prayer which has the potential to destroy or to heal us; to attract to us what we believe, fear and expect. Our thoughts are similar in nature to electricity. When we flip on a light switch in a room furnished with bulbs, the room is illuminated. Each time we have a thought a circuit in our brain flashes a beam so bright that it is visible to certain sensitive people. When I witness such a flare over someone's head I'm aware that he or she has had a sudden thought or inspiration.

Thought is a potent form of energy. It is the common denominator which governs and influences our lives. Every thought we have manifests eventually as a form of some kind precisely equaling its original pattern, the thought itself. In the Introduction to this book I noted that we are all immersed in a *Sea of Mind*. It is as invisible as the air which we breathe, but it exists, nevertheless, just like that air and it is always with us, flowing through and around us. This Sea of Mind is what is known as God. Thought is the element which makes us co-creators with the Universe or God. Each thought becomes a part of that vast *Ocean*. It may float about for some time until the proper time arrives for it to be accepted or applied; until the cause which is the thought becomes an effect or creation, but because of the universal Law of Attraction it will always manifest as a form, condition, object, situation, event or circumstance. A negative thought can become a weapon such as a boomerang which succeeds in hurting or destroying its target, subsequently returning to its home base almost as a guided missile to complete its destructive mission. That is exactly what every negative thought about anyone or anything does. If it is about yourself, it doesn't have too far to travel, therefore the immune system is alerted and harmful chemicals are excreted throughout your body. Another example: Because thought is such a powerful form of energy, imagine that negative energy flowing from you in a grayish stream to that person and returning to you as a black cloud. On the other hand, the energy from a loving, positive thought emanates from you as a gleaming, white stream which returns to you and heals you.

Your body will gladly accommodate what you order because the subconscious records and must act upon all input. For example, sneeze and think, "I must be catching cold…" You are mobilizing all the forces which have the power to fulfill your desire. Ernest Holmes said, "We should carefully consider whether we are willing to experience the results of our thoughts." So, it makes sense to keep our thoughts positive and pleasant about ourselves as well as everyone and everything. It was Michel de Montaigne who said, "The pleasantest things in life are pleasant thoughts, and the great art of life is to have as many of them as possible." And Dr. Deepak Chopra whom I love to quote, said, "At the very instant you think, 'I am happy,' a chemical messenger translates your emotion, (which has no solid existence whatever in the material world,) into a bit of matter so perfectly attuned to your desire that literally every cell in your body learns of your happiness and joins in." Imagine your cells jumping up and down with joy! Isn't that exciting?!

Here's another *Switch Word* which you can use to stop the effects of negative thoughts and/or suggestions as they occur: *Cancel!* When you are aware that you have allowed a negative thought or image to invade your brain, *Cancel* it immediately. *I Cancel all negative thoughts.* You can repeat it several times, if necessary. Reinforce it with, *I refuse to accept anything of a negative nature into my consciousness,* and/or, *I don't accept that!* when someone suggests something negative to you. Most treatments are invoked mentally. How you respond is your personal choice.

The bottom line here is: You must first be willing to take responsibility for your own health and welfare, even if you are under medical supervision. As previously discussed, one of the most enlightening and empowering potentials of our minds is the capacity to influence healing on others as well.

Group Power

We've all heard of prayer meetings where a group of people sends out healing to recipients often with successful results. There definitely is power in numbers. After hurricane Frances in September of 2004 destroyed the roof of our two level clubhouse, my classroom was moved to one in the lower level while reconstruction was in process. One afternoon during a session, the workers were hammering directly over our heads. I told the class that I would concentrate on moving them to another place and another less noisy task. It worked! Just as I was about to conduct the Guided Meditation, they returned with a vengeance. I then suggested that there is power in numbers. "Everyone close your eyes and concentrate on moving them away from here," I said. "Say mentally, 'These workers are moving to a quieter task,' and imagine that happening." At that time there were 35 people involved. They all complied, and within seconds it was as if the workers had vanished from the area altogether. This is another example of our mental potential.

If you are asking, "How can I become a more positive thinker? How can I change and improve my life? How can I boost my mental potential?" Read on.

Chapter XXXIX

MEDITATION; LIFE PRESERVER

"That which we persist in doing becomes easier; not that the nature
of the task has changed, but our ability has increased."
Ralph Waldo Emerson.

Achieving Peace of Mind

"Man must be arched and buttressed from within,
else the temple wavers to the dust."
Marcus Aurelius.

WOULDN'T IT BE wonderful to possess that often elusive entity, peace of mind? But, what exactly is it and how can we achieve it? For me personally, it's the acquired capacity to refrain from worry and anxiety when I hear unfavorable news from or about someone. I just give everything over to God for the best possible outcome and I know it's a done deal. It's being serenely content and delighted to be living alone and loving my own space. It's knowing that whatever I endeavor and wherever I may be, my God is with me. My daily meditation since 1965 has availed me with an ineffable peace, with this enduring faith, this optimism. Being capable of observing what transpires in our world from a Universal standpoint precludes me from judging and from living in fear of what the future might bring. I am at peace with the dazzling and complex machinery of life. Because my meditation serves as a bridge to connect me with my Higher Self, it inspires in me the assurance that everything is as it should be and all is well in the Universe even if it appears otherwise. I know that the Universal Law of Karma is the ever-present equalizer. So, I equate peace of mind with happiness. As long as I have God with me, within me and around me and I can arise in the morning after having enjoyed a deep, peaceful night's sleep, humming whatever tune impresses me, I am happy, no matter what. When my initial journey into meditation began I was surprised at the exponential improvement in my attitudes and behavior within just a few months. As I assessed the merits of the situation, I realized that I was a fledgling who was spreading its wings for the first time and taking flight. It seemed that a whole constellation of miraculous changes was occurring within me and around me. I had learned to reprogram my ingrained negative subconscious belief and behavior patterns with positive affirmations which I later entitled *Positive Mental Treatment* thereby forging a *Positive Mental Attitude* into the forefront of my brain. All the old detrimental debris or trash was hypothetically swept into the far recesses of my brain. It will forever remain there as a permanent reminder of what I once was. It was my implacable determination to change which spurred me on. I knew that I couldn't forgo my meditation practice for even one day, lest I regress to that mean-spirited, neurotic hypochondriac that I so needed to vanquish. If I missed one day, that sludge could ooze right back to its origin.

Most people would like to achieve a state of inner peace and serenity, but they are hopelessly shackled by the hectic life of daily responsibilities and stressors. Some of them slog through life existing in woeful resignation; raising and supporting a family, struggling in often intolerable working conditions, suffering a contentious and noxious relationship and sleep deprivation, unaware that the **Road to Utopia** is attainable with a minor reorganization of their daily routine. Many of the most common diseases which beset modern society are the direct product of these stressors. Those of us who have become meditators are so much better equipped to shield ourselves under an umbrella of security from negative responses to the pressures of daily life. When life presents me with wrinkles, I just iron them out, present them to God and carry on with confidence, assured that I have been provided with the opportunity to learn, progress and evolve to higher levels of consciousness. But, I live alone so I'm free to do my own thing. I'm retired except for the fall and winter seasons when I teach my classes for three semesters; but that's only once a week. The season here in our community is more hectic because of the entertainment factor, the responsibility of preparing for and conducting my classes, meetings and the *snowbirds* who flock down to the Florida paradise. That's when I must summon all of my inner resources to buffer the additional stress.

The Requirements

"There is no need to run outside for better seeing; nor to peer from a window. Rather abide at the center of your being; for the more you leave it, the less you learn."

Lao Tzu.

Once you proceed to meditate for the first time you may find that you are distracted by external and internal stimuli. If you have ever heard *experts* claim that you must "quiet the mind," to meditate, in most cases that is virtually impossible. Threads of thoughts and vagaries are incessantly imposing themselves, floating sluggishly within the brain seeming to emanate from many sources at once. It's quite phenomenal since you are not always inviting them. The great majority of those thoughts are most commonly negative and anxiety producing due to old ingrained habits because most negative thinking is based on fear of some kind. The secret is, merely let them float in and out with a detached attitude. Just maintain your composure and continue to focus your inner attention in the area of your third eye, at the center of your forehead. Your goal is to gain an intimate association with meditation, remaining totally quiescent; harnessing the ability to commune with your inner being.

You will eventually attain an altered state of consciousness; an Alpha brain wave level. Even seasoned meditators like me experience distractions, though most of the unconscious thoughts are not unpleasant or disruptive. They can be intuitive and inspirational as I have shown in Part I. Your body will instinctively and customarily demand attention with little twinges of pain, slight muscular tics, itching, etc. You can learn to ignore and even control these petty annoyances. As for external stimuli, when you have become more experienced in focusing deeply within swathed in a veil of silence, you will discover that your expertise blossoms. You'll gain the capacity to disregard any interruptions. Of course, all of this demands practice, self-discipline and patience.

In order to become a meditator and achieve the most beneficial effects of meditation, there are several prerequisites besides the aforementioned. You must be motivated because you are aware that you need a radical shift in the current of your life. Are you willing to learn and determined to continue and persevere? Do you have the volition and resilience to devote yourself to change and to bring it to fruition? Sometimes it seems that time, like a fleet-footed, skittish, gazelle barely leaves tracks, but you can make the time if you seriously consider the link between meditation and your health and that of your loved ones. Regular meditation offers us a mosaic of palliative and therapeutic possibilities. Integrate it into your schedule at the same time every day and it becomes routine. You actually anticipate retreating to your inner sanctuary at least once a day.

The Rewards

The body contains all the essential ingredients to heal itself, but we must be willing to cooperate by not focusing negative attention and energy on an illness or affliction. Meditation has the extraordinary power to prevent illness, because when we are completely relaxed our immune systems are mobilized. Our contribution is as simple as disciplining ourselves to meditate every day, clinging to it with a resolute tenacity. The rewards we receive because we are being proactive with our health are worth the time and the delicious endeavor.

If you have been a meditator in the past and have abandoned the practice, I recommend that you reevaluate your priorities. Your health and welfare should be the major ones, yet some people neglect their health for self-indulgent, hedonistic pursuits. As long as you are not harming yourself or anyone else in the process you don't have to forgo them altogether. Fun and amusement are essential ingredients in our lives. Without them our lives would be dull. So, it's time to resume that *Life-Preserver*, meditation, and you will once again encounter its magical properties. Suppress the impulse to rationalize why you can't resume and admit that there is still room for improvement. Given the proper setting, the necessary implementation and a receptive attitude of confidence and anticipation, you can change your life like never before because meditation has a ripple effect. It offers a potpourri of benefits.

You will notice a significant improvement in your attitudes. Everyone in your life begins to behave differently toward you. Gone are the petty bickering, jealousies, resentments, and animosities, because you are motivated by a newfound attitude of self-respect and love; patience and tolerance towards all. Because of the Law of Attraction, you attract to you what you are. Like attracts like, though it may not seem so at times. There are always intrinsic similarities between you and those with whom you are in close relationship.

When you train every muscle group in your body to respond to the word Relax; just that simple achievement can make a profound difference in your health. As you continue to relax and un-stress yourself in daily meditation, utilizing the techniques which are put forth in this chapter, you will find that your concentration becomes more acute and your memory and perceptions are spiked. If you have active children, you'll discover that you respond to the tumult with more disciplined ease. Modern life bludgeons us with clamor. You'll react to it with more composure. Many, if not all of your psychosomatic complaints such as headaches, colds, insomnia, hypertension, respiratory ailments, and so many other mental and physical disorders begin to decrease and even vanish. Your response to pain diminishes as well. Your life takes on an ever-rising upward spiral.

In 1986 Blue Cross and Blue Shield studied 2,000 meditators in Iowa and found that they were much healthier than the American population as a whole in 17 major areas of disease; mental and physical. The meditating group was hospitalized 87% less often for all kinds of tumors. Respiratory and digestive disorders, including clinical depression were equally reduced. So, this proves that prevention does indeed become a major factor. Many of my students have reported that since they have begun to meditate every day, sometimes more than once, they have been able to reduce and even forgo blood pressure medication and their sleep habits have also improved. In 2003 I was hospitalized for an agonizing 18 hours with food poisoning which I mentioned in Part I. My record of avoiding hospitals for 38 years was blemished. Since then I am determined to avoid becoming a patient again.

A study done in England calculated that each year of regular meditation erases roughly one year of biological aging. For example: a typical person of 60 meditating for five years or more would have the physiology of a person of 48. In other words, it slows down the aging process.

After you have been meditating for some time, talents which you denied having, which have been lying dormant within you will suddenly spring forth. You'll become more productive, enthusiastically launching new ventures. You'll wonder where the energy was hiding. If your libido has been in a slump for some reason, it will be revived and stimulated. During meditation and in your normal daily routine you'll become aware of a heightened sense of intuition. If you mentally ask questions on any prevailing issue in your life, you can receive inspiration and guidance because you are elevating and expanding your consciousness; burnishing your perceptions and accessing your Higher Self. If you remain mindful and don't allow yourself to be distracted, the answers will often flow in from unexpected sources. I demonstrated that in Part I.

As an added bonus, you will notice that some of your habits are beginning to change. Cravings for artificial fixes such as alcoholic beverages, caffeine, cigarettes and other addictive drugs are gone. Your appetites for meat and sweets, all junk foods and carbonated beverages will be tempered and often eliminated. You will no longer need to be concerned with weight because your wholesome and regulated dietary regimen will stabilize it. This healthful lifestyle which incorporates a balanced nutritious diet, exercise and satisfying social interaction is the direct offshoot of daily meditation. So, meditation then becomes the consummate panacea. If all of this sounds too good to be true, the first two parts of this book prove otherwise.

I have formulated a most effective, therapeutic meditation technique which I have recorded on cassette tapes and now on CDs. (This is the method which I use every day, including *treating* for other people and pets.) It is comprised of complete relaxation, guided imagery and visualization for self-healing; transcendental meditation and *Positive Mental Treatment*. It may sound quite comprehensive, but it merely takes 30 to 40 minutes of your time. If you prefer the more simplistic method, you can merely repeat a mantra which will ultimately result in the transcendental phase of meditation which is the most common, generally adopted form. For successful meditation, special rituals, equipment and lotus postures are not really necessary. Of course, that is a matter of personal choice.

Meditation Procedure

*Select a comfortable seat in a secluded area in your home. If you don't live alone, instruct your housemate or family that you are about to meditate and you would appreciate no interruptions. This is your time. Don't allow yourself to feel selfish or guilty. You deserve to be indulged and cloaked in a veil of calm, and your family will learn to respect that fact. If possible, disconnect the telephone.

*The best time to meditate is on an empty stomach before any physical exertion, routinely at the same time every day.

*Remove shoes. Wear unrestricted clothing or none at all.

*Sit with your lower spine flush up against the back of your seat with feet flat on the floor.

*Place hands comfortably in your lap with palms facing up. If you wish to contain the energy within you, bring the pads of your thumbs and forefingers together.

*Keep your head upright with chin gently tucked in to prevent your head from bobbing forward or back.

*Gently close your eyes.

*Everything is done mentally, and you never move any part of your body.

*Say *relax* 3 times. (Pause after each *relax* and allow your body to respond.)

*Next say, *I am peaceful, calm and serene.* (Draw out *calmmm* and *sereeennne* for a pleasant high sensation.)

***Exhale** through your lips, emptying your lungs and sucking in your abdomen; then promptly **inhale** through your nostrils, re-inflating your abdomen. **Hold the breath for a count of 5,** then **exhale** very slowly through lips while you repeat *relax* 3 times, allowing your body to respond. **Repeat the *Relaxation Response* 2 more times.**

Now you are ready to begin the next procedure. But, before I continue with the rest of my method, I'll enlighten you regarding transcendental meditation. Any word or phrase which ends in *m* or *n* makes an especially effective mantra because it resonates in the brain. You can use *one, calm, serene, shalom* or any word or phrase which appeals to you. Or, you can discover your very own personal mantra. You need only to close your eyes and ask, *What is my personal mantra?* The very first word or phrase with which you are impressed; that is it! Be mindful when it surfaces. It may consist of one or more syllables. Mine has two syllables and it works perfectly for me.

*After you have relaxed, tell yourself that you will return in 10, 15 or 20 minutes, whatever suits you. Your inner alarm will alert you at the designated time.

*Repeat the mantra mentally on the exhale, breathing normally. After you've repeated it for a few moments you should click off into an altered level of consciousness. It may seem that the mantra is repeating itself without your input.

*When you are no longer aware of your body or other external stimuli, you have transcended, risen above the physical, material world.

*There may be those rare and wonderful times when you ascend to a euphoric, blissful paradise; an exhilarating spiritual phenomenon which may leave you almost breathless with its vivid radiance and beauty.

*When we meditate, we register on an electroencephalograph, (EEG) printout an Alpha brain wave level of consciousness which can be extremely therapeutic in and of itself.

The Rest of My Method

Once you have relaxed yourself completely, prior to chanting the mantra, you are primed for the following steps. Your eyes remain closed throughout this exercise. (Some of this was presented in Part II.)

The Consciousness Awareness Exercise:

*Place your consciousness, (your mind,) into your feet. Say mentally, *The joints of my feet are soothed, lubricated, cleansed and healed.* (You are traveling mentally up through every **joint, gland, muscular group and organ** in the same manner. It's essential that you remember to repeat the *treatment* for each segment of your body. (The **muscles** are *relaxed* and the **joints and organs** are *soothed, lubricated, cleansed and healed.*)

*When you arrive at the **bladder and pubic area,** men include the **prostate** as well.

*Remember the **abdominal cavity-- the intestinal tract; the diaphragm** which is a muscle; the **digestive tract; stomach, liver, pancreas and gall bladder.**

*Men and women; when you arrive at the **breasts,** imagine the *Healing Hands,* one on each **breast** and mentally chant the healing mantra, *Hummmm,* allowing the healing vibration to penetrate the **breasts.**

*Imagine the *Healing Hands* around the **heart muscle,** and chant *Hummmm.*

*Now you are in the **respiratory tract** including the **throat.**

***Unclench your teeth.** Relax the **jaw.**

***Feel** the flesh surrounding the **cheekbones** releasing away from the cheekbones.

*Imagine the *Healing Hands* one on each **ear** and chant *Hummmm.*

*In the **mouth;** the **gums** and **teeth** are strengthened.

*In the **sinus** and **nasal** passages; the **sinuses** are draining perfectly whenever necessary.

*Imagine the *Healing Hands* one on each **eye** and chant *Hummmm.*

***Relax the brow. Feel** the **scalp** releasing away from the **skull.**

*Go into the **brain**. Say, *My memory and brain power are better and better, stronger and stronger, improving and increasing every day in every way.*

*Now, think of the **nape of your neck**. Imagine a **tightly closed fist** there. That **fist** represents the **tension** which generally affects the neck. Each **finger** in that **fist** represents a **nerve**. Visualize those **fingers opening** and **wiggling loosely** at the **back of your neck**. (If you are doing that correctly, you should feel the **tension easing out** of your **neck** and **upper and lower back muscles**.)

*Travel down the **spinal column through every vertebra and every disk into the rectal area**.

*Travel back up to the **kidneys** and mention the **spleen** which is the blood reservoir.

*Up to the **shoulder joints; down the arms, and into the hands.**

*Before you *treat* your *physical* **hands**, perform what follows: Visualize the *Healing Hands* around any other part of your body which requires special attention, and mentally chant the mantra *Hummmm*. Those imaginary **hands** can be **tiny** enough to surround a **gland** and/or **massive** enough to encompass your entire **body**.

*Now, you are ready to focus on your **physical hands**. Say, *These joints are soothed, lubricated, cleansed and healed. If there are any deposits in these joints which do not belong, they are pulverized into dust and carried out through the blood stream.* Imagine that happening.

*Now imagine that you are **holding all the healing energy in the palms of your hands**. It is a **sparkling, creamy white lotion**. You imagine that you are **pouring** that **sparkling, creamy white lotion**

over your head. It **cascades down** through every **gland, joint, organ** and **system of your body,** *soothing, lubricating, cleansing, healing* and **carrying out with it all the impurities and negativity.** It arrives at your **toes** and **exits as a black cloud.** All of the **negativity is concentrated in that black cloud.** The **black cloud** begins to float up into the air, **dwindling** as it rises and ultimately **dissipating into space, all the negativity with it.**

*You take a **slow, deep breath of relief and release and remain as you are in silent meditation.**

*Your inner attention should be riveted on the *third eye* area at the center of your forehead as previously mentioned.

*Breathing normally, mentally repeat your chosen mantra on the **exhale.** Continue with the mantra for a few minutes. Then, remain as you are and begin to repeat the **positive affirmations** which are specifically designed to **reprogram your subconscious thought and belief patterns from *negative to positive.*** These affirmations, (*Positive Mental Treatment,*) may sound like lies at first, so refrain from thinking that. If you do, you are defeating your purpose which is to achieve a *Positive Mental Attitude.* Try not to allow prejudice and past convictions to adulterate your efforts. Repetition is the secret to success. (Because you only have a few minutes to repeat the mantra, relax yourself and resume for a longer period at another convenient time in your day.)

A more effortless option is to listen every day to my CD.

Modified Positive Mental Treatment/Affirmations

(My CD contains the full spectrum of affirmations as well as the entire *Consciousness Awareness Exercise* and more.)

These words are the only truth about myself. I know that I have the power within me to relax and heal myself at any time.

I am always in complete control and command of my nerves, emotions, thoughts, words, deeds, mind, body and habits.

My immune systems are strong and healthy, always functioning perfectly, normally and naturally.

Every cell, fiber, gland, organ and system within my body is always functioning perfectly, normally and naturally.

All action is positive, perfect and complete within me.

I am restored, repaired, renewed and healed permanently, perfectly and completely.

I am completely metabolized, stabilized and centered.

I am always in perfect balance, harmonium and equilibrium of mind and body.

I refuse to accept any negatives as a part of me.

I am filled with boundless strength, energy, vigor and vitality; in the highest of spirits, the highest vibrations, joyful and enthusiastic with a zest for life.

I am guided and inspired into right and perfect judgment and decisions.

I love, respect, and forgive myself and everyone. Everyone loves, respects, and forgives me. (Optional:) *I know God loves and forgives all.*

Good alone goes from me and only good can return to me.

I am filled with infinite patience and understanding for myself, everyone and everything.

I refrain from passing judgment on anyone lest I shall also be judged.

I treat everyone as I would be treated.

I am always peaceful, composed, secure and confident.

All of my thoughts are positive and constructive. Every day I am motivated to be creative and productive.

I am philosophical about life, aware that whatever I experience is for my good and for my progress.

I flow gently with the stream of life and I shed adversity pleasantly and calmly.

The Universe always provides me with all of the abundance and prosperity that I need and more so I can share it with others.

I continue to elevate my consciousness mentally, physically, and spiritually.

I am a positive, peaceful, poised, protected, patient, powerful, perfect individual.

These words are the truth about me. I know they are so.

Thank You.

(Every time we say *I am* we are confirming our bond and stewardship with God.)

If you wish, you can copy those affirmations which are germane to your specific needs and rehearse and memorize them and then recite them in your meditation.

Chapter XL

THE TRUTH ABOUT ACCIDENTS

The following segments serve as stepping-stones to the development of the *Shield of Protection* previously mentioned.

LET'S FIRST CAST a shard of light and a disclaimer on a popular tenet held by our society. There is no such thing as an *accident*, a vehicle over which we have no control; something caused by fate or God's wrath, or which befalls us "out of the blue." Because of Karmic Laws and the Law of Attraction, belief in *accidents* and coincidences is subject to unenlightened interpretation. There is a reason behind every occurrence.

A so-called *accident* is the result of psychological, memory retentive or past-life Karma. Let us postulate: the first time a child falls and hurts itself, this experience is indelibly imprinted in the memory, becoming an integral component of the consciousness, creating an unconscious fear. We can say that an *accident* is an effect for which there first must be a cause.

There are many other causes of *accidents*: personal carelessness; harmful personal habits; the unconscious desire for self-punishment and/or to punish someone near and dear to us for whatever underlying reason; to avoid doing something which we believe is unpleasant; anger, anxiety, stress, agitation, fear; (mostly psychological.)

Our previous lifetimes often bequeath us with harsh Karmic debts. When we honestly and candidly consider why we have been the victim of an *accident,* and we cannot determine any obvious reason for it in our present lifetime, it may be the result of a careless or vicious act in the past. We may have caused a similar circumstance affecting one or more lives and/or damaging property.

We include under the heading of what we accept as *accidents* all of the following mishaps as well: mugging, theft, fire, assault, battle injury and natural catastrophe. Anything which may be injurious to us, our loved ones or our material possessions may be considered an *accident.*

If a negative unforeseen event should occur and you feel you must discuss it, you can call it an incident or a mishap, but not an *accident.*

The Energy Field

According to quantum physics, the constant flux of molecules and atoms which comprise all matter, including living organisms, is a source of dynamic energy. This perpetual motion creates an electromagnetic field of energy which flows through and surrounds all matter. It emanates a radiance in living organisms and a simple sheath in inanimate matter. In the psychic arena, it is known as the aura. When a person is in good health the aura is bright and full, reflecting the individual's vitality. An irregularly shaped or angular aura may reveal inner turmoil or anxiety. A grayish, wavering aura suggests ill health.

Some psychics can perceive the aura and describe its colors which are often blended as in a rainbow. Some of them can read a person's life pattern; thoughts, emotions, personality and characteristics. Around thinking organisms, the aura mutates according to variations in thoughts, emotions and attitudes. Edgar Cayce, the Sleeping Prophet called the human aura the *Weathervane of the Soul.* He couldn't have conceived a more accurate term. He was able to see auras from childhood and believed that everyone saw them.

The Breath of Life

Breathing is an automatic function of the body; just another major task which the subconscious and the autonomic nervous system perform for us. We take it for granted just as we do seeing, hearing, walking, etc. When we walk we don't stop to consider which foot goes first or in which direction. So it is with every breath we take; inhaling and exhaling unconsciously. Most of us are chest breathers which can be detrimental to our health in many ways. The only time we breathe abdominally is when we sleep, providing we are not on our stomachs. Chest breathing is a learned process. When we were infants we instinctively knew how to breathe correctly. Observe a baby lying on its back. You will see the little tummy rising and falling as it respires. Wearing tight clothing, belts, bras, girdles, etc., has contributed to the habit of chest breathing. Stress response and sucking in a protruding abdomen are also responsible.

Are you a sloucher? If you are, your breathing apparatus is also being restricted along with the normal function of the heart. So, be mindful at all times of your posture. If you're not taking full, deep breaths every so often, you could be suffering from oxygen deprivation.

If you are a chest breather, you can learn to breathe correctly. It takes conscious application and perseverance. When you practice diaphragmatic and abdominal breathing and integrate it into your daily life, it once again becomes an instinctive habit. You will be oxygenating your brain, heart, blood and every cell in your body, and stimulating every other organ. You will be helping to prevent pneumonia and other respiratory diseases by exercising the lower lobes of the lungs which are neglected with chest breathing. Also, if you or someone you know suffers from panic or anxiety episodes, taking slow, deep breaths can alleviate the symptoms. They help to stimulate the parasympathetic nervous system which calms you and lowers the heart rate. Wherever you are when you feel the sensation arising; at home, at work or while driving, disrupt it by performing the slow, deep breaths. (If you're driving I suggest you keep your eyes open!)

Strive to become mindful of the breathing process. Are you breathing too frequently through the mouth? When your awareness kicks in, switch to nasal breathing whenever possible because the interior membranes of the nose contain cilia, those tiny hairs which filter out unhealthy particles. Don't hold your breath when you exercise unless designated. Inhale through nostrils when you stretch or extend and exhale through slightly parted lips when you bend or contract.

Perform the following deep breathing exercises several times during the day and eventually abdominal breathing will again become an ingrained habit. You will notice a marked improvement in your health and you will feel more invigorated than you have ever felt. (Here's a tip: You'll know when you are chest breathing if your shoulders rise when you inhale deeply.)

Daily Breathing Exercises

*Place your left hand on your chest.

*Place your right hand, fingers spread out, gently pressing on the abdomen; thumb on the diaphragm.

*Exhale by blowing out through slightly parted lips, emptying lungs and sucking in the abdomen.

*Promptly inhale deeply and slowly through nostrils, drawing in as much air as you can. Fill up the abdomen first. Feel it expanding under your fingers as if a balloon was inflating inside of you. Likewise with the diaphragm as your thumb feels the resistance.

*Now, proceed to exhale by slowly blowing out through slightly parted lips. Feel the process reversing itself as you deflate first from the lungs; then the diaphragm, and finally from the abdomen. (This is the natural process.) You should feel the muscles tense and contract.

*Repeat the breathing process from 3 to 8 times. Stop if you begin to feel lightheaded. With daily repetition you will be able to increase these exercises.

*A good way to practice this is lying on your back in bed with a pillow under your knees. This is the technique we use before we relax and meditate, but we don't hold the breath for a count of five as we do in the meditation process. If you feel tense or anxious at any time day or night, especially if you are breathing in short gasps, you may take 1 to 3 deep, slow breaths as just mentioned and let every part of you go limp and relaxed. Each time you exhale very slowly, say *Relax* mentally, three times.

Once you have mastered the correct breathing technique you no longer need to use the hands. You have retrained your autonomic nervous system to breathe normally. I cannot stress strongly enough the importance of diaphragmatic/abdominal breathing. (It's the lungs which actually inflate with oxygen, but the stomach muscles contribute to the action.)

The Shield of Protection

Now, while you are performing the breathing exercises, when you inhale, imagine your aura as a bright light surrounding you at arms length. (That is precisely what is occurring.) It can be a white light or any color which appeals to you. When you exhale, normally the energy field recedes, but you imagine it maintaining its radiance and fullness.

As you continue with the breathing exercises and visualization, not only will your vigor and vitality be renewed, but you will be reinforcing the natural protective shield surrounding you, which is your aura, your electro-magnetic field of energy. Your *Shield of Protection* can be anything which you can most effortlessly visualize. You may imagine it as a large plastic bubble, the bright light mentioned above, or you may do as I do. I mentally encircle myself, anybody or anything who or which I wish to protect. There are times when I imagine and feel myself encompassed by the awesome energy of the aura. I use the following *Switch Words* most frequently and they work for me. However the *Shield of Protection* fails me when I allow myself to become frustrated, careless, neglectful, or act unconsciously. (If I ever gave you the impression that I was flawless, I apologize. I confess that there have been times when my suit of armor exhibited a chink.)

Switch Words

Guard, Together, Thank You: For personal protection, whatever you are doing; (or for someone else.) For example: Before you turn on the ignition in your vehicle, say *Guard, Together, Thank You*; *Attention, Together, Thank You,* and also imagine you and your vehicle surrounded by the *Shield of Protection.*

If you or anyone else is using a sharp knife, climbing a ladder, etc., doing anything which may endanger you or them, do as previously suggested. If you find yourself in a hazardous situation, wherever you may be, protect yourself. If you are shaving, showering, walking up or down stairs, etc., invoke the *Shield of Protection* and the *Switch Words*. You may repeat them as often as necessary for your own security and peace of mind.

You have the power within you to protect yourself, your loved ones, and your belongings and property from negative occurrences. As you visualize and strengthen your aura you may also repeat this affirmation: *I am always guided and protected by God's Shield of Love, Light and Protection from all harm and danger; all things of a negative nature. Thank You.*

<u>Treatment</u> for <u>Living</u> <u>Quarters</u>: *There is a Shield of Love, Light and Protection surrounding this apartment, (or home and/ or property,) everyone and everything in and on it. Thank You.* (If it's an apartment, include.... *and this building.* Mentally encircle the premises with the *Shield of Protection.* (As with everything, these affirmations should be repeated daily for reinforcement and to create a chain reaction.)

You must maintain unwavering faith at the outset with all treatments that what you are doing is cementing your efforts. You and the Universe have a common objective—to fulfill your desire. The strength of your faith and the intensity of your belief that you are always protected not only bolsters your resolve, but also helps to fortify your protective *Shield.* Negative thinking, anger, frustration, doubt, fear, submission to stress, exhaustion and weakness, to the distraction and debilitation of illness and to harmful personal habits tend to weaken and perforate that protective *Shield,* your energy field. You are in control, so remain mindful at all times and determine to sustain a healthy aura no matter what occurs. Your deep breathing exercises, visualization and faith are the secret to success. With constant repetition of the treatments and the *Switch Words*, your sense of security and peace of mind will be augmented.

My own experiences with the *Shield* and *Switch Words* are quite miraculous. Previously, in Part I, I related how I was impelled to move from my small flower shop to a larger one and wasn't aware at the time of the significance. Apparently the *Shield of Protection* was enforced while I still maintained occupancy. Once I relocated, my new premises became my target for protection. The electrical fire which consumed the building where my former shop was located originated in the wall of that shop. Intuition and the *Shield* worked hand-in-hand to save me from disaster

On Halloween, practically every other store window on that block was marked with wax. Mine were "passed over."

When Neal was in Viet Nam, every day in my meditation and every night without fail, I put him in God's Hands and encircled him with the protective *Shield*. I never worried or feared that he was in danger, nor did I imagine him in any kind of jeopardy. If I had I might have inadvertently caused it by attracting to him what I feared. I knew in my heart and soul that wherever he was, he was safe; protected from harm.

A bizarre sequence of events occurred one Saturday night when we lived in New Jersey. Charlie and I were dining and dancing at our country club. A neighbor who lived on the corner a couple of houses from ours was walking his dog. Every time they arrived at our driveway the dog persisted in pulling him into our back yard. He kept tugging the dog away, but eventually he complied and followed him. They spied a burglar perched on the small roof over the back door of the house just before he smashed the window. The dog made such a ruckus that he scared off the perpetrator. The neighbor called the police and they caught the guy who had foolishly remained in our neighborhood. The *Shield* definitely had something to do with that. I was also convinced when I heard this story, that our Missy who we had lost from throat cancer, was still fulfilling her duties as our watch dog.

My favorite place to meditate is on my sofa in the den. For 20 years a large, square wooden clock hung on the wall over me. One day while in meditation I heard a sharp crack which I ignored. When I finished, I rose and scanned the room for the source of that sound. That clock was hanging suspended from one thin wire. My handy man repaired it, but weeks later the same thing happened while I meditated. Both times I was situated under it. My *Shield of Protection* saved my life, because that clock surely could have killed me. Finally, I took the hint and retired that old clock and replaced it with a smaller, lighter one.

By the time hurricane Wilma swept through Florida in October, 2005, I had been fortifying my condo and our building with the protective *Shield* every day for 20 years. I had nothing to protect my condo from a hurricane except for the *Shield* and my faith in it. Our area was hit quite severely. The destruction was widespread. Roofs were ripped away; windows shattered; walls caved in; trees shredded and uprooted; pavement buckled; cars smashed and overturned. Our building was spared and so was my condo. A trickle of water seeped into my enclosed patio which damaged nothing. Some condos in my building suffered broken glass and water damage. A few drainpipes were felled, but the roof and air conditioners remained unscathed. That hurricane was the ultimate test of the *Shield of Protection*. When I related this story to my class one day, one of my students asked, "Do you have a vacancy in your building?"

Chapter XLI
FINDING MISSING THINGS

I'VE MENTIONED THE *Switch Word* phrase *Reach, Together, Thank You* earlier in these pages. It has been instrumental in locating missing and misplaced items, not only for me, but for family, friends and students of mine. (Once again, James Mangan, this is a tribute to you for introducing me to your miraculous *Switch Words*.)

One night when we lived up north, I was working on some floral arrangements at home when I received a panicky call from my Mom. "My wallet was stolen from my purse!" "How did that happen?" I asked. "I was running late for work, so instead of locking it in my locker, I put it on a shelf in a storage closet," she said. "I don't care about the ten dollars I have in my wallet; I just want everything else returned." I explained to her how to use the *Switch Word* phrase, *Reach, Together, Thank You* and told her I would also treat. The treatment: **We want Strick's wallet returned now. It is returned. Reach, Together, Thank You.** (We can repeat a treatment as often as necessary, but as I pointed out previously, each time we must let it go.) Only ten minutes had elapsed when the phone rang again. "You'll never believe this," Mom excitedly reported, "I just received a call from Albert's Restaurant. Their toilet was running and when they went to check it, they found my wallet laying on top of the ball-cock. It's wet, but thank God the only thing that's missing is the ten dollars!" Why? Because she had downplayed the cash and expressed her desire. The Law of Attraction satisfied her wish.

I joined a group of women one afternoon for luncheon in a Chinese restaurant. While we were dining, a woman sitting opposite me who I had just met, grabbed her left ear and gasped, "Oh, my God! My earring is missing!" She explained that those earrings had been an anniversary gift from her late husband and it was very valuable. "Don't worry," I said casually, "It is returned." She glared at me as though I had lost my mind. She then anxiously proceeded to search the premises and hastened out to scour her car. Meanwhile, I seized the opportunity to treat with the *Switch Word* phrase and let it go. When she returned, my friend Alma assured her, "Don't worry, Norma knows what she's talking about."

The next morning when I stepped out onto our sun-drenched parking lot a shimmering glint flashed in my eyes. I looked down and stooped to retrieve what appeared to be a golden worm-like object. As I held it up staring at it curiously with questions clawing at my brain, I determined that it was a child's bracelet. Suddenly, a spark of recognition flared in my mind. The remaining earring the woman wore was a gold snaky chain loop! "This must be the missing earring!" I exclaimed aloud. I phoned Alma and she gave me her friend's phone number. That woman was nonplussed. "I'll never doubt again," she declared and effusively thanked me.

My nephew Marco called me one day to share a story with me. He and his wife were frantically searching their apartment for their missing keys, becoming increasingly frustrated. Their daughter, Danielle who was four at the time, with arms akimbo, piped up, "Mommy; Daddy; why are you so uptight? Why don't you say *Reach, Together, Thank You?*" Of course, the keys were swiftly retrieved.

Marco told me that when Danielle wants to find a toy, as she moves around her room, she mumbles the *Switch Word* phrase.

One afternoon I was returning home from our clubhouse and found Alma and her hubby, Seymour and some neighbors scanning the terrain and ruffling the shrubbery. When Alma spotted me approaching she said with a note of desperation in her voice, "Oh, here comes Norma; thank God! She'll find it!" "What happened?" I asked. "I was leaning over the banister on the catwalk above and my diamond and emerald ring slipped off my finger and we can't find it!" she cried. "Please Norma, find it for me. I'm frantic!" "Okay, relax," I said as I took a deep breath, relaxed myself and mentally repeated the *Reach, Together, Thank You* treatment. I extended my right arm and proceeded to divine for the ring by scanning the bushes with my right palm. As I returned to one area, a warmth and tingling pervaded my hand and it dipped down. It recurred each time I scanned that spot. Finally, convinced that was a positive sign, I reached down into the hedge without looking and plucked the ring right out of the soil.

(You, too, can try this in a similar situation.)

Everyone was dumbfounded. Alma and Seymour were very grateful, especially Seymour since she had a history of losing jewelry, eyeglasses and other items and he could no longer report losses to the insurance company.

I receive numerous phone calls from people and testimonials from students who have had what they report as amazing success with *Reach, Together, Thank You*. After all, nothing is really lost. It's still here somewhere on this earth waiting to be retrieved; so never say lost. It's merely missing or misplaced, and most of the time it's mocking us, lurking in our subconscious.

Chapter XLII

PAVING THE ROAD TO A BETTER LIFE

**DISCIPLINE YOURSELF TO relax completely and meditate once or more often every day for 15 to 30 minutes, (or listen to my CD.)

You'll be recharging your batteries, and with complete relaxation and meditation, the following suggestions will become a substantial and integral part of your life. Try to be grateful and thankful for your daily blessings and for all the blessings in your life and your appreciation will grow along with a more positive attitude. (Before I perform my stretching exercises and arise from bed in the morning this is what I say: *I thank You God for all of the blessings You bestow upon me every day of my life and this wonderful day ahead. I know You are guiding and protecting; healing and providing for me and my loved ones every day and I thank You for that. I shall continue to do Your bidding for the rest of my days and eternally with love and faith and humility. Thank You.)* That sets me up for the remainder of the day.

**Eliminate old negative thinking, habits, beliefs, expectations, reactions, responses and attitudes. Frequently stop to evaluate your attitudes towards yourself, other people, things, your life, situations, events and circumstances. Once you become aware of how many things irritate and annoy you; how many hostilities you harbor; how many fears and insecurities you have; try to honestly and frankly alter those attitudes and emotions. Remember that every attitude, every emotion affects your body and radiates all around you as well. If you become zealously dedicated to meditating daily, repeating the affirmations, your attitudes will automatically undergo an astounding transformation; (or listen to my CD.) Negative attitudes and emotions like anger, resentment, fear, irritation, prejudice, hostility, jealousy, etc., are like magnets. They attract to you *like* effects and reactions. (Try to fill your being with love, patience and understanding. When you meditate send out love to all; *I embrace the world, everyone and everything in and on it with my love.* Here you might visualize your arms encircling the globe.)

**Stop believing in drafts, sneezes, and temperature changes as portents of colds, flu or worse. When you or someone else sneezes, after the *blessings* say, *Good; we're clearing out the cobwebs* or *the sinuses,* or *Sneezing is nature's way to clear the head,* or *Out with the bad in with the good.* Sneezing is healthy. Never stifle a sneeze. *Cancel* negative suggestions about sneezes. A little fresh air is good; the more the better. Be thankful that you can expand your lungs and fill them with deep breaths. Sit up straight, or while standing, throw your shoulders back and feel invigorated as you drink in the fresh air. If you believe it is healthful even from an open door or window, it can't hurt you. What you believe and expect is what you get! Stop believing that a perspired body is vulnerable to a temperature change. The more we dwell on heat and cold, the more they can affect us. (The Polar Club swims in freezing temperatures and they're not affected because they believe it's a healthful activity, and the practice is currently becoming more popular world wide.)

I live in Florida where the summers are hot and humid to extremes. So, I perform my errands without a thought about the temperature and happily return to my air-cooled apartment. If I allowed myself to focus on the heat, it would become intolerable. I do, however prefer warmth to the sharp, biting cold of the northern winters. Our ingrained belief patterns have a profound effect on us. That's why *Positive Mental Treatment* is so indispensable. It morphs our negative consciousness into a more positive one. (I'm fully aware that I have repeated this and many other suggestions several times, but they serve to emphasize and reinforce.)

Some examples of how our cellular and subconscious memory systems provide us with what we believe and expect: At a banquet a woman sitting opposite me began to sneeze incessantly. When the outburst finally ceased, and she blew her nose noisily, she proudly announced, "I always sneeze 26 times after a big meal." A friend was convinced that she was allergic to bananas, eggs, and a host of other foods which she had been avoiding for years. After a close call with death, while in a rehab for several months she couldn't be choosy so she ate them without any after effects. People have naively told me, "Oh, I catch a cold every April and November!" I've heard people say, "My arthritis acts up every time it rains."

In the 1970s I experienced a surprising and discomforting effect whenever I ate cherries, apricots or peaches. My throat and the membranes connected to my ears would tickle. There was no chance that I was going to give up the fruits that I loved, so I began to treat: *I absolutely refuse to accept this situation. I am in complete control and command of my mind and body. I will eat cherries, apricots and peaches again with no negative effects.* One day soon after, we were at a banquet and the dessert was Peach Melba. I devoured it with gusto without the slightest tickle. That was that!

**Don't let your spirits be dampened by a cloudy, rainy day.

Remind yourself or anyone else who complains or blames the weather for their problems that it takes all kinds of weather to keep nature happy, healthy and thriving. Because it's cloudy and rainy doesn't mean it's nasty and miserable. Every day is beautiful and special because you are here to experience and enjoy it.

**When you obsess upon every minor ache or pain, you are fueling the fire. Stop letting your imagination control you. Repudiate it! Refuse to accept whatever it seems to be. Stop studying and reading, listening to and watching; (on TV, etc.,) symptoms of fatal and other diseases and disorders. Avoid identifying with such symptoms. (Hypochondriacs do that. I ought to know.) When you are exposed to them say, *I don't accept...* and/or *Cancel, cancel!* Avoid viewing hospital series on TV.

If you feel a headache coming on, inhale slowly and deeply while shrugging your shoulders up to your ears. Hold the breath for a few seconds and as you exhale very slowly, repeat the word relax three times. As you do that, drop your upper torso toward the floor with knees slightly bent. Every muscle in your face, scalp, neck and body should feel completely relaxed, loose and limp including your arms which are dangling loosely. If you drool, you'll know that you are indeed relaxed.

**Think of the body as a piano, an instrument of rhythm. If it is finely tuned and cared for, it serves us well, with little or no discord. But, if one chord is out of tune, the entire rhythm, balance and harmony are disrupted resulting in cacophony.

Stop creating negative conditions and situations for yourself, family and others with suggestions like, "Be careful, you might fall!...Get run over!... Get killed!...Have a heart attack!...Catch cold!" Everyone is susceptible to suggestions, especially after repetitive mental conditioning. Instead of warnings and worrying, say, **Easy does it, and invoke the *Shield of Protection.* When someone you know is about to drive away, say, **Drive mindfully,** instead of *carefully.* No harmful, negative suggestions there. Stop babying yourself and loved ones. You are all much hardier than you think.

**Continue to do your deep breathing exercises. Exercise those joints. Move and shake every part of your body daily. Stretch body and limbs for flexibility. For good cardio-vascular health adopt a daily exercise regimen. A weight bearing aerobic exercise like walking is the safest and most recommended; also moderate weight lifting for the upper limbs and torso to strengthen bone structure and develop muscle tone.

**We can affirm five positive statements and one negative one and the negative statement will take precedence over those positive ones. Why? Because our memory bank, the subconscious, is saturated with all the trash which has been programmed into it since our inception. So, we must remember to *Cancel* every negative thought when it occurs.

When you are thanked for a service or a kindness, respond with, **My pleasure, instead of *No problem.* The word *problem* is registered in the subconscious. When you say, *Don't forget to…* instead of **Remember to…,** the word *forget* is remembered.

**If you are told there is no cure for something or that you have a progressively debilitating ailment and "You'll just have to live with it;" do not accept the verdict! You can exercise control over it if you don't let fear and defeat take over. If you have the will and the courage to live a life of value and quality you can prevail and triumph. There are so many natural alternative methods which you can try. It's your life after all! Previously, you have been given some healing methods. Use them. I was inspired with this, one of my favorite

affirmations for healing while writing this book: *My body heals itself and God's perfect Life within me makes it so. I am healed; I am restored. Thank You.* (Recall Harold's story in Chapter XXX. He was given a disastrous verdict, refused to accept it and ultimately conquered it.) Another affirmation which helps: *I am a pure and perfect spiritual being. That's all I am, can be or ever will be. Thank You.*

**When someone asks you how you are, reply with, *I'm fine...feeling great or good...no problems that can't be solved...* or *getting better every day.* If you feel that you are lying, these little lies become truths if repeated often enough, just as your daily affirmations do. It's all a part of *Positive Mental Treatment.* (I normally respond with, *I'm just wonderful!*)

People don't really want to hear sad tales of woe and constant complaints, and repeating them can only help to magnify them, depress you and them and perhaps even alienate them. You want to attract positive, loving attention and recognition. You'll be noticed, admired and attract more of the right kind of friends to you if you are always cheerful and optimistic with a natural, loving attitude towards all. A smiling, pleasant disposition is contagious. Pretend that you really have it. Act the part and it will become you. Your family will be happier and more loving as well.

**If you have a depressive disposition, or if you should awaken in the doldrums, look at yourself in the mirror and force a smile! A happy face can make you feel happy. (Researchers say smiling causes bio-chemical changes in the brain that create a feeling of happiness. The act of smiling can make you feel better. Turning our mouths upward changes the way the air flows through our heads, cooling the brain. Experts say a cool brain is a happy brain. And smiling relieves stress by relaxing the muscles in the neck.) While you're smiling at yourself, say your name mentally or aloud and tell your image that you are *handsome/ beautiful/ wonderful/special/ healthy/feeling great/ happy/ it's a great day*…any of the aforementioned.

When you answer the phone cheerfully say, **Good morning,** and the rest of the day sing **Hello!**

If you live alone, continually bless your home and everything in it, for it responds to and reflects your innermost feelings and emotions, not only to yourself, but to those who enter it. The walls, the ceilings, the floors vibrate with the interplay between the dramas and the joys. Play music on the stereo, CD or radio and **sing! No matter how low or lonely you may be feeling you will discover the difference in your vibrations and those of your surroundings.

**When you or someone in your home breaks or spills something, smile and deal with it calmly and rationally. When minor details don't seem to be going your way such as tangles, knots, etc.; don't lose control, swear or curse. You are fanning the flames and hurting yourself in the process by discharging adrenalin. Is it worth it? Stop for a moment; take a deep breath, relax yourself and say, *I am guided into right and calm action at this very moment.* That's a viable formula for any challenge which confronts you. Develop a sense of humor about mishaps, mistakes and momentary memory lapses and you'll be much healthier. Learn to laugh at yourself; it makes life much easier.

The *Switch Word* to dispel any kind of frustration is *Together.* With frequent use its effectiveness increases. Repeat it many times, if necessary. You may also chant it silently or aloud.

**When you walk down the street, smile; hold your head high, swing your arms and keep your step springy. (This is what law enforcement officials suggest to repel possible muggers.) You'll feel better and the response from other people is generally a positive one. You'll help cheer up their day, as well. (I confess that I received dour, suspicious looks from some folks who are distrustful when I smile and greet them; bless them.)

**Remain aware of; observe and commune with nature and your surroundings. Drink in the beauty around you. No matter how squalid or dismal the environment may seem, there is always something lovely to behold. Look up at the sky if necessary. Emerson said, "The sky is the daily bread of the eyes." There is always something fascinating up there. Remember to keep one eye on the ground, though.

**Try to perform a kind service for someone every day. A simple telephone call or a greeting card to cheer someone who is ill or lonely can be so welcome and appreciated. If you know someone who lives alone, especially an older person; ask him or her if they have a telephone *Buddy* with whom they speak every morning. If not, ask them to call you every morning at a designated time. Obtain a door key and the phone number of a close relative or neighbor. If you are up in years, live alone and don't presently have a telephone *Buddy*, try to make a contact with someone in the same manner who you can call every morning.

**Work on eliminating your bad and harmful habits one at a time. Don't undertake breaking the smoking habit and losing weight at the same time. Stop smoking first.

**If you feel that you would like to venture into creative pursuits, go for it! Dare to explore heretofore uncharted territory. If you are dissatisfied with your present employment situation, summon the courage to investigate new and perhaps more fulfilling options and enterprises. Hone and resume former talents which you might have abandoned because of pressing responsibilities. After all, you too are an essential element in the scheme of things, and your health and contentment should be carefully considered.

**Whatever your age, if you don't have a love partner, make it a regular habit to pleasure yourself. Sure, it's not the same as lying next to a warm, supple body fondling and being fondled, but do the best you can with what you have. (Even though I was born in 1925, I am still horny and easily aroused.) Most women sustain their sexual desire and libido, while sadly many men sometimes lose it due to prostate disorders and medication. Again, that old cliché, *Use it or lose it.* That applies to just about every aspect and activity in our lives.

**Live for today. Don't get bogged down in worry and apprehension of what tomorrow and the future might bring. Take each day as it comes. To ease your mind, make it a daily practice to list your agendas for the following day the preceding evening or in the morning. Remember to consult it, though. You don't want to forget an important appointment. Whatever you can accomplish is a plus. What you don't get to, schedule for the following day. Just know that it will get done, and don't fret over it.

Another Emerson quotation: "Finish every day and be done with it. You have done what you could. Some blunders and absurdities no doubt crept in; forget them as soon as you can. Tomorrow is a new day; begin it well and serenely and with too high a spirit to be encumbered with your old nonsense. This day is all that is good and fair. It is too dear with its hopes and invitations to waste a moment on the yesterdays." Here's another apropos quote by an unknown source: "Yesterday is history. Tomorrow is a mystery. Today is a gift; that's why we call it the present."

**In Part I of this book, I stressed the importance of listening to your intuitive impulses. Your first impression or hunch about anything at all is usually the correct one. Act upon it. That "still, small voice within" always guides you into right and perfect action and decision. Be mindful when it surfaces and don't ignore it. If anyone tries to sway you when you have a strong hunch about something, stick to your convictions.

**Worry wastes energy, doesn't accomplish anything and can affect your immune system and impair your health. When a stressful event looms in your life, or if you find yourself in a difficult situation, there's a good chance that you can spare yourself the ordeal if you meditate and *treat*. As I've mentioned previously, I also affirm, *I give this entire matter over to God for the best possible outcome and for the good of all concerned. Thank You.* Then, I can relax and know that it is done as I have stated. If you tend to take your troubles to bed with you, that treatment can provide you with a restful night's sleep because you're giving them away. Also, there's a difference between worry and concern. Worry can be a chronic, perpetual emotion which causes a positive response to freeze, immobilizing us into helplessness and hopelessness. Concern, on the other hand, can be temporary and spur us to take action. Remember also that the thoughts which we persist in entertaining are attracting to us like results.

**We persistently replay in our minds the grievances we have with other people; the wrongs we feel they have perpetrated upon us; the echoes of voices from the past until our insides begin to churn. Granted, sometimes it's not easy to desist and detach, but if I'm aware that it's happening, I treat: *I love, respect, forgive, and bless ___?___ ,and I give him/her over to God for Divine Guidance. I love, respect, forgive and bless myself. I am free of all negative thoughts and feelings. Thank You.*

**If you act happy, smiling, humming, singing and laughing more, you will cultivate a happiness personality and it will become an intrinsic and permanent part of you. All of these activities help to boost your immune system. You definitely can brighten your day with a smile. And, laughter can lower the levels of hormones associated with stress, besides secreting endorphins, our mood elevators. So, even if you've heard those old jokes that comics tell dozens of times or more, force yourself to belly-laugh. Enjoy! Dr. Deepak Chopra says that if you start off your day with laughter, you'll digest your food better. Just close your eyes and *ha, ha, ha* as loud as you can for a few moments.

Researchers suggest that frowning can make you feel unhappier than when you wear a neutral expression. Psychologists report that people tend to have more positive attitudes toward those who are spoken of with a smile. Look at the eyes, not the mouth, to determine whether a smile is genuine. When a smile is sincere, there are crinkly crow's feet around the eyes. It's natural to expect a reaction to your smile. In fact, infants who don't receive attention in return for their smiles, smile less than babies who do.

**The choices we make can significantly influence and impact our lives, and I don't mean choosing one brand of cereal over another. We've been endowed and blessed with the gift of free will and choice. The energy which enforces that gift is the power of thought. So, choose carefully and judiciously the image you wish to present to the world. Ask yourself, "What values define my life?" Be honest and forthright and take it from there.

**Only you are in full charge and command of what transpires in your life. Only you can change yourself; no one else can do it for you. If you expect someone close to you to improve, begin with yourself. Integrate into your life the suggestions and concepts put forth herein, and you'll discover that your transformation is not only a benefit to you but to everyone around you.

**Pessimists versus Optimists:_The pessimist peers into a partially filled refrigerator and perceives it as half empty. The optimist looks into it and sees it as half full. On the other hand, the metaphysical practitioner peers into the same refrigerator and imagines it over-stuffed with food and plenty.

To take this one step further; the pessimist thinks of his/her pain-ful or deteriorated condition as utterly hopeless and depressing. The optimist maintains hopefulness and tries to fight it or learns to live with it. But, the metaphysical practitioner knows it doesn't belong to him/her and mentally visualizes wellness and perfection with ultimate healing in mind; sees him or herself healthy and active again.

**Studies show that survivors share three specific personality traits which help them resist the effects of stress: They are *committed* to their endeavors. They feel in *control* of their lives. They view change as a *challenge* not a threat. (The three Cs.) Patients who survive are those who question, demand and educate themselves as to their treatment. They exercise some measure of control over their health and main-tain a positive attitude.

**Avoid saying *my* arthritis; *my* asthma; *my* allergies; *my* migraines, etc. You are owning it; therefore holding on to it! If you must speak of it, preface it with *the* instead.

**Instead of thinking or saying, "I've got lots of problems;" change that to, "I have many challenges in my life, and that's good. They provide me with the opportunity to learn and grow." When we think of challenges, we think of *facing the challenge; overcoming the challenge; hur-dling the obstacles; fighting and slaying the dragon.* This provides us with a complete change in our attitude. We no longer feel helpless or defeated.

**Every setback, failure and disappointment is a rainbow with a pot of gold at the end, so if we realize we've learned something and glue our sights to our goals with faith, patience and determination, we will reach that pot of gold. If for every step backward we take two giant steps forward we will succeed.

Try not to waste your thoughts. While driving, walking, doing dishes or any other uninteresting, menial task, don't allow your mind to wander into worry thoughts, or other negative images. Daydreaming and meandering are okay as long as you are contemplating nature or something beautiful or creative. At such times you often receive inspiration and psychic impressions. Try meditating while you walk, mentally reciting your affirmations, and/or beginning with your feet, travel through your body with a modified *Consciousness Awareness Exercise:* Tell each part it is **soothed, lubricated, cleansed and healed. When you become totally absorbed in doing that, the time will fly by and you will have done something productive and worthwhile to improve your health besides walking.

Grumbling about inflation; rising prices, failing business, job loss, the economy and stock market fluctuations and losses impedes your divine prosperity heritage. You are focusing your attention on loss instead of gain, attracting lack and limitation into your life. Be grateful for what you have instead of lamenting and regretting what you don't have. Affirm and believe that the Universe provides you with all you need and much more; that you are successful and prosperous. Miracles begin to occur commensurate with your desire. My favorite affirmation: ***God always provides for me all that I need and much more so I can share it with others. I am successful and prosperous in every aspect of my life. Thank You.*

**Change is a major part of life, for without it our lives would remain stagnant and dull. We are endowed with the gift of change so we can learn and grow spiritually and intellectually. The universe is based on perpetual change. We cannot escape it. Sure, our bodies exhibit changes as we age, but if we accept those changes with understanding and equanimity as a part of our life here on earth we preserve our health. Remember, there is so much we can do to prevent disastrous changes from impacting our lives.

**When a fountain is first activated it sputters as it struggles to gain momentum. Gradually, the water ascends until it gushes forth in a display of visual splendor. That's a metaphorical example of what is happening to your soul as you continue to elevate and expand your consciousness.

**Expect miracles. What you expect is what you get!

On Being a Mature Adult

(Note: Being a somewhat liberated woman, I am parenthesizing male references.)

*Exhibit emotional and psychological balance. ("The happy person knows that every day is a new lifetime to enjoy." Maxwell Maltz.)

*Maintain a positive attitude. ("It is our attitude at the beginning of a difficult undertaking which more than anything else will determine its outcome." William James.)

*Exhibit courage when challenges arise. ("You gain strength, courage and confidence by every experience in which you stop to look fear in the face. You say to yourself, 'I have lived through this horror; I can take the next thing that comes along.'" Eleanor Roosevelt.)

*Persevere and complete any task. ("One is judged by what (he) finishes not by what (he) starts." Unknown Source.)

*Put an end to procrastination. ("Don't put off until tomorrow what you can do today." Unknown Source.)

*Be a respectful, loyal friend. ("Treat your friend as a spectacle. Stand aside; give (his) merits room; let them mount and expand." Ralph Waldo Emerson.)

*Nurture the ability to forgive and let go. ("When we forgive ourselves and those against whom we harbor resentment, animosity or anger we cleanse and purge the toxins from within." Norma Locker.)

*Give, serve and share unselfishly. ("What is a true gift? One for which nothing is expected in return." Confucius.)

*Treat everyone equally with kindness, love and understanding. ("All have not gold to give, but all may yet be kind. Where'er you are, where'er you live, give thy love to all mankind." R.W. Trine.)

*Be sincere; be yourself; be honest in all relationships, business or otherwise. ("I hope I shall possess firmness and virtue enough to maintain what I consider to be the most enviable of all titles---the character of an honest man." George Washington.)

*Be faithful in love. ("A union between two people is sacred. It must be honored, respected and preserved." Norma Locker.)

*Have the humility to express appreciation; to be grateful and thankful. ("When you are the recipient of a service, a kindness or a generosity, you have earned it. Accept it humbly and offer your gratitude generously." Norma Locker.)

*Exhibit patience and self-control. ("A (man) who is master of (his) patience is master of everything else." Lord Halifax.)

*Adjust to and accept change with equanimity. ("The art of life lies in the constant readjustment of our surroundings." Okakuro Kukozo.)

*Make careful and judicious choices. ("In the long run, we shape our lives and we shape ourselves. The process never ends until we die. And the choices we make are our own responsibility." Eleanor Roosevelt.)

*Temper your reactions to stressors, adversities and disappointments. ("If you are distressed by anything external, the pain isn't due to the thing itself, but to your estimate of it. This you have the power to revoke at any time." Marcus Aurelius.)

*Release your hold on grief and bereavement. ("Grief is the agony of an instant; the indulgence of grief, the blunder of a lifetime." Disraeli.) ("After we've endured all the stages of grief, it's all right to cling to the memories, the loneliness and the sorrow for awhile. But, there comes a time when we must let go or destroy ourselves. In other words, grieving for the moment is normal, but we shouldn't make it our career. Forcing ourselves to become involved with upbeat people and creative pursuits can save us." Norma Locker.)

*Be independent and self-reliant, but have the humility to ask for help when needed. ("When we have lost our way, asking for directions is permissible. The ego will survive." Norma Locker.)

*Continue to educate yourself regardless of age. ("Anyone who stops learning is old, whether at 20 or 80. Anyone who keeps learning stays young. The greatest thing in life is to keep your mind young." Henry Ford.)

*Maintain a sense of humor. ("You don't stop laughing because you grow old. You grow old because you stop laughing." Michael Pritchard.)

*Admit when you are wrong. Apologize freely for mistakes and omissions and desist from making idle excuses. ("People who persist in having their own way when they are wrong destroy their personal worth in the process." Maxwell Maltz.)

*Avoid gossip and criticism of other people. ("Like sand castles, a reputation takes a long time to build and a moment to destroy." Unknown source.)

*Remain aware and respectful of nature and everything. ("Love every leaf, every ray of God's light. Love the animals...the plants...everything. If you love everything, you will perceive the Divine mystery in things. Once you perceive it, you will begin to comprehend it better every day. And you will come at last to love the world with an all embracing love." Dostoyevsky.)

*Respect other people's opinions and credos. ("As long as we don't demean or malign anyone, each of us has the right to express our opinions and beliefs without fear of criticism. Bigotry and self-righteousness are cruel relatives." Norma Locker.)

*Avoid confrontation and conflict through patient and loving communication. ("The heart of a fool is in (his) mouth, but the mouth of a wise (man) is in (his) heart." Benjamin Franklin.)

*Replace bad and harmful habits with better ones. ("Back of 99 out of 100 assertions that a thing cannot be done, is the unwillingness to do it." William Feather.)

The True Meaning of *Wealth*

Wealth is not only a matter of financial security. You are wealthy if : *You have your health. *You can awaken in the morning feeling rested and refreshed and arise without too much effort. *You can move and stretch your limbs and exercise. *You can hear. *You can see and read and continue to learn. *You can speak and express your feelings and communicate with others. *You have the love and support of family and friends. *You have one significant other whom you love and who returns your love. *You can feel; you can touch and hug. *You can create in any way your guides and your soul direct you. *You have a glorious sense of humor. *You can still play and have fun. *You are interested and curious about worldly events. *You are gainfully employed and love what you do. *You are independent, yet not too proud to ask for help when necessary. *You can adapt to life's challenges with equanimity. *You can appreciate the beauty around you. (If all of the above apply to you, you are the wealthiest person alive!)

Chapter XLIII
IMPROVING SELF-IMAGE;
SELF-CONFIDENCE;
SELF-ASSERTION

"No one can make you feel inferior without your consent."
Eleanor Roosevelt

*RELAX YOURSELF IN any uncomfortable situation.

*I love, respect and forgive myself. Everyone loves, respects and forgives me. (Optional: I know that God loves and forgives all.) Thank You. That affirmation should be repeated many times during the day. Another worthwhile treatment: There is no one in the world just like me. Anything I set my mind to, I can do. I am special.

*Remind those who are close to you, (family, close friends,) that you would like to improve your self-image. Ask them to compliment you and to comment positively and constructively on any task you complete, (or on any expended effort on your part.) Also, enlist their help to encourage you to attempt tasks which you avoided trying in the past, and to reassure you. Emerson said, "Do the thing you fear and the death of fear is certain." Most of what you do with your life is your own choice. Norman Vincent Peale wrote, "Force yourself through a fearsome thing or to overcome a fear. Once you have, your self-esteem will grow. Self-doubt will vanish. Break the habit of turning away and back from a challenge." If someone threatened your life or offered you a huge sum of cash, the incentive would surely compel you.

*Evaluate your capabilities and your qualities. List them. Recall past successes. List them. You'll surprise yourself, I guarantee it.

*Expect each day to be a good one. Start off your day slowly and easily. Allow enough time in the morning to avoid rushing. Always be on time. Tell yourself upon retiring, *I did my best today and tomorrow I'll do better.*

*Imagine, (visualize) yourself receiving respect and admiration, and in the positions you would like to achieve. Imagine yourself as confident, competent and composed. See yourself excelling at something; one of your goals. Achieve one goal at a time. Work at it mentally and physically until you have achieved it. Become an actor. Act as though you cannot fail. Start things you put off. Complete what you start.

*Carry yourself straight and proud. Stand erect. Walk erect and swing your arms. Smile. Brighten up your appearance.

*Work at improving whatever you do best. If you are creative or talented in some way, use it, especially if you do it well, and share it with others to receive praise and compliments. This bolsters your self-image.

*Stop trying to please the world. Learn to please yourself first, not selfishly, but don't allow yourself to be swayed from your preferences and goals because someone may criticize you. Do what you really want to do, not what everyone expects you to do.

*Try not to avoid unpleasant situations. Mentally rehearse yourself actively rehearsing then actually perform it. Begin with the simpler ones; then gradually increase.

*Try to improve something every day. Whatever you do be proud of it, as long as you have honestly done your best. Don't hesitate to toot your own horn, tactfully. If you are employed, let your boss know how much work you've been doing.

*Do a good deed every day. (Perform a service for someone.)

*The more self-conscious you are about certain parts of your body, the more attention you tend to attract to that area. Accept and love yourself as you are, but if you feel insecure and guilty about your weight, embark on a gradual change and persevere to maintain it.

*List what you wish to accomplish daily and weekly. Review at the week's end to evaluate your accomplishments. Don't rationalize why you haven't done something. You present yourself as undependable and incompetent. Accept full responsibility for your actions. Don't cast blame on others. (Whatever you don't accomplish one day, save for tomorrow. Remain calm and philosophical about it.)

*Don't be overly dependent upon anyone. Make your own decisions and have the courage to venture out on your own.

*Use at least 75% of your spare time on constructive activity. Share the remaining 25% of your time with others; (involvement.)

*For depression and a sense of lack of self-worth, enroll in an art class; drawing, painting, sculpting; any art form which can absorb you and fill you with a feeling of self-pride and achievement.

*Admit when you're wrong or make a mistake, but don't degrade yourself by dwelling on it. You will gain more respect if you don't constantly demean yourself. Yet, try to avoid a supercilious attitude. Maintain a humble but confident demeanor. (Reach a happy medium.)

*Be mindful of phrases such as, *I should have... Why didn't I?* or, *How stupid of me.* They are self-deprecating and mask the enhancement of your self-image. Dwelling on past mistakes can be detrimental to your emotional and physical health as well. Promptly *cancel, reverse* and *rephrase* a negative thought or statement into a more positive one...*Regrets won't get me anywhere. I'll know better next time;* or; *Everybody makes mistakes, that doesn't mean I'm stupid. I'm as good and intelligent as anyone else;* or; *So, I made a mistake. I learn from my mistakes.*

*Listen well and attentively to others. Encourage people to talk about themselves. Look a person in the eyes, (or at the tip of the nose, at least.) Act genuinely interested. Remember to use a person's name often. Discuss their interests. Be aware of the feelings, vibes you generate to others. Are they negative or positive?

*Be a good, affectionate, loyal friend. Be yourself; honest, open and aboveboard; dependable and truthful in your relationships.

*List the people to whom you feel inferior and the reasons you feel that way; the things you like and dislike about each one. Then evaluate what you have written. You may find that your shape and other traits about you are similar to theirs, yet they're confident and successful. You may find qualities in them which you would like to see in yourself.

*If you are seated and someone standing over you conversing with you makes you feel inferior, uncomfortable, or perhaps reminds you of your childhood when you were similarly scolded or reprimanded by a parent or teacher; offer him or her a seat, or stand up yourself so you can feel on equal footing with that person.

*When someone steps into your space, tactfully step back to a space where you feel more at ease. If that person persists in moving toward you, smile and stretch out your arm to stop him.

*Think of someone you admire for being a self-confident extrovert. Picture yourself as that person after you have entered an alpha, (meditative) state. Visualize yourself speaking, behaving and succeeding as this person does. Actually imitate him/her in every way you can imagine. (Acting again.)

*Keep yourself informed to become more interesting, but try to avoid controversy. Observe other people who seem to exude confidence and self-assurance. How do they smile, make eye contact, open and close conversations; relate to others?

*When you begin to practice assertiveness, begin with people such as clerks, mail persons, and other humbly employed people; then work up to more influential ones. Speak up! Complain to the proprietor when service is poor or undesirable. If food is unsatisfactory, send it back. If you ruined it yourself, admit it. If you are not receiving satisfactory feedback from a company representative, ask to speak to the supervisor or manager. Always go to the top. If a product is unsatisfactory return it by mail with an expressive note, or in person when possible.

There's a movement afoot which advocates the termination of complaining. They expect us to accept the status quo. We have a right to express our distaste or disappointment with a service or a product. There's a difference between assertiveness and aggressiveness. If you assert yourself tactfully, no harm is done and in most cases you will triumph.

*When making an appointment with a doctor who is new to you, ask the pertinent questions: **Can you see him at your convenience? **How holistically oriented is she? **Does he speak in layman's terms and does he speak with a strong accent? **Is she connected to a local hospital?

Be assertive enough not to behave submissively. Doctors are not gods. If you feel that a doctor behaves arrogantly, find another one. Bring a list of your dietary supplements and meds to your doctor. If his attitude is indifferent or negative, he is not the right doctor for you. According to Dr. Bernie Siegel patients who are assertive, ask questions, make demands and stand up for their rights are the survivors. Submissive ones generally don't make it. Which one would you rather be? Before submitting to prescribed medication, ask if there is anything that might perhaps work as well.

If you must be hospitalized, also ask questions so you can exercise a measure of control over your treatment. If you are conscious remain aware of any visible infractions of medical hygiene. Don't be concerned about your personal reputation. It's your body and your life, after all.

*Have the courage to disagree with someone. Explain why you don't like a person's behavior or attitude, not why you don't like him or her, while maintaining a calm, controlled demeanor. (*In my opinion...* or, *I disagree with you...* or, to your boss, *I don't exactly agree...,* and ask if you can offer your own suggestions.)

*Have the courage to approach your employer, or even your teacher with new, creative ideas, but do it discreetly and privately.

*Don't allow a pushy, aggressive person to overwhelm you. At a meeting someone might try to dominate the procedure and make all the decisions. If you disagree, speak up. Stand up for what you believe is right. Make that person listen to your ideas, too. Don't allow yourself to be undermined. If someone is hogging the conversation, interrupt if necessary, politely, but emphatically. If you are interrupted, interject firmly and loudly, "You interrupted me. I'd like to finish if you don't mind. Thanks."

*Train yourself to improve your skills. Enroll in courses or study on your own.

*Don't gossip. Avoid resentment and jealousies. Bless those who seem obnoxious or hostile, instead of complaining at home or to friends. If you believe that people are out to get you I suggest that you give it up because that is the kind of behavior you will attract. If you treat everyone with a warm, trusting attitude, they will respond likewise.

*The best affirmations to improve your self-image: *I am always guided into right and perfect speech, thoughts, actions, judgments, reactions and responses;* and, *I love, respect and forgive myself and everyone. Everyone loves, respects and forgives me.* Repeat them as many times daily as possible.

*If you encounter a task which you have never attempted and if it is daunting to you, say, *I can do this.* You'll be astonished at your sudden ability to triumph and succeed.

Making Decisions

"(Men) often become what they believe themselves to be.
If I believe I cannot do something, it makes me incapable of doing it.
But, when I believe I can, then I acquire the ability to do it even if I did not have it at the beginning."
Mahatma Gandhi.

*Indecisiveness can create confusion and tension within the mind and body. When a person is indecisive the body receives messages which can short-circuit the nervous system...*yes, no, yes, no,* etc. This may lead to hypertension, and secrete chemicals which can produce digestive discomfort and disorders, among other things. Some people become so frustrated and agitated they hyperventilate. So train yourself to make a decision and stick with it.

*Relax yourself and repeat: *I am guided into right and perfect judgment and I always make the right decisions at the right time. I can do this!*

*Use the *Switch Word* phrase, *Reach, Together, Thank You* when you are faced with a decision: *We want to make the right decision now. Reach, Together, Thank You.*

*Practice quick decision-making in minor every day events, like selecting from a menu, or choosing an outfit to wear to a party, where the consequences are minor. Because some people are intimidated by a comprehensive menu they order whatever someone else orders. Grocery stores offer a plethora of choices of too many items, nowadays. When you need to select a cereal, for example, plan ahead of time and pluck the item from the shelf with determination and clarity of purpose. (Suggestion: Always read the ingredients on grocery items if you care about your health.)

*Avoid asking other people's opinions until you've made up your mind about something.

*Concentrate only on the question which needs a decision. Try not to worry about possible consequences.

*Before making a major decision, (like buying a new car,) research it thoroughly. Ask yourself the pertinent questions. Visualize every desired detail. Learn all you can about whatever decision you must make.

*Again, listen to your intuition. Tune in to that "wee, small voice" within you. Act on your very first impression; it's usually the right one. Don't allow anyone to change your mind. Emerson said, "There is guidance for us, and by lowly listening we shall hear the right words." (If you ask a question, the answer will come, sometimes from a most unexpected source as I have shown earlier in this work.)

*Force yourself to make a choice. Stick with the decision you make without feeling regrets. (William James wrote: "There is no more miserable human being than one in whom nothing is habitual but indecision.")

*Know that whatever you do decide, as long as it isn't a life/death situation, that is the best decision at the time and everything eventually works out for the best in the long run.

Chapter XLIV

ACQUIRING A "SLEEP CONSCIOUSNESS"

"Have courage for the great sorrows of life and patience for the small
ones, and when you have finished your daily task,
go to sleep in peace. God is awake."
Unknown Source.

*IF YOU HAVE trouble falling asleep and remaining asleep
throughout the night, think of sleep and only sleep.

*Verbal reinforcement: Tell yourself and others any or all of the fol-
lowing even if they are lies at the time: *As soon as I hit the pillow,
I'm out for the night... I never have trouble sleeping...I love my
sleep and I'm a good sleeper...I need 8 or 9 hours of sleep every
night and I get it...Sleep is important to me and I sleep well.*

*Bed is only for two things, sleeping and sex, (or if you're not well,)
and not for snacking, watching TV, reading, emailing or texting.

*If you take your troubles to bed with you, suggest to yourself: *We
want the perfect solution to this situation in the morning; or; We
want this situation solved or resolved for the good of all con-*

cerned; Reach, Together, Thank You. Or, do as I do, I just give everything over to God: *I place this entire matter in God's Hands. It is resolved. Thank You.* Then you can relax and pop off to sleep. Forget about it; it is done. The solution will be provided at the right time for you. The *Switch Words* for stopping disturbing thoughts and popping off to sleep are: *Cancel, Together, Thank You; Off, Together, Thank You.*

*When you sleep on your side, bend your knees. Your top leg should be flung over your lower leg, not on top of it. The arm on top should rest loosely on your hip so the spine is straight and the heart is not compressed. The other arm will naturally find its comfortable position. Never sleep on your stomach, because you are restricting your respiration and compressing your heart. If you prefer to sleep on your back, protect your spine with a soft pillow under your knees.

*Keep warm for arthritic pain with an electric blanket, thermal underwear or a sleeping bag.

*In bed tell yourself: *We want to sleep in a deep, peaceful, undisturbed sleep with the limbs and the entire body resting in a relaxed, comfortable, painless position all through the night. Care, Together, Thank You.* You'll be amazed at the response.

Chapter XLV

"ORGAN" LANGUAGE

MOST PEOPLE AREN'T aware that what we say and how we say it can affect our lives and our health. The following words and phrases, if repeated habitually can actually be mentally, emotionally and physically injurious to us. We adopt certain pet expressions which we unconsciously use repetitively. We think them as well as utter them. Most of them are directed at our organs and other body parts, accumulating as drops of acid, eroding that part of the body toward which they are directed. The more emotion behind the words, the deeper the scars.

The secret to breaking any bad habit is being mindfully aware when it occurs. The best *treatment* for the following words and phrases is to eliminate those that apply to you from your vocabulary altogether. Remember to *Cancel* any of them when someone directs them at you. Within the parentheses are the words and phrases to substitute for, reverse and negate the harmful ones. If you don't recall the correct disclaimer, at least remember to say **Cancel**. You'll recognize and chuckle at some of these even if they're not in your vocabulary. Remember, the subconscious takes every message seriously and must act upon it.

(Some of the most damaging phrases are directed at the *Heart*.)

*My *Heart* isn't in it. I haven't got the *Heart*...(*I don't care to do it.)* *It breaks my *Heart*. I'm *Heartbroken*. It's a *Heartache*... gives me a *Heartache*. My *Heart* bleeds for...I'm sick at *Heart*...*Heartsick*: (*I feel sorry for...It bothers me. It's a shame. Cancel!*) I'll have a *Heart attack! I'm eating my Heart* out! (*Cancel, Cancel!*)

*I'm *Tired!...Exhausted!* (*Cancel. I want to rest or relax. I need to get some sleep.*) I'm *Sick* and *Tired;* worn to a *Frazzle*. (*Cancel. I'm strong, energetic and healthy.*)

*I *Died*... nearly *Died! I'm Passing out.* (*Cancel, Cancel.*) I'm *Dying to...(I'd like to... I want to...*) That's what *Kills me!*...My feet are *Killing me!* (*Cancel! Pain can't kill me. I can deal with pain.*) ...*starving to Death!* (*Hungry.*) ...worried to *Death!* (*Concerned.*) ...scared to *Death!* (*Frightened.*) ...too cold; I'm *Freezing* to *Death!*...too hot; I'm *Boiling...Roasting... Smothering* to *Death!* It's drafty; I'll catch a *Cold*...my *Death* of *Cold/ Flu/ Pneumonia!* (*Cancel. I'm always in control; comfortable. Temperature changes can't affect me.*) (Why must we have a death wish?)

*...*gnawing* at me. (It bothers me.) ...*eating me up alive!* (*Cancel. Relax. I can easily deal with it.*)

*I *can't catch my breath*, I'm so busy. (*Relax. I'm busy but I'll manage.*)

*I can't **Stand**...I **Hate...Loathe... Despise...!** (*I don't care for...I'm not too fond of...don't really like...too well. Bless it/him/her/them.*) (Note: On what do we **Stand**? This is also one of the most common, destructive phrases.)

*I'm **Steaming!...Burning up or Burnt up over**...get so **Annoyed!** That **Irritates** me!...**galls** me! (*I feel angry. It bothers me. Cancel. Relax.*)

*It **Pains me** to...**Hurts me** to...(*I don't like to...*) I'm so **Hurt!** (*Cancel. Nothing can hurt me.*) I **Ache** to see...I'm **Aching** to...(*I'd love to see...I want to...*) It's a **Painful** experience. (*Cancel.*) (Wonder why you're in pain?)

*It **Breaks me up!** (*It bothers me....makes me laugh.*) I'm **falling apart...coming apart at the seams...can't get myself together.** (*Cancel. Together. I'm fully capable, strong and healthy.*) (When you imagine these you can see the humor in them.)

*...God damn **Pain in the Neck!...the Ass! Get off my Back!**...my **Aching Back!** (*Cancel!... a nuisance. Stop bothering me.*) (More very commonly repeated phrases. When someone says **pain in the ass** I counter that with *Look out; hemorrhoids!*)

*...makes me **Sick to my Stomach. ...Nauseous.** I'm **Fed Up!** (*Cancel. It bothers me. I can take it. I'm resilient.*) I **don't give a Shit!** (*Cancel. My bowels are functioning perfectly.*)

*It makes my **Head swim!**...don't know how I **hold my Head above water!**...gives me a **Headache!** (*Cancel. Relax. I can cope!*) ...can't get my **Head together**...can't **Think straight.** (*Cancel, Relax. I think clearly. I am organized.*)

*...can't *See my way clear*....can't *See* why...(*Cancel, cancel!*)
(With what do we *See?*)

*I can't *Handle*... can't *Deal* with...can't *Grasp*... (*I am fully capable and in control.*) (With what do we *Handle, Deal* and *Grasp?*)

    I have included some of the most common detrimental phrases here. Some of them may seem ludicrous to you, but psychologists are fully aware of the impact they can impose on our health. Give them serious consideration; identify those that you use habitually, and concentrate on excluding them from your daily use. I haven't included all of the terms to reverse the negative to positive; but you can compose your own. Suggestion: (*My eyesight and vision are perfect.*) I also didn't add the apparent physiological effects. It doesn't take a college degree to determine what they can be.

    A little girl's father had been killed and her uncle was serving in the Persian Gulf war in the 20th century. She was limping in obvious excruciating pain which was evident in her face. Therapists elicited her language pattern which was ...she was afraid her uncle would be killed like her father. They asked her how she felt about that. "I can't *stand it!*" she exclaimed. Her body was obeying her language pattern, making it so painful to stand. When she learned to release the emotion and permit herself to stand and love that he was over there, and bless him with health and safety, she was able to stand without pain after suffering for weeks.

    J. W. Teal said: "It is the habitual thought that frames itself into our life. It affects us even more than our intimate social relations do. Our confidential friends have not so much to do in shaping our lives as the thoughts which we harbor."

Chapter XLVI
REMAIN YOUTHFUL AT ANY AGE

*LIVE AN AWARE and purposeful life. Be kind and helpful to your fellow human beings. This gives you a feeling of accomplishment and satisfaction and can prevent excessive self-pity and self-involvement.

*Take pride in yourself; your appearance. Care for your complexion; your teeth and gums; your body; (personal hygiene.)

*Relax and meditate to prevent and overcome stress responses, distress, depression and other emotional disturbances.

*Beginning with your younger years, continue to work on remaining fit with regular exercise. That can enrich your health for your entire life. A study by the National Institute on Aging found that seniors who exercise regularly may live better and longer. Having many disabilities in later years is not due so much to the aging process, but to the reversible deterioration of muscle mass resulting from a sedentary lifestyle.

*The quality of life should remain our primary goal. We can choose a healthy lifestyle. Improve your eating habits. Lower your fat, sodium and sugar intake. Adopt a high-fiber diet including lots of vegetables and fruit. Choose whole grains over processed white flour products. Break bad and deleterious habits. Keep your body hydrated with fresh, pure water, but do it wisely. Alcoholic beverages tend to dehydrate. Avoid or moderate your intake of carbonated beverages. If you are over 40, introduce dietary supplements into your daily regimen, because the body begins to lose the ability to absorb all of the nutrients from food, and most people don't maintain a completely balanced diet. Begin with a good, well-balanced multi-vitamin/mineral as your basic supplement; then add whatever extras you may require for eyes, for energy, for bones, etc. Research on line and consult your health care practitioner or your pharmacist if you take prescription drugs or even over-the-counter medication. Studies have shown that people who eat properly, avoid junk foods and fast foods and supplement their diets maintain proper weight for their height and remain energetic, healthy and youthful.

*Dare to be different; to venture into uncharted territory. Flirt with new ideas. Accept new challenges; take chances. Don't allow rejection or ridicule or fear of ridicule or failure to deter you. Ignore the contradictory advice and deterrents offered by family and friends. You don't have to fit yourself into anyone else's stereotyped mold. Try new things, even sexually, but be safe and prudent.

*Touch, hug and you'll be touched and hugged in return.

*For retired people you now have the opportunity to realize the dreams that you've been shelving when you were deluged with responsibilities. List your favorite projects and aspirations and proceed to achieve them. If you are especially expert or skilled, or perhaps had taught something, share it with others at senior centers or recreational clubs. Teach young people what you know and learn from them as well. Surrounding yourself with youngsters; babysitting or volunteering at youth centers and schools can help to keep you young.

*Respond positively when asked, "How are you?" Don't make that person regret having asked you. Even if you're not feeling great, it's okay to lie. You can reply, *I'm getting better every day. I feel wonderful* may be a lie, but if you repeat that often enough, you'll soon begin to believe it. It's verbal reinforcement of *Positive Mental Treatment.*

*Avoid thinking or saying, "If I'm around for my next birthday," or "Who knows where I'll be next year?" Joyfully anticipate every birthday. When discussing your age, say I'm 30, 40, 65 or whatever, but omit the word *old.* When discussing someone's age, ask *What is your age?* or *What birthday is this?*

*Motivate and educate yourself. Explore your creative talents. If you feel you have no talent of any merit, meditate for a few moments. Ask, *What hidden talents do I have?* At the close of every day ask yourself, *Have I learned something new today?* Mental pursuits, whether creative or just reading, studying or working puzzles, prevent the brain from degenerating. Go back to school. Keep a journal of your daily thoughts, activities and experiences.

*Be responsible for keeping something alive and healthy besides yourself. Gardening, raising herbs, caring for plants and/or a pet can cast a beacon of light on your life.

*Volunteer your services to hospitals.

*If you don't know how to dance, enroll in a dance class.

*Learn to play a musical instrument. If you know how, begin again.

*When you travel keep diaries, take photos, videos, slides and speak to groups sharing them with others.

*Act in amateur plays if there's some latent ham in you.

*Forgive yourself and everyone against whom you've ever held a grudge. Cleanse your mind, body, heart and soul of damaging negative emotions.

*Exult every day in the glory of creation; the wonders of nature and life.

*Indulge yourself with weekly, bi-weekly or monthly massage therapy; whatever your income allows. Bob Hope extended his life with daily massages. When my massage therapist visits me every month I receive a full hour, full-body massage. It is not only therapeutic; it's a heavenly experience.

*Love deeply. Everyone needs to love and be loved. It doesn't have to be a romantic love. When you give love you receive it in return. Be kind and charitable. It adds quality years to your life.

*Accept loss philosophically. Life is a series of cycles; birth, growth and death. When you can accept that it's a loved one's body that died, and realize that the true essence, the spirit vibrates with life and energy, you can still communicate with one another. Longing for and missing that physical presence is normal for awhile, but as I pointed out previously, don't make it your career. Your body will be grateful. When I was discussing the merits and benefits of smiling one day in my class, a woman approached me during recess and lamented, "How can I smile? My husband died twelve years ago." At a restaurant I met an acquaintance who I hadn't seen for quite awhile. When I mentioned it, she said, "Since my husband died four years ago, I haven't been going to the clubhouse or doing anything for amusement." These women chose to exist in a virtual vacuum. How sad!

*It has been statistically proven that very devout people, those with an abiding faith in a Higher Intelligence or God; who have a spiritual foundation, live longer and happier lives. I've enjoyed the privilege of knowing a few such delightful people who lived 100 contented years.

*Maintain a sense of humor.

*It's advisable to live one day at a time, but plan from year to year, not only day to day. Accept long-term commitments. An unknown writer said, "If you have finished everything you set out to do, then you are finished." Living in the past gets you nowhere.

*Studies have shown that we don't die of old age, we die of disease. Believe that growing older has value, that it's an adventure to be anticipated. Old age is a state of mind, and age is only a number. I believe that with every fiber of my being. Those clichés will always be timely. Our attitude toward aging and the changes that normally occur with aging can have a powerful effect on us. If we believe that 80 is old we are doomed to becoming old! If we think and act youthfully, whatever age we are, that resonates as a permanent reality and we can remain that way for the rest of our lives.

*Keep that child within alive forever. Don't fall into the self-pity trap. Don't allow society's concept of aging to influence you. You are what you believe. Believe that you have drunk from the proverbial Fountain of Youth.

As we grow older we experience a decline in our powers of attention and concentration; two very important memory tools. On the other hand, the rate at which we forget things we've already learned doesn't change with age. Given the use of good techniques, practice and daily stimulation, there's no reason why we can't improve our memory by 50%." Samuel Johnson said, "The art of memory is the art of attention."

Memory Treatment:

My memory and brain power are better and better; stronger and stronger; improving and increasing, sharper, keener, more alert, aware and perceptive every day in every way. I have perfect observation, concentration, memory, attention, comprehension, retention and total recall of anything at anytime. Thank You.

Celebrate

Celebrate the privilege of your life on earth; the precious miracle of your birth; your dignity and your self-worth; the potentiality of you.

Celebrate the beauty that surrounds you; friends and family that gather 'round you; all the lovers that have found you; everything you've learned to do.

Celebrate your hopes and dreams; your self-control and self-esteem; the Divine in you that reigns supreme; that will forever remain true.

Celebrate your freedom, your independence; the special gift of common sense; that adjunct to intelligence upon which you always drew.

Celebrate the years which have passed, and all the knowledge you've amassed; the wisdom you've earned unsurpassed; how you've improved and how you grew.

Celebrate yourself my friend; you have only yourself to commend; to your progress there is no end.

Celebrate your uniqueness too, for there is no other just like you.

Serenity

Waves of peace wash over me.

I surrender to celestial strains humming in my bosom.

I am a leaf undulating on the crest of a wave; serene and trusting in the universe to carry me home.

Flowing gently with the stream of life; I am there, one with it all.

It Only Takes a Moment

It only takes a moment to hurt someone we love; that barb, that stinging word they wish they'd never heard.

Those words uttered in anger can never be recalled.

They hang suspended in the air, a cloud of doom which breeds despair.

It only takes a moment to apologize; yet there are those who let their pride prevent the peace which they denied.

It only takes a moment to make amends for hurts; to say, "I'm sorry; I was wrong; I shouldn't have been so darn headstrong."

A plea for a reprieve only takes a moment; and a moment is all we need to make forgiveness our creed.

To forgive is a noble deed; two wrongs don't make it right.

The moment we let go, our souls progress and grow.

Chapter XLVII
EPILOGUE

"Cherish your visions; cherish your ideals; cherish the music that stirs in your heart; the beauty that forms in your mind; the loveliness that drapes your purest thoughts, for out of them will grow all delightful conditions, all heavenly environment. Of these, if you but remain true to them your world will at last be built."

James Allen.

Relative to Part I

AFTER GRAPPLING WITH challenges that seemed insurmountable; suffering apparently incurable afflictions and sloshing in a swamp of ignorance about metaphysical ideologies; my life began to assume an ever-rising crescendo of change. At the age of 40 the revelation that there is a God; a powerful force; an invisible omniscience which provides me with all that I desire and demand; even if it is counterproductive to my growth as a spiritual being, was a catharsis. *Tapping* that *Reservoir* and availing myself of the dynamic diversity of metaphysical gifts rehabilitated my soul. I had discovered the key which unlocked the treasure chest of my universe.

Perceptions which in the past hadn't been recognized or acknowledged escalated and became a routine part of my life and that of my family. Our attention was firmly rooted in these newfound, exciting psychic adventures. Miracles began to manifest in our lives as my perspective changed from negative to positive. I learned not to leave anything to chance and summoned all of my inner resources with meditation. All I had to do was plant the seed of *Positive Mental Treatment* and germination and fruitfulness were guaranteed. Our faith in God's powers and provision burgeoned with each demonstration. The stage was set for renewed life. I wanted to spread the word to the world. As we zealously embarked on these new ventures, we garnered more knowledge and became totally absorbed in developing spiritually and psychically.

Relative to Part II

What's It All About? It's about redefining our essential purpose on this planet and in the universe and acknowledging the magnitude of it all. It's about accepting and admitting that there is more to our existence than many of us have ever imagined. If you have been saturated with traditional religious discipline throughout your life, it might be a fearsome undertaking for you to explore its mysteries. Organized religion taken to extremes is the bane of our society. Everyone has the inborn right to worship as they please as long as they realize that theirs is not the only way. Those that have accepted biblical scriptures as the only written word of God are deluding themselves. They were written by men to conform to the dogma and lifestyle of the era. Consider how many re-interpretations and deviations of the bible have been conceived through the ages.

My God is not prejudiced nor does He/She/It preach hate or condone wars. My God loves all of Its creations unconditionally whatever their gender, race, lifestyle, destiny or choices. My God observes us in our progression or regression without judgment or punishment. I believe that the antithesis to God was conceived by men who desired to control the masses with fear. Those who seem to be evil are merely misguided, primitive souls. The term God was derived from Good with the omission of an O. If God is the omniscient, omnipotent, Supreme Creator of all that exists in the universe, who created this devil? It would be a dichotomy, and that is not possible in this cosmic universe. When we speak of lower forces in the spirit world, our reference is to misguided, un-evolved souls. That is why we invoke God's Shield of Love, Light and Protection before we enter into the realm of the unknown and the often unseen.

How can anyone decry the amazing intellectual and spiritual messages which came through to us? It was only beneficial material which elevated us to higher levels of spiritual and psychic consciousness. If that was against God's plan for us, it would not have been such a significant and uplifting experience. We were assured that we are unique beings; that life is infinite; that we are accountable to no one but ourselves; that we are all connected and that this is not a random universe. It's my soul and your soul, but it's One soul. We know where we are destined to go and what and who we really are. Each of us is a sentient being with divinely imbued faculties.

I endeavored to emphasize throughout this book that you, too, can journey into the mystical world by placing your faith in Divine Guidance and protection. If you are passionate about engaging in new avenues of exploration; go for it! When you do, it would please me if you would share your most impressive paranormal and metaphysical experiences with me. Then I would feel that what I have put forth herein was meaningful and useful.

So tread fearlessly with confidence into the secrets of our reasons for being, if that is your desire, and the faith that God is with you guiding and protecting you in your quest for consciousness expansion and soul enhancement. If that is destined for you, you will be compelled and you will learn.

Relative to Part III

The *Road to Utopia* can be paved with gold if we adhere to the precepts required by our soul for our general health, inner peace and evolvement. Love and forgiveness; living in harmony with the world around us, are the stepping-stones which can elevate us to unimagined heights. An accident did not place us here on this planet. Our own personal, unique mission is imprinted in each soul. We can easily access the relevance of that purpose by exploring our inner resources with meditation. With *Positive Mental Treatment* we are insuring the birth of our ultimate transformation; assuming responsibility for our own health and welfare even while undergoing medical treatment. All we need to know lies within us. From there we carry on abiding by the knowledge we have garnered; living the virtuous life that our soul has dictated.

GLOSSARY OF METAPHYSICAL AND PSYCHIC TERMS

ABSOLUTE: Another term for God.

AKASHIC RECORDS: *Imperishable film* or images of each soul's life records; every thought, desire and act which constitutes the Karma.

ALMIGHTY: Another term for God.

ANGEL: A highly evolved entity whose duty it is to be of specific service to each of us.

APPARITION: The appearance of an immaterial, intangible, incorporeal form or figure.

APPORT: The materialization or appearance of an object which has been transported from one place to another by spirit entities; (a form of physical phenomenon.)

ASTRAL BODY: The emotional body which departs and survives on the Astral plane after physical death occurs.

ASTRAL PLANE: The lowest level of consciousness just above that of the earth or physical level. When we sleep and after death, this is the next dimension we visit.

ASTRAL PROJECTION: The function of traveling voluntarily or involuntarily in the Astral body.

ASTROLOGY: The science of interpretation of the movements and influences of planets, stars and the sun as relates to one's life and past lives.

AUGURY: An omen, token or indication of an event.

AURA: The electro-magnetic field of energy penetrating and surrounding all matter.

AURIC BODY: One of six emanations surrounding the human body, each with its own color and purpose.

AUTOMATIC WRITING: Writing produced by one who is in a state of meditation or trance which is said to be guided by spirit entities or the medium's subconscious.

AUTOSUGGESTION: Repetition of affirmations in a relaxed, meditative, self-hypnotic or alert state. (*Autogenics and Positive Mental Treatment* are related.)

BI-LOCATION: The ability to be in two or more places at once and to be witnessed.

BIO-FEEDBACK: The use of the EEG and EMG machines; (Electro-encephalograph, Electromyograph,) to train individuals to relax, meditate and control bodily functions; to eliminate pain, stress and physical conditions through muscular or voluntary mental control. Computers are currently utilized to display results.

BLACK MAGIC: The negative or evil use of mental or Cosmic power to produce pain, harm or other negative results in a victim's life. (Black witchcraft; black voodoo.)

BLISS: A mental, spiritual state of extreme ecstasy or rapture.

BOOK OF LIFE: Another name for the Akashic records.

CHAKRAS: The seven psychic centers in the human body. Each one is identified by a color or combination of colors. Lowest: *Spinal:* red; *Pubic:* (sex organs;) orange. Central: *Spleen:* (solar plexus;) yellow. Highest: *Heart:* green; *Throat:* blue; *Pineal:* (third eye; center of forehead;) indigo-(violet-blue;) *Pituitary:* (crown;) violet. They coincide with the seven endocrine glands in those locations.

CHANNEL: (See *Medium.)* One who receives messages, impressions; allegedly from spirit entities or from living, (mortal) beings from a distance; also from extra-terrestrials.

CLAIRAUDIENCE: The ability to hear psychically, or without the use of physical hearing apparatus.

CLAIRSENTIENCE: The ability to feel psychically, or without the use of mental senses. Experiencing the pain, physical condition or anguish of another whether in spirit or mortal. The sensation of being touched.

CLAIRVOYANCE: The ability to see things, spirits or people psychically, or without the use of the physical eyes.

COLLECTIVE MIND or UNCONSCIOUS: The theory that all minds in the world are connected at the subconscious level.

COLOROLOGY: The science pertaining to the effects and values of color on human behavior.

COLOR THERAPY: The science which uses color to affect emotions and heal.

COMMUNICATION: (On the psychic, mental levels;) between minds, psyches; between Spirit minds and mortal minds.

CONSCIOUSNESS: Mental awareness.

CONSCIOUSNESS AWARENESS: Focusing on and mentally entering every part of one's body for relaxation and healing.

CONJURE: To cast spells.

CONTROL: An entity in spirit who assumes control while a medium is in trance in order to relate and interpret messages purported to come from other discarnates. An intermediary in spirit.

COSMIC CONSCIOUSNESS: (Or Christ consciousness:) The ultimate Karmic level attained through living purely and spiritually.

CRYSTAL BALL: An instrument of focus through which the psychic function is concentrated.

DÉJÀ VU: (Already seen: French.) Often confused with glimpses into past lives which is not always the case. The feeling that a place looks familiar and that you have been there before can originate from past experiences buried in subconscious memory; sights seen in movies, on TV, books, photos, etc. Sometimes Astral travel while asleep produces *déjà vu* sensations.

DIMENSIONS: (See *Planes.*)

DIRECT VOICE: The voice of a spirit entity speaking while a medium is in trance, or speaking through a séance trumpet. The voice has no timbre whatsoever of the medium's voice.

DISCARNATE: An entity who has departed the physical body after its death. A spirit.

DISTANT/REMOTE HEALING: Healing energy directed mentally to a subject who is not present. There is no limit as to distance.

DIVINING ROD: An instrument, twig or any other object which is used to locate something not visible to the naked eye.

DOWSING: Locating objects, minerals, water, oil, etc., psychically with the aid of an instrument such as a *divining rod* or *pendulum.* One can even use a hand to locate any of the above mentioned.

ECTOPLASM: The etheric material which emanates from the solar plexus of a medium. It supplies energy and substance for activity and materializations.

EMPATH: One who exhibits a super-sensitivity to the problems and illnesses of others to the extent of manifestation in their own bodies and lives.

ENERGY HEALING: When a healer directs energy into a subject. Sometimes the healer uses his/her own energy.

ENLIGHTENMENT: An intellectual or spiritual understanding. When one becomes aware of mystical knowledge. The state of knowing and comprehending the meaning of higher consciousness. A spiritual rebirth.

ENTITY: For our purposes: Any individual who has made his/her transition to the other side.

EPIPHANY: A sudden intuitive perception of, or insight into reality, or the essential meaning of something often initiated by some commonplace occurrence.

ESP: (See *EXTRA-SENSORY PERCEPTION.*)

ETHERIC BODY: One of the spirit bodies which is the double of the individual. This is the emanation which is often observed hanging around grave sites. It dissolves as the cadaver disintegrates.

ETHERIC BRIDGE: Links the physical body with the psychic mechanism. Links physical or waking consciousness with psychic consciousness.

ETHERIC DOUBLE: (Same as *Etheric Body.)*

ETHERIC FIELD: The emanation of energy radiated by the *Etheric Body.*

ETHERIC PROJECTION: The ability to project the *Etheric Body* to other places, taking all mental faculties with you and recalling what has transpired. (Miscalled *Astral Projection* by some.)

EVIDENTIAL: Pertaining to the confirmation or proof produced and discovered after a message has been received psychically or through a medium. The validation of past life accounts.

EVOLVEMENT: Elevation and expansion of the consciousness. Moral and spiritual progression of the soul.

EXORCISM: The religious ritual of driving a negative entity out of a human body or out of a place. Any unwelcome spirit visitor, or earthbound spirit, (ghost,) can be exorcised, (sent on its way to the light.)

EXTRAS: Images of deceased persons appearing in a snapshot or photograph without physical or mechanical means.

EXTRA-SENSORY PERCEPTION: (Preferred interpretation: *EXTENDED SENSE PERCEPTION*, because there is no extra sense.) The normal, natural function of every human being, and not extra at all; perhaps more highly developed in some than others.

FAITH HEALING: When the healer and subject believe implicitly, (faithfully,) in the applied healing.

FANTASIES: Extravagant or unrestrained mental images which have no solid foundation.

FIELD OF ENERGY: The Aura which can be strengthened to use as a *Shield of Protection* or a powerful, resistive wall of energy. Some Far Eastern masters have this highly developed power which enable them to fend off attackers.

FORTUNETELLER: Anyone who gives messages of a psychic nature, especially one who can foresee the future.

GHOST: The thought form of a previously incarnate individual which remains earth bound, linked with its old haunts, sometimes seen to repeat its last act over and over. Also known to perform feats of physical phenomena drawing its energy from humans.

GLOSSALALIA: (Gift of tongues; speaking in tongues.) In a highly emotional state, usually trance-like and during ecstatic prayer; people sometimes experience an involuntary babbling which seems to be of a tongue totally alien to any familiar earthly language; purported to be Spiritual language.

GOD POOL: The eternal place to where the soul returns after being released from all Karmic responsibilities.

GUARDIAN ANGEL: The religious term for Spiritual Guide. Angels do exist and they perform specific duties for us.

GUIDE: An entity on the Astral Plane whose duty it is to aid, comfort, protect and enlighten the individual to whom it is assigned. Each of us has several Guides specific to our personal interests and professions.

GUIDED IMAGERY: (CREATIVE IMAGINATION; VISUALIZATION:) All connected. The practice of mentally entering one's body and visualizing certain suggested symbols or thought forms for healing purposes. *Creative Imagination* can be used for anything, especially in the arts. *Visualization* can also be used that way; especially effective in athletics.

HAUNTINGS: The phenomena produced by the presence of Ghosts in any location; rappings and other physical phenomena; also materializations.

HEALING HANDS: Can be the use of physical hands for the purpose of healing, or imagining *Healing Hands* being directed to specific areas in one's own body, or to a present or distant subject.

HIGHER SELF: God's spirit within each of us.

HOST: A human being whose energy is being used by a Ghost to manifest itself.

HYPNOIDAL STATE: (Also *HYPNOGOGIC:*) The in-between level of consciousness just before awakening from sleep or just prior to dozing. Best for psychic impressions and meditation. (Alpha brain wave level.)

HYPNOSIS: The condition in which a subject's mind is in a highly suggestible state; the conscious level asleep and the subconscious open to suggestion by a hypnotist, or one's self.

HYPNOTISM: The science dealing with the above.

HYPNOTHERAPY: The branch of *Hypnotism* dealing with the emotional or physical healing of a subject; also used to conquer bad habits.

ILLUMINATION: A flash of insight into a higher realm or level of consciousness. Spiritual enlightenment.

ILLUSION: Something that deceives by producing a false or misleading impression of reality, such as a mirage.

IMMORTALITY: The principle that there is no death but that of the physical body. The eternal being and continuance of life.

IMPRESSION: The reception or perception of a sensation, thought or idea emanating from the psychic senses, from guides, familiar spirit or one's *Higher Self.*

INCANTATION: The chanting or uttering of words used to cast a magical spell.

INCARNATE: In the physical form or being. A human being or animal.

INSIGHT: Perception into the unseen or inner world. Deep understanding of the spiritual nature of things.

INSPIRATION: Spiritual guidance or perception into creativity of some kind, or the answer or solution to a problem.

INSTINCT: The pre-programmed subconscious function of biological forms of life. Inborn impulse or natural inclination.

INTERPRETATION: The function of the conscious mind to explain or define psychic impressions or symbolism. Varied interpretations may be given for the same thing by different people, depending on the individual's background, beliefs or experiences.

INTUITION: The natural function of every human being which enables one to perceive facts through feelings or vibrations without the use of reasoning processes.

INTUITIVE: One who has and uses the above faculty. Some are more fully developed than others, able to perceive and diagnose illnesses.

KARMA: The Sanskrit term for the physical laws of cause and effect; action and reaction. Every effect must be preceded by a cause. There cannot be a reaction unless there has first been some kind of action. (See Part II, *We Have Lived Before.*)

KIRLIAN PHOTOGRAPHY: Developed by Simion Davidovitch Kirlian, Russian electrician, purported to reveal in colored photos the electro-magnetic field of energy or Aura flowing through and surrounding all matter and living beings.

KUNDALINI: Snake-like manifestation; (Spiritual energy,) which rises through the *Chakras* as one evolves spiritually.

LEVITATION: The faculty of shifting one's weight psychically in order to cause the body to become lighter and rise into the air. Also the rising of objects into the air aided by the psychic energy of a person or group; sometimes with the aid of discarnates.

LIFE REVIEW: Holographic account of each person's life on the other side as well as all previous lifetimes spent in human form. Every thought, act and experience is reviewed when we make our transition. (See *Akashic Records* and Book *of Life.*)

LUCID DREAMING: Dreaming while in a half-sleep, alpha or hypnoidal state just before awakening. This does not produce the REM state of deep sleep dreaming. The dreamer can often control the content of the dreams and create at will.

MANTRA: A word, phrase or sound which is chanted or intoned vocally or silently, (mentally,) in order to induce deep meditation. An aid to transcending the physical realm. Also used to elevate vibrations and develop the psychic centers, (*Chakras.*)

MASTER: A highly evolved spiritual teacher on earth or one who is on an elevated plane or level of consciousness in the Spiritual realm, (on the other side,) whose duty it is to enlighten and guide those who have been striving to improve themselves through meditation and spiritual study.

MATERIALIZATION: The formation of spiritual matter through the use of ectoplasm emanating from a medium's solar plexus. The physical form which results from such emanation.

MATERIALIZATION MEDIUM: One who, while in trance produces ectoplasm and psychic energy for spirit entities or matter to take form and materialize.

MEDICAL INTUITIVE: One who can discern, perceive medical conditions in people unconsciously, consciously or psychically. Some can also recommend treatment.

MEDITATION: The practice of deep thought or contemplation by removing one's conscious thought and entering into a subconscious, (alpha brain wave level) of consciousness. Reflection upon a continuous thought or mantra. Complete relaxation and contemplation. Deep concentration.

MEDIUM: The human instrument who communicates with other dimensions of consciousness such as the spirit world. One who enters a trance state and receives and often relays messages from those who are in spirit. One who gives spiritualistic or psychic readings.

MENTAL PROJECTION: Voluntary Mind Travel, still being aware of one's body, surroundings and thoughts.

MENTAL TELEPATHY: The phenomenon of the meeting of two or more minds. Since we are all connected mentally and spiritually, we can be privy to other people's thoughts.

METAPHYSICS: The science which deals with the mind, body and spirit and the connection between them. Humankind's relationship with God and the universe. Involves philosophy, psychology, (human behavior, the nature of humanity, the nature of being;) physics, cosmology, consciousness, the paranormal, health and healing.

METAPHYSICAL HEALING: Any healing performed using mental and spiritual concentration.

MIND TRAVEL: Mental Projection to other locations.

MIRACLE: An effect in the physical world which seems to surpass all human or natural powers. (Everything is natural when fully understood.)

MYSTICISM: The doctrine of spiritual enlightenment and illumination which fosters a deep union and understanding of the Divine. The attainment of the elevation and expansion of consciousness through meditation thereby transcending the physical, material world in order to gain knowledge of the secrets of the universe.

NEAR DEATH EXPERIENCE: (NDE:) A patient dies for an indeterminate length of time, leaves the body and returns to life able to report what has transpired. Some claim they have seen heaven or the other side, their deceased family, etc. Some return with changes in personality and deep spiritual and intellectual transformation.

NIRVANA: A place or state of consciousness whereby one is released from mortal cares. In Buddhism, the freedom from Karmic responsibilities when one's soul rejoins the God pool.

NUMEROLOGY: The science which deals with numbers and their hidden relationship and influence on one's life, past lifetimes and characteristics.

OBEAH: A form of belief involving sorcery practiced in the West Indies, South America, southern USA and Africa. A fetish or charm is used in this practice.

OCCULT: That which is hidden or mysterious; beyond the bounds of ordinary knowledge. Most of the terms in this glossary can be defined as *Occult*.

OMEN: A sign or an event believed to portend something good or evil.

OUT OF BODY EXPERIENCE; (OOBE:) Astral or etheric projection; bi-location. The phenomenon of leaving one's body voluntarily or involuntarily and being aware of self, thoughts and surroundings.

OUIJA BOARD: An instrument which is used for communication or psychic development with a planchette which spells out messages purported to be from the spirit world, but predominantly guided by one's subconscious and psychic energy.

PALMISTRY: The science dealing with the lines and mounts of the palm and fingers relative to and influencing one's life, characteristics, health, etc. The secondary hand reveals that with which one came into this life. The dominant hand reveals what one has done or will do with his/her life, and what will ultimately transpire.

PARANORMAL: Above or beyond what is considered the normal. Of or pertaining to perceptions or events occurring without scientific explanation.

PARAPSYCHOLOGY: A branch of psychology which deals with the investigation and research into psychic phenomena of all types.

PENDULUM: A weight or object attached to a thread, string or fine chain which responds to one's psychic vibrations. Can be used over a list of items, names, places, numbers, etc., to receive correct answers and information. Also used to locate missing persons while held over a map. A plumb bob makes an excellent pendulum.

PERCEPTION: The ability to see on the psycho-physical level more than meets the eye. Intuitive recognition or cognition.

PHANTASM: An apparition or specter. (Also *PHANTOM.)*

PHANTASMAGORIA: Commonly occurs while in a hypnoidal state, just prior to dozing. One is aware of disconnected, incomplete, flashing images, sometimes reminiscent of a moving picture. On occasion voices may be heard as if emanating from a crowd of people. These are usually fragments from one's own subconscious mind and psychical perceptions which remain beneath the surface of consciousness.

PHRENOLOGY: The science dealing with the shape of the skull; the bumps and depressions and the characteristics involved.

PHYSICAL MEDIUM: One who has the psychic power to cause objects to move or levitate. A spiritualistic medium who supplies psychic energy for spirit entities to move or levitate objects; to materialize themselves or deliver *apports.*

PHYSICAL PHENOMENA: The actions, movements and occurrences produced by or through a physical medium or poltergeist. (*Psychokinesis; telekinesis.*)

PHYSIOGNOMY: The science dealing with the characteristics of the face. Every aspect of the face is considered including the eyes and ears.

PLACEBO: Anything in which one places his/her faith—the health practitioner, the treatment, holy water, an amulet, a medication, etc. which results in a positive outcome. (The opposite of *placebo* is *nocebo*, when one believes in a negative result.)

PLANCHETTE: A small heart-shaped object which accompanies a *Ouija Board.* When touched by the fingertips psychic impulses from the subconscious cause it to move when a question is asked.

PLANES: Levels of consciousness pertaining solely to the spiritual realm; also known as dimensions. As the soul progresses or evolves, it is elevated to higher levels and becomes more rarified. No matter how high a plane a spirit attains, if necessary it can densify and communicate through a medium.

POLTERGEIST: (from the German; mischievous ghost:) Causes physical phenomena to occur, mostly of a negative or harmful nature, such as objects being thrown, damage, hurting people; fire and water phenomena, etc. This is usually unconsciously caused by frustrated psycho-energy emanating from young people; adolescents, teenagers, or adults who have deep-seated sexual aberrations.

POSITIVE MENTAL TREATMENT: (Autogenics; see *Auto-suggestion:)* The mental or verbal repetition of positive affirmations designed to achieve a *Positive Mental Attitude.* It can also be used for self- healing.

POSSESSION: When a person is dominated or actuated by a spirit, especially an evil one, he/she is said to be *Possessed.* This can only occur if one is not God-oriented and/or has an irrational fear of demons or a devil. Opening one's psyche to the unknown without proper instruction and/or in solitary can be dangerous. We attract what we fear.

POST-COGNITION: (In card guessing:) If you guess the card which comes after the one upon which you are concentrating and that occurs more often than anything else, you excel in *Post-cognition* which is a form of clairvoyance.

PRE-COGNITION: The psychic perception of something which has yet to occur, as in *precognitive* dreams, visions, feelings or hunches.

PREDICTION: The foretelling of that which is yet to occur.

PRE-NATAL CONDITIONING/PROGRAMMING: While still in the mother's womb, the fetus receives impressions and impulses transmitted by its mother; her emotions and thoughts, as well as sounds emanating from the mother and elsewhere once hearing is established. If every mother-to-be were aware of this, she would meditate, remain as calm and peaceful as possible and absorb culture and knowledge and transmit it to the fetus. Playing light classical music can also have a calming effect on the fetus.

PRESAGE: Something which predicts a future event. An omen. To forecast.

PRESENTIMENT: A feeling that something evil or foreboding is about to happen.

PROGNOSTICATE: The act of forecasting from present signs or indications.

PROGNOSTICATOR: One who forecasts or predicts.

PROPHECY: Something which foretells or predicts that which has yet to occur; purported to be Divinely inspired.

PROPHET: A person who foretells the future.

PSYCHIC: One who has the ability to perceive through senses other than the physical ones. One who is gifted with non-physical perception.

PSYCHIC BRIDGE: An imaginary arc or connection between the pineal and pituitary glands which can be developed through certain exercises. The triangle which is formed between the head, throat and heart centers or *Chakras*. (Imaginary psychic connection.)

PSYCHIC HEALING: Any healing which is performed through mental concentration.

PSYCHIC PHOTOGRAPHY: (Thought photography:) The type of photography which is influenced by a psychic solely by thought or concentration. Ted Serios had the ability to produce images on film or plates without the use of a camera.

PSYCHIC SURGERY: Alleged surgery performed without the use of instruments by a medium usually untrained in surgical or medical procedure.

PSYCHISM: The art, study and interest in psychic ability. Psychic ability.

PSYCHOKINESIS: (PK:) The movement, alteration or levitation of matter caused by the psychic energy of one or more individuals through deliberate concentration or involuntarily. This phenomenon can also occur in a séance situation.

PSYCHOMETRIZE: Attempting to tune in to vibrations, thought and energy patterns from an object or person by touch to receive impressions and messages from same. A metallic object retains these impressions longest and strongest.

PSYCHOMETRY: The art of *Psychometrizing.*

PSYCHONEUROIMMUNOLOGY: The study of how the brain can influence the endocrine and immune systems. The ability of the mind to heal oneself. The influence of will power on a person's health and survival.

RACE SUGGESTION: The influence of the power of suggestion on individuals, groups and society in general. The influences to which we are exposed from birth by parents, other relatives, friends, teachers, clergy, peers, the medical profession, (the scientific establishment,) all of the media, literature and government. All environmental influences and external stimuli which are experienced through the senses and registered in the subconscious, *(memory* bank.) Negative or positive programming resulting in subconscious conditioning.

RACE CONSCIOUSNESS: The belief, acceptance and reactions of the world population; society in general, in the aforementioned influences. The more people who believe, the greater the acceptance or faith in what is learned; the more powerful the influence. In *Race Consciousness,* the media, the scientific establishment, the clergy and religious groups, and literature such as the bible invoke the most profound influence. Example: Another terrorist attack on our nation:

If enough people believe that this is possible, when the critical mass number is reached, we can create that reality. Conversely, if enough of us believe that this is impossible, we can create that reality, as well.

RADIESTHESIA: The science dealing with *dowsing* and *divining* through psychic impulses.

READING: Messages or impressions delivered by a psychic. Messages delivered by a palmist, phrenologist, astrologist, card reader, etc. Spiritualistic messages. Any analysis given by the aforementioned.

REALITY: Our mortal, physical perception is flawed because what we believe and perceive as *reality* is actually a false impression. The only true *Reality* is what is known as God.

REGRESSION: Deals with the experience of mentally going back in time under hypnosis or through auto-suggestion; also into past lifetimes.

REINCARNATION: The philosophy that life is a continuum and that the soul passes from one lifetime to another until it has progressed to the highest state of purity so that the soul can once again return to the *God-pool* eternally.

RETRO-COGNITION: (In card guessing:) If you guess the card which precedes the one on which you are concentrating, and this occurs more often than anything else, you excel in *Retro-cognition*. This is also a form of clairvoyance.

SÉANCE: A spiritualistic meeting or circle of people usually headed by a trance medium for the purpose of communicating with discarnates; also for psychic development and phenomena.

SÉANCE BATTERY: An experienced séance participator who sits next to the medium for the purpose of providing psychic energy and to officiate when the medium enters the trance state.

SEA OF MIND, SEA OF ENERGY, FIELD OF MIND: The invisible energy which flows through and around everyone and everything in the universe. Definitions of what God really is.

SEER: A prophet. One who is endowed with moral and spiritual insight or knowledge.

SEEKER: One who questions, studies and researches the meaning of life and what the universe holds in relation to his/her own life.

SENSITIVE: One who is attuned to that which is not seen or felt by physical means.

SHAMAN: (Among certain tribal peoples:) A person who acts as intermediary between natural and "supernatural" worlds, using magic to cure illness, foretell the future and control spiritual forces.

SHIELD OF PROTECTION: Deep breathing exercises and visualization of the aura expanding on the inhale and remaining full and powerful on the exhale strengthens the aura. This becomes one's *Shield of Protection*; a natural, psychic defense against harm or any negativity. (God's Shield of Love, Light and Protection.)

SIGNS: Omens; portents. Physical means of communication by spirit entities.

SILVER CORD: The spiritual *umbilical cord* which connects the spirit body to the physical. It is said to sever only when physical death occurs to free the spirit.

SIXTH SENSE: Refers to the psychic ability or ESP. There is no extra, sixth sense. ESP is a natural, inborn function of everyone.

SOLAR PLEXUS: The network of nerves in the diaphragm of a human being which is the central *Chakra* or psychic center. The area through which ectoplasm is produced and emanates when a medium is in trance.

SOOTHSAYER: A person who foretells events.

SORCERY: Black magic; witchery.

SOUL: Another term for the subconscious or subjective level of mind. It must obey what is given it by the conscious level of mind. It is the storehouse of all knowledge; that component of God within each of us which sustains and animates us and which continues eternally.

SOURCE: Another term for the *Creator* or God.

SPECTER: A visible, incorporeal spirit, ghost or apparition; especially of a terrifying nature.

SPELL: An incantation. A word or phrase supposed to have magic powers.

SPIRIT: In metaphysics, the word for God or one's Higher Self. The vital principle, essence or energy which survives after physical death occurs embodying memory, personality and thought.

SPIRITISM: The belief in, and the study of the survival of the Spirit after death.

SPIRIT PHOTOGRAPHY: The practice of photographing apparitions, ghosts, spirits, by *ghost-hunters,* and *parapsychologists,* best accomplished with infra-red light and highly sensitive photo equipment.

SPIRIT SURGERY: (or *HEALING:*) Surgery or healing purported to have been performed by "Spirit doctors."

SPIRIT SURVIVAL: The doctrine that the spirit departs the body after its death and makes the transition into another dimension of consciousness continuing as the personality of the individual.

SPIRITUAL HEALING: Any healing done invoking the name of God.

SPIRITUALITY: God consciousness. Some people who practice traditional, organized religions are not always spiritual because they adhere to certain dogmas and traditions.

SPIRITUALISM: The religion devoted to the belief in the survival of the spirit after death of the body. The practice of communicating with discarnates.

SPIRITUALIST: One who practices the above religion and who can also deliver messages from discarnates in a church or séance environment.

SPIRIT WRITING: Written messages purported to have been produced by discarnates without the aid of physical means.

SPONTANEOUS HUMAN COMBUSTION: A phenomenon whereby a person or parts of a person have been turned to ashes apparently from the inside of the body. Nothing surrounding the body has been burnt. It remains a mystery to this day.

STIGMATA: Marks, bleeding or apparent impressions upon the skin of hysterical, highly emotional or religious people, produced psychologically. The Roman Catholic Church believes that this is evidence of the crucifixion if the hands and feet manifest marks and bleeding.

STREAM OF CONSCIOUSNESS: Inspiration; allowing creativity to flow freely and naturally; unconsciously while in a relaxed mental state. Poets, artists and writers are familiar with this phenomenon. Some believe that they are impressed by spirit guides.

SUBLIMINAL: Produced through the subconscious level of the mind; beneath the surface.

SUPERNATURAL: Above or beyond the natural; miraculous; supernormal. There is no such thing, as everything is natural when fully understood.

SUPERNORMAL: Above or beyond the normal. (See above.)

SYMBOLISM: Represented by symbols, signs, colors, figures, numbers, etc. Often received as psychic impressions or visions and open to interpretation.

TABLE TAPPING: The practice of sitting or standing with hands on top of a table and causing the table to vibrate or levitate via psychic energy. One of the legs of the table taps out *yes, no* or *maybe* in response to questions. For ex.: two taps for *yes,* one tap for *no,* three taps for *maybe.*

TAROT CARDS: Picture cards of a specific nature used in fortune-telling.

TEACHER: One in the spirit world who is more highly evolved than a guide and less than a Master.

TEA LEAF READER: One who has the psychic ability to read and interpret the remaining tea leaves at the bottom of a cup.

TELEKINESIS: The same as *PK; Psychokinesis.*

TELEPHONE COMMUNICATION: Soon after a person has passed over he/she sometimes has the ability to make one telephone call to a loved one. This phenomenon has been documented.

TELEPORTATION: When objects move from one place to another without physical means by disappearing and reappearing somewhere else, as in the case of apports. Frequently caused by poltergeist activity.

THE OTHER SIDE: The unseen dimension where the spirit goes after physical death. Some call it heaven.

THIRD EYE: Another term for the pineal gland which is the seat of the psychic center; located at the center of the forehead.

THOUGHT FORM: Any manifestation which is the product of thought or imagination. The forms which are seen as ghosts, apparitions and spirits are produced by thought. Some are the products of our own thoughts, but most are the products of the entities and what they want us to see.

TRANCE: When the conscious mind is in a deep sleep, producing a theta brain wave rhythm, sometimes even a delta brain wave rhythm which is an unconscious state. The deep sleep of a medium which usually produces the best psychic phenomena; spirit communication, telekinesis, etc.

TRANSCEND: Mentally rising above the physical, material world. When a mantra is repeated in meditation one can experience an altered state of consciousness, sometimes rising to a state of bliss or nirvana.

TRANSCENDENTAL MEDITATION: A mantra is repeated in a meditative state causing the meditator to transcend, as above.

TRANSFIGURATION: The alteration of the face and body of a medium when a discarnate enters the body. The transformation of the physical characteristics into those of the entity which has taken temporary possession.

TRANSITION: When the body dies and the spirit departs to the next dimension; the other side.

TRANSMIGRATION: The doctrine which is adopted by many Far Eastern cultures and primitive tribes in regard to reincarnation which holds that the soul can return into lower forms such as animals, insects, and even objects, regressing and progressing at will. This is a primitive, degrading doctrine contradicting the true progression of the soul.

TRUMPETS: Often collapsible, cone-shaped objects with one to five sections or tiers, usually aluminum, galvanized or plastic, or fashioned from any lightweight, sturdy material. They are used at séances as instruments which levitate and enable spirit to communicate.

UNIVERSE; UNIVERSAL MIND: Alternative terms for God.

VISIONARY: A person with unusually keen foresight; one who sees visions.

VISIONS: The images received clairvoyantly by a psychic or prophet.

VOODOO: Black magic; sorcery.

VOICE PHENOMENA OR RECORDINGS: Voices and sounds received via tape recorder or crystal radio which seem to be messages from other dimensions or discarnates, produced without the séance or trance situation.

WARLOCK: A male witch.

WHITE LIGHT: In healing one's self or directing healing to another, *white light* can be visualized and used as a healing tool. Any brightly colored light can be just as effective as long as the intention is present.

WITCH: One who uses black or white magic employing incantations, potions, and/or other methods.

WITCHCRAFT: The art and practice of the above.

WRAITH: Apparition of a living person or one supposed to be living; reputed to portend or indicate his death; a visible spirit.

CREDITS AND BIBLIOGRAPHY

Bohm, Dr. David: *Wholeness and the Implicate Order*, London; New York: Routledge Classics.

Cayce, Hugh Lynn: 1964. *Venture Inward*, New York: Harper and Row, Inc.

Cerminara, Gina: 1967. *The Edgar Cayce Story: Many Mansions*, New York. Signet Mystic Books.

Chopra, Deepak, M.D., 1989. *Quantum Healing: Exploring the Frontiers of Mind/Body Medicine*. New York; Bantam Books.

Dyer, Dr. Wayne, 1989. *You'll See It when You Believe It*, New York: William Morrow and Co.

Greenberg, Jay, 2007 (60 Minutes, TV.)

Holmes, Ernest, 1966. *The Science of Mind*, New York: Dodd-Mead and Co.

Mangan, James, 1972. *The Secret of Perfect Living*, Englewood Cliffs, New Jersey: Prentice-Hall, Inc. (Now Upper Saddle River N.J.: Pearson Education, Inc.)

Montgomery, Ruth, 1967. *A Search for the Truth*, New York: William Morrow and Co.

Oyle, Irving, M.D., 1979. *The Healing Mind*, Berkley, California: Celestial Arts Publishing Co.

Stevenson, Ian, M.D.: 1987. *Children Who Remember Previous Lives: A Question of Reincarnation*, Charlottesville, Virginia: University Press.

Sugrue, Thomas: 1990. *The Story of Edgar Cayce: There Is a River*, Virginia Beach, Virginia: A.R.E. Press.

Sutphen, Dick: 1987. *Lighting the Light Within*: Malibu, California: Valley of the Sun Publishing Co.

Teilhard de Chardin, Pierre: (Unknown source.)

Teutsch, J.M. and Champion K.: 1975. *From Here to Greater Happiness,* Los Angeles, California: Price/Stern/Sloan Publishers, Inc.

ABOUT THE COVER ARTIST

RICK MIDLER IS an Emmy award-winning artist, writer, director, musician, puppeteer, and lover of nature and family. His paintings have been sold in solo exhibitions and group shows throughout the world. As a Creative Director for clients such as Snickers, FedEx, HBO, AT&T and M&Ms, Rick has created some of the most famous and successful advertising campaigns in the last decade. His work has been honored by the Andy's, Addy's, Clio's, the Emmy's, the London Festival, the National Academy of Television Arts and Sciences, the Radio Mercury Awards and at Cannes. He has been published in AdAge, Creativity Magazine, Communication Arts, Shoot Magazine, The One Show and in the New York Times. Rick Midler was born in Clifton, NJ and currently lives in Park Slope, Brooklyn with Samara, Judah Maximillion and Elijah Beau.

For more information, please contact: rick@rickmidler.com

BOOKS & CDs by Norma Locker, Msc.D.

The MIRACLE Years:
What I Learned about God, Miracles, Life, the Paranormal,
and Why We Are Here.

To purchase *The MIRACLE Years,* go to: www.NormaLocker.com

###

"When you listen to *A Unique Meditation Experience,* you are traveling throughout your entire body for blissful relaxation and healing with my guidance. The affirmations reprogram your subconscious thought and belief patterns from negative to positive thereby instilling in you a positive mental attitude which changes your life profoundly as they have and continue to do for me." Love and blessings to miraculous YOU, Norma Locker.

To purchase *A Unique Meditation Experience,* go to:
www.NormaLocker.com

CPSIA information can be obtained at www.ICGtesting.com
Printed in the USA
LVOW10s1224200116

470623LV00001B/19/P